X

The Quotable Edison

UNIVERSITY PRESS OF FLORIDA

Florida A&M University, Tallahassee
Florida Atlantic University, Boca Raton
Florida Gulf Coast University, Ft. Myers
Florida International University, Miami
Florida State University, Tallahassee
New College of Florida, Sarasota
University of Central Florida, Orlando
University of Florida, Gainesville
University of North Florida, Jacksonville
University of South Florida, Tampa
University of West Florida, Pensacola

THE
Quotable Edison

Edited by Michele Wehrwein Albion

FOREWORD BY PAUL ISRAEL

UNIVERSITY PRESS OF FLORIDA

Gainesville · Tallahassee · Tampa · Boca Raton
Pensacola · Orlando · Miami · Jacksonville · Ft. Myers · Sarasota

Frontis: Edison in 1881.
Courtesy of the Thomas Edison National Historical Park, 14.910.16.

16 15 14 13 12 11   6 5 4 3 2 1

LIBRARY OF CONGRESS CATALOGING-IN-PUBLICATION DATA
Edison, Thomas A. (Thomas Alva), 1847–1931.
The quotable Edison / edited by Michele Wehrwein Albion;
foreword by Paul Israel.
p. cm.
Includes bibliographical references and index.
ISBN 978-0-8130-3559-8 (alk. paper)
1. Edison, Thomas A. (Thomas Alva), 1847–1931—Quotations.
I. Albion, Michele Wehrwein. II. Title.
TK140.E3A25 2011
621.3092—DC22 [B]   2010040990

The University Press of Florida is the scholarly publishing agency
for the State University System of Florida, comprising Florida
A&M University, Florida Atlantic University, Florida Gulf Coast
University, Florida International University, Florida State University,
New College of Florida, University of Central Florida, University
of Florida, University of North Florida, University of South
Florida, and University of West Florida.

University Press of Florida
15 Northwest 15th Street
Gainesville, FL 32611-2079
http://www.upf.com

For my husband, Jim, who is known for a few quotations
of his own, and for Sarah, Matthew, Zoe, and Noah

Contents

Foreword

Thomas Edison was not a man of letters. Though his business correspondence is voluminous, only occasionally do his letters produce a pithy quotation. And while he filled hundreds of notebooks, his technical notes and drawings do not readily lend themselves to quotation. Instead, most of the well-known Edison quotations are to be found scattered in the pages of newspapers and magazines. As the director and general editor of the Thomas A. Edison Papers Project at Rutgers University, I am well aware of how much work tracking down these quotations involves. We frequently receive requests to verify quotations attributed to Edison, but too often we have been unable to answer these inquiries because so many of these quotations are taken from the Internet, where they are found without any source attributed to them. Thanks to Michele Albion, who undertook the herculean task of tracking down these and other quotations, we now have an essential ready reference. But this book is more than a way to verify Edison quotations. By bringing together Edison's statements on specific subjects, it provides insight into his views and ideas as well as giving us a sense of his personality.

Among the many quotations are several concerning Edison's own role as a subject of journalistic inquiry. Speaking to William Croffut, the reporter from the *New York Daily Graphic* who dubbed Edison the "Wizard of Menlo Park," he remarked, "I like to talk about a thing I am interested in, and I have served newspapers too long as a telegraph operator not to feel an active sympathy with their efforts to get the news."[1] As a Western Union operator, Edison had specialized in receiving Associated Press stories for delivery to the local newspapers. During these years he got to know the newspaper business through his association with editors and reporters, some of whom had begun their own careers as telegraph operators. As an inventor, Edison would establish friendships with several newspapermen who repeatedly came to his laboratories to conduct interviews. The journalists who interviewed Edison found him "a most entertaining talker. He has a charm of narrative which is delightful, and to hear Edison tell a story is to enjoy a bit of comedy and to hear an anecdote that is of itself good and is well acted."[2] Edison was a voracious reader and enthusiastic theatergoer (Shakespeare was a particular favorite), and his familiarity with English prose, poetry, and drama flashes through even his technical writing. He knew how to use words with economy, clarity, and some grace.

Because he was an inventor, journalists found that Edison invariably had something new to talk about. Just as the media appreciated the value of Edison and his inventions as a subject, he appreciated the ways in which the media enabled him to better promote himself and his new technologies. Thus, in the early years of his career, most of these interviews turned on Edison and his inventive work. But increasingly, reporters began to ask his opinions on a variety of scientific and technical subjects, especially on the possibilities of future inventions. Edison was, of course, a key figure in the development of several of these technologies, most notably the phonograph, motion pictures, the telephone, and electric light and power. But he was also a symbol of American technological ingenuity and an important voice of technological utopianism. Edison viewed technology as a liberating force capable of creating utopia or at least providing the primary mechanism for the progressive improvement of human society. This was a reassuring message for a society that seemed to be undergoing rapid technological change, coming as it did from the person most associated in the public mind with science and technology.

After announcing his "retirement" in 1907, Edison increasingly became the nation's philosopher-inventor. He became more expansive and speculative in talking to reporters as he became less concerned with promoting his own inventions. Reporters responded to his growing interest in social issues by seeking his opinion on any and all subjects. Edison was asked to comment on a host of social, cultural, political, and economic questions of the day. Interviews ranged from the future of electricity and the role of inventions in the Great War to questions about diet and the existence of God. He spoke on labor relations, business practices, and education. He gave opinions on the role of women, the character of other nations, and the nature of art and music. In these interviews, Edison voiced both Progressive ideas and common prejudices of the day. Michele Albion helps to humanize the famous inventor by including both aspects of Edison in this volume.

But what still attracts us to Edison are the ways in which he continues to strike a chord with our modern culture. Like Edison, we continue to be imbued with the idea that new technologies or the scientific methods used to develop them can provide solutions for social problems. Thus, we turn to Edison for quotations regarding the possibility of solar power or electric automobiles as we seek to cope with global warming. His views on the nature of invention and creativity continue to provide lessons for us because we, too, believe that technological innovation remains important to improving the human condition. As the inventor who first turned invention into research and development at his laboratories and took his ideas all the way into the marketplace, Edison was in many ways the first modern innovator. It is for this reason that he continues to speak to us today.

PAUL ISRAEL

Preface and Acknowledgments

I have my own business problems to attend to, and I don't
want to be set up as an authority on every question.

Thomas Alva Edison, 1921

Thomas Alva Edison is an icon, America's—and perhaps the world's—most famous inventor. His very name is synonymous with ingenuity. His most famous innovation, the light bulb, is the very symbol of a new idea. Before he was forty years old, Edison achieved the ultimate triumvirate of inventions. His phonograph, electric light, and improvements to the motion picture camera brought sound, light, and motion to humanity. Nearly a century after his death, no one inventor from any nation approaches his lifetime of 1,093 patents. Perhaps no one ever will.

Edison's fame was firmly established while he was still in his thirties. He cultivated media coverage, drawing attention to his innovations through charm and a willingness to indulge the press. As the decades passed, he began to speak to issues outside his area of expertise, increasingly making pronouncements and predictions about subjects ranging from politics to clothing. Despite his protestations, he enjoyed his status as "an authority on every question."[1]

·

Edison was born in Milan, Ohio, in 1847, the seventh child of Nancy and Samuel Edison. He grew up in Port Huron, Michigan, where his formal schooling ended after a teacher called him "addled."

Thereafter, his mother taught him at home using books from the family library.

As a young boy, Edison sold newspapers and candy on railroad cars. When he saved a small boy from an oncoming train, the boy's father taught him telegraphy. He became an accomplished "man of the key" and spent his young adulthood as a traveling telegrapher, working throughout the Midwest and the South. In his spare time, Edison educated himself in electrical science and conducted experiments.

By 1868, Edison was a full-time inventor. Several of his innovations proved successful and enabled him to acquire the financial backing necessary to become an independent inventor. In his newly established workshops, Edison made improvements to stock tickers and telegraphic communication.

A decade later, the inventor established Menlo Park, a research laboratory and machine shop in New Jersey. There he made improvements to Alexander Graham Bell's telephone, and in 1877, invented the phonograph. The machine, the first to successfully record and replay sound, resulted in immediate fame for its inventor, who was henceforth known as the "Wizard of Menlo Park."

A year later, he garnered even more fame by inventing the first practical incandescent light. Yet another first, in 1882, he established Pearl Street, the world's first central electricity-generating station, which transmitted electricity to an entire New York neighborhood.

Any other man might have retired, but not Edison. He returned to perfecting the phonograph, experimented with early film and motion picture cameras, and launched into his one abysmal failure, an effort to mine iron ore. Even this setback was temporary, as mining operations were converted to a lucrative cement manufacturing business.

Despite his advancing age and his personal opposition to war, Edison acted as an adviser to the U.S. Naval Consulting Board during World War I. His research made him realize the vital importance of rubber for war industries. Later he devoted himself to finding a practical source of domestic rubber to be used in the event of future wars. He was still working toward this end when he died in 1931.

·

This project started out as something else entirely. It was John Byram, the editor-in-chief of the University Press of Florida, who suggested a book of Edison's quotations. He had admired Alice Calaprice's remarkable *The Expanded Quotable Einstein* and wondered if Thomas Edison would merit a similar book. I immediately thought back to my days as curator at the Edison and Ford Winter Estates. I had often been frustrated by requests to authenticate Edison's witticisms. Later, when researching my first book, *The Florida Life of Thomas Edison*, I developed a deeper appreciation of Edison's homespun aphorisms on everything from inventing to the political leadership of Italy.

As Paul Israel states in the foreword, Edison was not a man of letters. His personal remarks are largely relegated to the margins of business correspondence; contained in his self-conscious and short-lived diary; or, in few rare instances, can be found in personal letters. By contrast, he frequently shared his opinions in newspaper and magazine interviews.

In amassing these quotations, I began with a few I had collected. Next Edison biographies, newspapers, and thousands of documents made accessible through the Thomas Edison Papers were reviewed. Tom Jeffrey, senior editor of the Edison Papers, kindly shared several pages of properly cited quotes compiled by the intern Lauren Maloney.

xvi · Preface and Acknowledgments

The majority of the sources required good, old-fashioned leg-work. Original versions of magazines, newspapers, and journals were hunted down, often with the aid of extremely talented and persistent librarians, archivists, and ephemera dealers. In the instances where original newspapers have not survived or were inaccessible, citations note the secondary source.

Web sites were considered carefully. While the Internet is a useful tool for disseminating knowledge, it is equally adept at spreading misinformation. According to numerous sites, Edison was:

A vegetarian. He was, in fact, a devout carnivore.

A misogynist. Sexist, yes, but for his time he was enlightened about women's rights.

An atheist. While Edison's beliefs were unorthodox, and he was not an adherent to organized religion, he believed in a divine creator.

The quotes in this book have been selected to present the breadth of Edison's personality. Some are eerily predictive of our world today, while others prove Edison to be a poor prophet. Many are humorous, insightful, or inspirational. Others may be disturbing. Edison's less appealing opinions and prejudices are included because they represent an integral part of his character. They should be evaluated in the light of his age and his state of mind at the time the statements were made. Many of these opinions changed over time.

Edison's quotations should also be viewed within the context of his time. Historical events, economic conditions, political movements, and scientific theories all influenced the inventor. Where these are not self-evident, background information is provided to help to place these concepts within a larger framework. Those seeking a deeper understanding will want to read one of the many excellent biographies on Thomas Edison.

In making selections, I was careful not to use paraphrased quotations. On several occasions I was sorely tempted, but they may not fully represent the inventor's opinions, and thus were omitted.

The quotes retain their original spelling, grammar, and punctuation. In some cases, nonstandard spellings of words (for example, "employe") represent common contemporary usage. Where press reports of the same event use slightly different language, it has been noted.

Although literally thousands of sources were scoured, undoubtedly many quotes have been neglected, not because they weren't worthy of inclusion, but because documented citations could not be found. For example, Edison is often credited with saying, "Opportunity is missed by most people because it is dressed in overalls and looks like work." While the statement sounds like Edison and likely is Edison, thus far it cannot be documented.

Further, some likely quotes were omitted because their original source could not be located. Many of the period's primary materials were mass-produced pulp publications. Though some are preserved in libraries and archives and online, many others have not survived. I hope there will someday be an organized effort to digitize late nineteenth- and early twentieth-century newspapers and magazines before they disappear entirely from the historical record.

Further, the Edison Papers, an ambitious project to make Edison's documents available to the public, continues to process thousands of Edison-related documents. Once these are entirely accessible, more Edison quotations will be rediscovered.

As I hope this volume will begin a continuing effort to compile Edison's quotations, readers are invited to send additional quotes. In order to verify these witticisms and comments, please include a source citation—even if it is incomplete. Quotations may be sent to: Edison's Quotations, P.O. Box 487, Dover, N.H., 03820, or to michelealbion.com.

I am deeply indebted to many individuals and institutions who have helped to make this book possible: Paul Israel and Tom Jeffrey at the Thomas Edison Papers; the University Press of Florida, especially John Byram, Michele Fiyak-Burkley, and my copy editor, Susan Murray; the Charles Edison Fund; the American Jewish Historical Society; Sue Vincent of the Dover Public Library in Dover, New Hampshire; the University of New Hampshire Library, the Seattle Public Library, and the Kent State University Library; and private ephemera collectors John Weedy and Michael Ward.

Leonard DeGraaf of the Thomas Edison National Historical Park patiently and expertly assisted with the selection of photographs from the park's archives.

Others who helped make this book possible include: Gail and Steve Syriala, Beth Tykodi, Pamela Oberg, and Marjorie Marcotte. Of course, my family deserves a great deal of credit. Thank you to Matthew, Sarah, Noah, Zoe, and Jim for your loving support and patience.

Chronology

1876   Establishes laboratory at Menlo Park, New Jersey. His first son, Thomas Alva Jr. ("Dash"), is born in Newark. Invents an electric pen.

1877   Invents the phonograph and a carbon transmitter for use in a telephone receiver.

1878   Edison's second son, William Leslie, is born in Menlo Park.

1879   Develops the first truly successful electric incandescent light.

1882   Opens Pearl Street Central Power Station in New York City.

1884   Edison's wife, Mary, dies.

1885   Purchases property for a winter home in Fort Myers, Florida.

1886   Purchases Glenmont located in Llewellyn Park in West Orange, New Jersey. Marries Mina Miller.

1887   Establishes laboratory in West Orange, New Jersey.

1888   Daughter Madeleine Edison is born.
Perfects production of cylinder phonograph records.

1889   Forms Edison General Electric, and invents kinetograph, an early motion picture camera.
Attends Paris Exposition.

1890   Son Charles Edison is born.

1892   Sells his interest in the electricity companies with the formation of General Electric by the merger of Edison General Electric and Thomson-Houston.

1893   Executes patent for giant ore crusher.

1896   Experiments with x-rays and x-ray fluoroscope.

1898   Son Theodore Edison is born.

1899   Fails in his efforts to develop a commercial process of magnetic ore separation. Organizes the Edison Portland Cement Company.

1902	Conducts road tests for electric automobiles.
1906	Develops molds to produce cement houses.
1909	Begins to develop disc phonograph records. Establishes Thomas A. Edison, Inc.
1910	Perfects a nickel-iron-alkaline storage battery.
1911	Organizes Thomas A. Edison, Inc.
1911	Tours Europe with his family.
1915–1918	Acts as an advisor to the newly established U.S. Naval Consulting Board.
1926	Steps down from Thomas A. Edison, Inc.
1927	With Henry Ford and Harvey Firestone, forms the Edison Botanic Research Corporation to develop a domestic source of rubber to be used in case of future wars.
1929	Welcomes President-elect Herbert Hoover to his Florida home on the occasion of his eighty-second birthday. Attends Light's Golden Jubilee at Henry Ford's Greenfield Village.
1931	Dies on October 18 at the age of eighty-four at Glenmont.

On Inventing

Edison became famous after he invented the phonograph in 1877. Two years later, on July 9, 1879, this iconic image of Thomas Edison as a wizard was published in the *New York Daily Graphic*. By the 1880s, Edison was known as the "Wizard of Menlo Park," a name that stuck even after he closed the Menlo Park facility and moved operations to West Orange, New Jersey. *Courtesy of the Thomas Edison National Historical Park.*

Edison was a true empirical inventor. Once he had an idea, he did not rely on theory. He experimented through trial and error until unparalleled success or stunning failure was achieved. This method was criticized by many. Fellow inventor Nikola Tesla complained, "If he had a needle to find in a haystack he would not stop to reason where it was most likely to be, but would proceed at once, with the feverish diligence of a bee, to examine straw after straw until he found the object of his search."[1]

When it came to the possibilities of human ingenuity, Edison fervently believed that anything was possible. Only an open mind and hard work were necessary to transform ideas into results.

On Inventing

No experiments are useless.[2]

December 7, 1870, letter to Daniel H. Craig

You cannot expect a man to invent and work night and day and then be worried to a point of exasperation about how to obtain money to pay bills. If I keep on in this way six months longer I shall be completely broken down in health and mind.[3]

July 22, 1871, letter to George Harrington

I have received so little encouragement . . . and so much opposition from the Scientific [*sic*] dept that it got my mind in a condition not active.[4]

Mar 7, 1878, letter to Henry Bentley

Let 'em steal the microphone if they will; that is only one little thing. Before another two years go by I'll give 'em phones and [phono]graphs enough to make 'em sick.[5]

Edison would later care a great deal about the theft of his patents.
June 9, 1878, *New York Sun*

It is unreasonable for men today to be afraid that they cannot find out any more. That all has been found.[6]

Circa 1870s–80s

I have the right principle and am on the right track, but time, hard work and some good luck are needed too. It has been just so in all of my inventions. The first step is an intuition and comes in a burst. Then difficulties arise. This thing a' that or that. "Bugs" as such little faults and difficulties are called, show themselves, months of intense watching, study and labor are required for a commercial success or failure is then reached.[7]

November 13, 1878, letter to Theodore Puskas

Of course it is only a laboratory process and you probably know that laboratory processes do not always work in practice; in fact not one process in 100 works in practice.[8]

July 14, 1879, letter to Freeman G. Lockhart

In fact I am resting from invention all together, and have been for nearly a year past, but I have not given it up. I may try again before long.[9]

August 31, 1883, *Detroit Free Press*

There are two ways of inventing. One is to make your machine first and then see if it will work; the other is to first find out whether it is possible to do the thing, then make your machine. The greater number of inventors adopt the first plan. . . . I always like to begin at the A, B, C in these matters. Any other system is a good deal like trying to read a language without having learned the alphabet.[10]

June 1888, *New York Sun*

I am not a scientific man. I am an inventor. There is a difference between them, although it may never have struck you. A scientific man busies himself with a theory. He is absolutely impractical. An inventor is essentially practical. They are both of such different casts of mind that you rarely find the two together. I do not think they can very well co-exist in one man. As soon as I find that something I am investigating does not lead to practical results, I do not pursue it as a theory. The scientific man would be content to go on and study it up purely as a theory. I do not care for that.[11]

November 4, 1888, *Brooklyn Citizen*

I can only invent under powerful incentive. No competition means no invention. Its [*sic*] the same with the men I have around me. Its [*sic*] not the money they want but a chance for their ambition to work.[12]

May 23, 1889

These ideas are occurring to me all the time. Some of them are for new inventions, others are proposed improvements in existing machines—both other people's and my own machines. I just jot them down here whenever they strike me, day or night, and keep them with the hope of getting leisure to develop them.[13]

February 1890, *Harper's Magazine*

Discovery is not invention, and I dislike to see the two words confounded. A discovery is more or less in the nature of an accident.[14]

February 1890, *Harper's Magazine*

In a discovery there must be an element of the accidental, and an important one too; while an invention is purely deductive. An abstract idea or a natural law, I maintain, may be *invented*; for, in my opinion, Newton invented but did not *discover* the theory of gravitation. He had been at work on the problem for years, and had no doubt invented theory after theory to which he found it impossible to fit his facts. Then he constructed the theory to which all facts corresponded, and thus invented it by deductive reasoning.[15]

February 1890, *Harper's Magazine*

It is too much the fashion to attribute all inventions to accident, and a great deal of nonsense is talked on that score.[16]

February 1890, *Harper's Magazine*

Nearly all great inventions are the results of logical and carefully made deductions from natural laws, and those which are the outcome of accident or chance are such rare exceptions that they confirm the general rule. . . . [T]he great majority of my inventions are the result of patient labor and experiments often continued for years.[17]

1890 interview

My mind is not of a speculative order; it is essentially practical, and when I am making an experiment I think only of getting something useful, of making electricity perform work.[18]

November 8, 1891, *New York Herald*

I don't soar; I keep down pretty close to earth. Of course there are problems in life I can't help thinking about, but I don't try to study them out. It is necessary that they should be studied, and men fitted for that work are doing it. I am not fitted for that. I leave the theoretical study of electricity to the physicists, confining my work to the practical application of the force.[19]

November 8, 1891, *New York Herald*

It seems to me that we are at the beginning of inventions.[20]

Unnamed newspaper, December 31, 1891

You mean the big ones? There are not very many of them. Here they are: District Telegraph—half of that is my invention.

January 18, 1892, *Cincinnati Enquirer*

Quadruplex system of telegraphy—that's all mine. Stock ticker—I am half inventor. Telephone—half of that again. Electric pen and mimeograph—mine. Incandescent lighting system—mine. Electric Railroad—I am one of the inventors of that. Phonograph—mine.[21]

On his inventions before 1892. January 18, 1892, *Cincinnati Enquirer*

To pioneer a thing is to get it on its feet.[22]

April 2, 1892, *Scientific American*

I never did anything worth doing by accident. . . . No, when I have fully decided that a result is worth getting, I go ahead on it and make trial after trial until it comes.[23]

July 1893, *Review of Reviews*

A great invention which facilitates commerce enriches a country just as much as the discovery of vast hoards of gold.[24]

October 10, 1895, *Philadelphia Bulletin*

It is a fundamental theory of mine that you can do the most good and make most money when your invention appeals to the public at large.[25]

April 5, 1896, *New York Times*

A man who can do something which no one else can do can get a lot for doing it.[26]

April 1898, *Ladies' Home Journal*

[L]et me see, what have I invented? Well, there was the mimeograph, and the electric pen, and the carbon telephone, and the incandescent lamp and its accessories, and the quadruplex telegraph, and the automatic telegraph, and the phonograph, and the kinetoscope, and—I don't know—a whole lot of other things.[27]

January 20, 1901, *New York Times*

Try anything, try *radium* if you like. I don't care if it costs a million dollars a cylinder. Just show me a*ny*thing that'll do the work, then I'll show you how to make it cheap enough for commercial use.[28]

Circa 1903

That's just where your trouble has been, you have tried only reasonable things. Reasonable things never work. Thank God you can't think up any more reasonable things, so you'll have to begin thinking up *un*reasonable things to try, and now you'll hit the solution in no time.[29]

Circa 1903

Negative results are just what I want. They are just as valuable to me as positive results. I can never find the thing that does the work best until I know everything that *don't* do it.[30]

Circa 1903

The telephone was no invention. It was a *discovery*. Don't you know how the telephone was found? One day Bell was fooling with some wires and diaphragms in his laboratory, and suddenly he heard the voice of an assistant over the wire from another room. The telephone was *all there*; the rest was simple. No, the telephone was no real invention; it was an accident. . . . Bell never *planned* to invent the telephone.[31]

Circa 1903

A practical theory is a good lead, but it is not a sure thing.[32]

October 21, 1906, *New York Times*

All my life I have been a commercial inventor. I have never dabbled in anything that was not useful.[33]

February 11, 1907, New York Times

There is a great difference between discovery and invention. The latter is generally attained by a process of pure cold reasoning from ascertained laws of science. A discovery, on the other hand, is often the result of pure accident. . . . But there is another kind of discovery that is the result of predetermined effort, starting from certain observed facts, and aiming at a definite object.[34]

May 19, 1907, New York Times

As an inventor I was engaged in the application of science to industry. Every investigation and experiment had a commercial, and what you would call a practical, object in view. I did not deal primarily with fundamental, scientific laws, but with concrete things that had a definite commercial value in the market to-day. Now I am running after entirely different game and I am not bothering my head as to whether it produces money or not, so long as it adds to the sum total of human knowledge and furnishes material for the inventors of the future.[35]

May 19, 1907, New York Times

Passing? Why, it hasn't started yet.[36]

Asked if the age of invention was passing.
January 12, 1908, New York Times

A man can't particularize. You can never tell what some apparently small discovery will lead to. Somebody discovers something, and immediately a host of experimenters and inventors are playing all the variations upon it. . . . A whole host of experimenters are at work to-day; what great things their discoveries will lead to no one can foretell.[37]

January 12, 1908, *New York Times*

You ask if the age of invention is passing? Why, we don't know anything yet. Tell me, what physical law do we know? Not one. So far as science is concerned we're still groping about in the dark. With this world of knowledge before us, how can any one say that the age of invention has passed?[38]

January 12, 1908, *New York Times*

I never leave a theory until I have either proven its correctness or demonstrated its error. I must either solve a problem or prove that there is no solution to it.[39]

February 11, 1908, *Dallas Morning News*

Everything, anything is possible. We know nothing; we have to creep by the light of experiments, never knowing the day or the hour that we shall find what we are after.[40]

October 11, 1908, *New York Times*

I've always got more than one thing in course of development, twenty things that I hope to do, or that I hope some one else will do. Scientific discoveries are coming so thick and fast, there are so many of us working like beavers at them, that it is appalling merely to think about possibilities in the future.[41]

October 11, 1908, *New York Times*

There is so much to do, though, such a lot of new discovery going on in the form of scientific experiment that promises new wonder, new sensation, new economy of life and time and money.[42]

October 11, 1908, *New York Times*

I shall do no more inventing for commercial purposes. All my life I have worried for the success of my inventions. . . . I have all the money I want.[43]

October 15, 1908, *Fort Myers (Fla.) Press*

It has been said of me that my methods are empirical. That is true only so far as chemistry is concerned. . . . So, when I am after a chemical result that I have in mind I may make hundreds or thousands of experiments out of which there may be one that promises results in the right direction. This I follow up to its legitimate conclusion, discarding the others, and usually get what I am after. There is no doubt about this being empirical; but when it comes to problems of a mechanical nature, I want to tell you that all I've ever tacked and solved have been by hard, logical thinking.[44]

Circa April 1909

We must develop the new senses before we can get more out of life. That man must do this is not in the least incredible. New conditions will bring new necessities, new necessities bring new discoveries, both through concentrated effort and what may be called accident—that is, the sort of accident which comes when men put themselves in the way of it.

The X-ray, and the ray of radium were discovered through this sort of accident. Neon, crypton, xenthon—all these were discovered accidentally to all practical intents and purposes.[45]

October 2, 1910, *New York Times*

There are bigger things remaining for discovery than any of the big things we have discovered yet.[46]

November 13, 1910, *New York Times*

Abnormal persons are never commercial inventors.[47]

July 1911, *Century Magazine*

Imagination supplies the ideas, and technical knowledge helps to carry them out.[48]

July 1911, *Century Magazine*

If he is a good inventor, [the inventor's chief goal] is to make his invention earn money to permit him to indulge in more inventions. If he is a one-idea inventor, the incentive is generally money only.[49]

July 1911, *Century Magazine*

I have tried so many things I thought were true, and found that I was mistaken, that I have quit being too sure about anything. All I can do is to try out what seems to be the right thing, and be ready to give it up as soon as I'm convinced that there is nothing in it.[50]

July 1911, *Century Magazine*

Some experiments don't cost much—hardly anything at all; just a little time and material. The working out or commercializing an invention costs money.[51]

July 1911, *Century Magazine*

Those long-haired fellows that act queer and figure out queer things, I don't call them real inventors. Once in a while they may hit something, but not often.[52]

July 1911, *Century Magazine*

I still get lots of suggestions from cranks. They want my idea on everything from a washing-machine to a rat trap. Most of them talk perpetual motion. The same old number of cranks. The same old notion. Can't be done. No perpetual motion, never! Can't get something out of nothing.[53]

December 6, 1911, *New York Times*

The worst thing about 1912 is the number of hoggish men it will have to tolerate. Men, I mean, who are so greedy that they'll starve an inventor so hard he can't work. . . . But the inventors can't produce. They're starved down. The men that handle their inventions starve them. That's why the greedy men are the year's worst blight.[54]

January 3, 1912, *New York Times*

The value of an idea lies in the using of it.[55]

Circa 1916

Why, man, I got a lot of results. I know several thousand things that won't work![56]

Response to his failures. September 1916, *Munsey's Magazine*

Any experiment that's reasonable is worth trying, I believe.[57]

June 22, 1919, *New York Times*

The only way to keep ahead of the procession is to experiment. If you don't, the other fellow will. When there's no experimenting, you go backward. If anything goes wrong, experiment until you get at the bottom of the trouble.[58]

July 10, 1920, *Fort Myers (Fla.) Press*

I would think more highly, perhaps, of the little I have done if I did not feel it to be only a promise of what lies before. There is still much to be done in the promotion of human happiness and comfort.[59]

September 12, 1922, *New York Times*

It is like playing poker with all blue chips; [New technology] is risky business, but it may come out all right. All gambling is risky, but you have got to gamble if you get anywhere.[60]

October 19, 1922, *New York Times*

[Electric labor-saving devices] can be done, and soon, although I don't know how soon. But I am not so sure that it will be a good thing. It will create much leisure, and it all depends on what people will do with their idle hours.

How will they use them? Will not the young men and women be harmed in the manner in which they dispose of their added leisure, rather than befitted? It will be a splendid thing for the older people, of course, for they will know how best to employ the added leisure hours. We've got to have work to keep going.[61]

October 18, 1923, *Boston Daily Globe*

Society needs no more inventions for a while. It has not caught up with Science as things stand now.[62]

March 15, 1926, *Time*

If you can't think a thing out yourself, get as many other people as you can to thinking on the subject. Somebody may find some facts that have eluded you and through them come to the solution. Who thinks a matter out is of no importance whatsoever. The important thing is that the problem should be solved.[63]

February 27, 1927, *New York Times*

After perfection of each invention the satisfaction is great. Then I plunge into another one, with all its trouble, to await another period of satisfaction.[64]

October 22, 1927, *New York Times*

Most inventors work to earn money to get a modest living for their families. All they want is enough money to experiment with.[65]

December 24, 1930, *New York Times*

I start off where the last man left off.[66]

October 25, 1931, *New York Times*

On His Own Inventions

In April 1878, Edison traveled to Washington, D.C., to demonstrate the phonograph. In addition to meeting President Rutherford B. Hayes, he visited Matthew Brady at his photographic studio. *Courtesy of the Thomas Edison National Historical Park, 14.650.1.*

No inventor, then or now, has ever achieved Edison's lifetime record of 1,093 United States patents. His first patent was awarded in 1868, when he was just twenty-one. The last came just ten months before his death in 1931. Four additional patents were awarded posthumously.

It is no exaggeration to say that the impact of Edison's inventions was revolutionary. His phonograph brought the world's first recorded sound. The incandescent lamp created light, and the movie camera transformed visual images from the flat page to realistic movement on the screen.

While his other inventions may be more obscure, they speak to the broadness of his vision and practicality. He sought useful innovations that could make the lives of human beings brighter, easier, and more joyous.

Improvements to the Telegraph

A telegraph operator as a youth and young man, Edison's first inventive work was in telegraphy, a system of sending messages over wires by Morse code. By the late 1860s, he was experimenting with improving the quality and speed of telegraph mechanisms.

Dot and Dash and Automatic Printing Translating System, Invented for myself exclusively, and not for any small brained capitalist.[1]

July 19, 1871, technical notes

I am pleased to inform you that my speaking telegraph is now *absolutely perfect*. It talks as plain English as you or I and quite loud. The bark of a dog, jingling of keys, clapping of hands, Breathing, Yawning, Chirp of a Cricket goes through perfectly. . . . You would be and I am myself completely astonished, the way it works.[2]

August 2, 1877, letter to William Henry Preece

On the Mimeograph

In 1876, Edison patented an "Autographic Printing" device, a machine that used stencils and a sharp stylus to make duplicate copies of documents. A licensee of Edison's patent later called it a "mimeograph."

> I invented a device for multiplying copies of letters. . . . It is called the mimeograph.[3]
>
> Circa 1880s

On the Telephone

Edison, himself, best described his role in the creation of a useable telephone:

> About the telephone, I want to say that Bell invented the receiver, that is the end that you put to your ear. He was trying to use that also as a transmitter, but it didn't work. I completed the device by inventing a carbon transmitter which made the telephone a financial success by making it commercially available.[4]
>
> January 18, 1892, *Cincinnati Enquirer*

In addition, he provided the standard greeting, "hello." Were it not for Edison, we might be answering "ahoy," as Bell had suggested.

> I do not think we shall need a call bell as Hello! Can be heard 10 to 20 feet away.[5]
>
> August 15, 1877, letter to Thomas B. A. David

> I see by the Scientific papers that Breguet, a celebrated instrument maker of Paris[,] has just discovered *my carbon telephone*.[6]
>
> Response to someone else taking credit for his invention.
> February 10, 1878, letter to Theodore Puskas

I think bells are a nuisance.[7]

> Edison never enjoyed answering the telephone.
> March 7, 1878, letter to Henry Bentley

The present state of science will not permit the working of any telephone over any cable a greater distance than perhaps 200 miles. New discoveries must be made to permit its use on the Atlantic cable.[8]

> August 6, 1879, marginalia on letter from Eugenius H. Outerbridge

I think the future of the telephone is going to be enormous in this country if the inventors and manufacturers don't disgust everybody trying to perfect it.[9]

> November 21, 1882, *Barnstable (Mass.) Patriot*

Did you ever talk through the telephone? Then you know what it is. So do I. I send some other fellow to do my talking, and I don't need to sit half an hour at a time saying, "Halloa." "What's that?" "Who are you?"[10]

> September 16, 1884, *New York Sun*

The day will come when every one will have his telephone.[11]

> Dec 31, 1891, unnamed newspaper

The telephone is used a million times an hour, showing that science has provided the telephone for the most rapid transmission of intelligence.[12]

> May 24, 1915, *New York Times*

It may seem strange to those who know of my work on the telephone carbon transmitter that this is the first time I have ever carried on a conversation over the telephone. Trying to talk 3,400 miles on my first attempt at a telephone conversation seems to be a pretty big undertaking.[13]

> Edison's first telephone call from San Francisco to New Jersey, which is closer to 2,500 miles. October 22, 1915, *New York Times*

On the Phonograph

Invented in 1877, the phonograph made the world's first recorded sounds by using a stylus to inscribe sound waves on thin sheets of foil. Later recordings were made on wax cylinders, and eventually discs. The phonograph brought Edison immediate fame, but he neglected his invention to experiment with the electric light. When he resumed work on the phonograph, he was able to make it a great commercial success as an entertainment device. His hope that the phonograph would serve as a business tool went largely unfulfilled. By the 1930s, competition and the emerging radio industry eclipsed his talking machine. The phonograph was always the inventor's favorite creation.

Poor churches in the country might have these machines rigged up over their pulpits. . . . Thus the poor churches would save their money and get rid of the poor preacher.[14]

> February 2, 1878, *New York Sun*

Why, I could put a metal diaphragm in the mouth of the Goddess of Liberty that the Frenchmen are going to put up on Bedloe's Island that would make her talk so loud that she could be heard by every soul on Manhattan Island.[15]

> Proposal to create a talking Statue of Liberty.
> February 2, 1878, *New York Sun*

You should hear the phonograph now, it's almost perfect.[16]

> February 12, 1878, letter to Benjamin Franklin Butler

I have been very busy working [on the] phonograph; hardly have time to eat.[17]

February 27, 1878, marginalia on letter from Henry W. Law

Phonograph is now *perfect.* . . . [Y]ou will get *whispering* perfectly and beautiful articulation even in hand turning, recognition of voice is easy.[18]

March 2, 1878, letter to Alfred Marshall Mayer

This machine can only be built on the American principle of inter-changeability of parts like a gun or a sewing machine. Hand made machines would create endless confusion.[19]

March 23, 1878, letter to George Samuel Nottage

Now, the lover, while waiting for his sweetheart to finish [getting ready] can place the phonograph sheet of the pretty things she has said to him before, and so occupy himself for a time.[20]

March 29, 1878, *New York World*

I've made some machines; but this is my baby, [patting the phono-graph] and I expect it to grow up to be a big feller and support me in my old age.[21]

April 2, 1878, *New York Graphic*

[The phonograph] is a very simple idea when you come to look at it, and the wonder is it wasn't discovered before.[22]

April 19, 1878, *Washington Post*

This will be useful for many purposes. A business man can speak a letter to the machine, and his office boy, who need not be a short-hand writer, can write it down at any time, as rapidly or slowly as he desires. Then we mean to use it to enable persons to enjoy good music at home.[23]

April 19, 1878, *Washington Star*

No machine has ever been got up that did not require years of improvement. I ought to be allowed at least two years to improve [the phonograph]. Now, old man, get out and let me go to work.[24]

October 20, 1878, *New York Sun*

The phonograph gets little attention from me nowadays.[25]

December 4, 1878, letter to Clarence J. Blake

[The phonograph is] [t]aking care of itself. Comatose for the time being. It is a child and will grow to be a man yet; but I have a bigger thing in hand and must get out [electrical systems] to the temporary neglect of all other phones and graphs.[26]

December 28, 1878, *New York Graphic*

They never will try to steal the phonograph. It's not of any commercial value.[27]

Circa 1880

I have never had the time to make [the phonograph] commercial yet. I fear to touch it. . . . Because as soon as I do and prove that there is money in it, about 400 people will come up and say that they discovered it twenty years ago. I want to get the entire credit for some one thing.[28]

November 21, 1882, *Barnstable (Mass.) Patriot*

You know that I finished the first phonograph more than ten years ago. It remained more or less of a toy. The germ of something wonderful was perfectly distinct, but I tried the impossible with it, and when the electric light business assumed commercial importance, I threw everything overboard for that.[29]

October 29, 1887, *Scientific American*

For musicians the phonograph is going to do wonders. . . . Each instrument can be perfectly distinguished, the strings are perfectly distinct, the violins from the cellos, the wind instruments and the wood are perfectly heard, and even in the notes of a violin the overtones are distinct to a delicate ear. It is going to work wonders for the benefit of music lovers.[30]

October 29, 1887, *Scientific American*

My phonograph will occupy about as much space on the merchant's desk, or at the side of the desk as the typewriter does.[31]

November 10, 1887, unnamed newspaper

Perhaps I am wrong in telling you anything about my phonograph, because what I claim for it is so extraordinary that I only get ridicule in return.[32]

November 19, 1887, *Scientific American*

Suppose you are sick, or blind, or poor, or cannot sleep. You have a phonograph, and the whole world of literature and music is open to you.[33]

November 19, 1887, *Scientific American*

Taken as it is I have great faith in the phonograph, and think it will become as useful as the telephone.[34]

May 24, 1889, *Pittsburgh Chronicle Telegraph*

The phonograph [works] have been shut down because we have nearly completed all the orders on hand, and the proprietor thereof, seeing that the country has resolved itself into a national lunatic asylum, decided to wait until the wave subsided somewhat.[35]

August 2, 1893, *Quincy (Ill.) Daily Herald*

I do not wish to talk about the past. I do not care to think of it, but now I see an opportunity to carry out my old ideas as to the phonograph, which is dearer to me than almost anything else I ever tried to do.[36]

April 5, 1890, *New York Times*

Why, I can sit by the hour myself . . . and listen to those [phonograph records], and I would not be human if I didn't want everybody to share my pleasure with me.[37]

April 5, 1890, *New York Times*

I promised complete novels and operas on the phonograph. I am keeping my word. I can now give you the opera of "Norma," music words, on five cylinders. . . . Very soon the old toothcomb music-box, with its three or four antiquated tunes, will be a relic of barbarism.[38]

April 5, 1890, *New York Times*

In addition, I intend to rescue the eyes from slavery. . . . Why should you have to read a book, or why, to save your eyes, should some tired member of your family have to read to you? . . . With the phonograph completed, anybody can get one of my cheap classics, slip it on one of those little phonographs, and half a dozen friends can listen at once.[39]

April 5, 1890, *New York Times*

[C]ommercial reasons when it comes to the phonograph don't count with me. It's the only invention of mine that I want to run myself.[40]

Circa 1899

I am now on Beethoven's Ninth Symphony and I expect to make the phonograph the greatest of all musical instruments. I will have plenty to do, but it will be done.[41]

January 3, 1915, *New York Times*

I'm always afraid of things that work the first time. When I made my first voice recording on the phonograph, shouting in it 'Mary had a little lamb, with fleece of whitest snow' and it reproduced perfectly, I was never so taken back in my life.[42]

July 10, 1920, *Fort Myers (Fla.) Press*

The day will come when we can have a grand opera for a dime.[43]

April 1922, *Current Opinion*

It has made life a little more attractive, and expedited business transactions.[44]

August 13, 1927, *New York Times*

I developed the phonograph in 1877 as a result of reason—of thinking about it. You might say that it was developed backward, because the idea of recording sounds came after the creation of sounds.[45]

August 12, 1928, *New York Times*

On the Incandescent Light

Edison's foray into electric lights began in 1878. His first real success came a year later, when, on October 22, a carbon filament was illuminated for more than thirteen hours. A few months later, he switched to carbonized bamboo filament and achieved 1,200 hours of light.

I am fearfully ignorant of the electric light business.[46]

May 24, 1878, note

I have it now! And, singularly enough, I have obtained it through an entirely different process than that from which scientific men have ever sought to secure it. They have all been working in the same groove, and when it is known how I have accomplished my object, everybody will wonder why they have never thought of it, it is so simple. . . . When the brilliance and cheapness of the lights are made known to the public—which will be in a few weeks, . . . I can light up the entire lower part of New York city, using a 500 horse power engine.[47]

September 16, 1878, *New York Sun*

[H]ave struck a bonanza in Electric light.[48]

September 22, 1878, letter to Theodore Puskas

All I want at present is to be provided with funds to pursue the light rapidly.[49]

October 3, 1878, letter to Grosvenor Porter Lowrey

Say nothing publicly about light[.] let them go ahead[.] I have only correct principle.[50]

On his competition. October 8, 1878, telegram
to George Edward Gouraud

The *[New York] Sun* article was *somewhat* exaggerated, but it is safe to say that I have some new ideas in regard to the electric light.[51]

October 10, 1878, letter to Henry Morton

When I remember how the gas companies used to treat me, I must say that it gives me great pleasure to get square with them.[52]

October 20, 1878, *New York Sun*

The electric light is the light of the future—and it will be my light—unless some other fellow gets up a better one.[53]

October 21, 1878, *New York Daily Graphic*

You light one of these by just turning a thumbscrew. No lighting of matches, no fumes, no danger of suffocation or damage if you leave it turned on full. And the beauty of it is that no electricity is wasted.[54]

October 21, 1878, *New York Sun*

Light tremendous excitement[.] Papers full[.][55]

October 24, 1878, telegram to George G. Ward

I don't know when I am going to stop making improvements on the electric light. I've just got another one that I found by accident. I was experimenting with one of my burners when I dropped a screwdriver on to it. Instantly the light was almost doubled and continued to burn with the increased power. I examined the burner and found it had been knocked out of shape. I restored it to its original form, and the light was decreased. Now, I make all my burners in the form accidentally given to that one by the screw-driver.[56]

November 17, 1878, New York World

My death could not destroy the utility of my invention. The [electric light] is proved to be of practical use.[57]

November 25, 1878, New York Sun

The lamp for the people must be so simple in its construction that any fool or mule can use it. I am making such a lamp. You turn your faucet, and there is your light. You turn your faucet, and your light is gone. There is no dickering and no feeling. Your light is there when you want it, and when you don't want it disappears. It is so simple in its design that a child can understand it and use it.[58]

November 25, 1878, New York Sun

The electric light is an accomplished fact, and it is more economical than gas.[59]

January 30, 1879, New York Herald

Just think of such a thing. The idea that a man can go to work and invent a whole new system, overturning an established business, especially such a complicated system as electric lighting, all within a few months![60]

January 30, 1879, New York Herald

The fact to be accomplished by me is the invention perfection and introduction into practice of a practicable system of illuminating by electricity which shall effect every object and take the place of the present method of lighting by gas.[61]

April 8, 1879, letter to Theodore Puskas

We are all on electric light now, and have no time to go on telephone work, etc.[62]

September 8, 1879, marginalia on letter from John E. Watson

I am working day and night on the electric light to the exclusion of everything else.[63]

September 8, 1879, marginalia on letter from John E. Watson

My light is perfected.[64]

November 18, 1879, marginalia on letter from Henry Cox

One of my lamps has waxed 208 hours. How is that for permanence [*sic*].[65]

January 1, 1880, letter to George Frederick Barker

So long as the Electric Light company is satisfied that the light is a success I care little for adverse criticism.[66]

January 2, 1880, *Quincy (Ill.) Daily Whig*

We put up about 80 lamps, the finest made, to ascertain the life of the lamps. They have all gone out. Their average life was 792 hours; the shortest 26 hours; the longest 1383 hours; a very satisfactory result for a 1st experiment. I have never concealed this fact when a lamp busted. I let it remain where the people could see it. My Laboratory is open + free to sneaks, ignoramus detectives, as well as gentlemen. I could have easily have made new lamps and replaced those destroyed had I wished to deceive the public.[67]

April 8, 1880, letter to Joseph Medill

We don't aspire to light street lamps, which is a small matter, but to light houses and homes.[68]

February 24, 1881, Cincinnati Enquirer

Gas is a barbarous and wasteful light. It is a light for the dark ages.[69]

April 27, 1882, St. Louis Post-Dispatch

I am so convinced of the [electric light] system's success that, as I said before, I have given up inventing and taken to business pure and simple.[70]

March 13, 1883, unnamed newspaper

The advantages of the incandescing light over gas is that it gives off but one-twelfth the heat of gas, yet gives off no poisonous gas, is perfectly steady and also safer than any other means of artificial illumination.[71]

July 13, 1883, Sunbury (Pa.) Democrat

None of my inventions has cost me as much time, labor and study as did [the electric light]; and though I myself never lost hope of ultimate success, some of my associates were often discouraged and despondent.[72]

1890 interview

I cannot waste my time over electric lighting matters, for they are old. I ceased to worry over these things ten years ago, and I have a lot more new material on which to work. Electric lights are too old for me.[73]

February 21, 1892, New York Times

I have always suspected that I was the inventor of the electric lamp, but now I am sure of it.[74]

Sarcastic remark upon winning an infringement suit.
October 1892, unnamed newspaper

While I cannot but rejoice at the place which the incandescent lighting art has made for itself among the inestimable comforts and conveniences of civilization, I feel that my share in the work is exaggerated.[75]

February 12, 1904, *New York Times*

I never got a cent out of my lights in Europe. . . . It's all right. I don't care. It doesn't worry or distress me. I never started out to be a business man. And, anyway, what I saw in Europe pays me. Yes; I'm paid; well paid for any little thing I may have done for Europe.[76]

October 29, 1911, *New York Times*

About the only help I had in the development of the electric light lay in the fact that the scientific world was all against me, and re-cited Ohm's law to prove the case.[77]

Edison believed knowledge of Ohm's law, which defines the relationship between power, voltage, current, and resistance, would have prevented him from achieving success.

October 11, 1914, *New York Times*

I don't believe—the electric light has ever stirred much sentiment in me. I had so much trouble and worry in connection with the perfection and introduction of the lights that I never had time for sentiment about them.[78]

October 11, 1914, *New York Times*

Electric lights, I think, have helped to keep the world awake, both physically and mentally. I hope so.[79]

February 27, 1927, *New York Times*

Without good lights the unexceptional will not reach a maximum of usefulness, although they may reach a maximum of foolishness.

A man can be an idiot in a dimly lighted dance hall; he needs good illumination if he wants to study anything worthwhile to produce.[80]

February 27, 1927, *New York Times*

All lights are wonderful. We need lights in the world. Light on everything.[81]

February 12, 1920, *Fort Myers (Fla.) Press*

On Electricity and Electrical Systems

Though the perfection of the incandescent light catapulted Edison to great fame, it was the systems he created to support the light, like generators and wiring systems, which made the light practical for universal adoption.

"[E]theric force" is just as much an unknown mode of motion as it ever was.[82]

Later known as high-frequency electromagnetic waves,
Edison discovered the phenomenon in 1875.
April 10, 1878, letter to George Miller Beard

The same wire that brings the light will also bring power and heat—with the power you can run an elevator, a sewing machine, or any other mechanical contrivance, and by means of the heat you may cook your food.[83]

October 12, 1878, *Times* (London)

I am all right on my lamp. I don't care anything more about it. Every bit of heat is utilized to produce light as far as art will allow. The theoretical and practical results are perfectly satisfactory. My point now is the generator.[84]

December 19, 1878, *New York Sun*

I have completed the standard generator which exceeds in simplicity and economy all generators previously devised by any one. . . . Nothing more remains but the construction of the standard lamp, and the working up of the mechanical details for a large central station.[85]

> May 10, 1879, letter to Theodore Puskas

[E]verything can be accomplished by electricity.[86]

> May 24, 1879, marginalia on letter from M. E. Gates

In the present state of science we cannot heat houses economically by electricity.[87]

> January 3, 1880, marginalia on letter from A. C. Carey

The moment I declared that I had subdivided the light, everybody thought they ought to see the light, burning in every house in New York within a few months. It's ridiculous. The newspaper came out and said the electric light was a failure because within six months or a year I hadn't started yet selling the light to everybody in New York.[88]

> April 27, 1882, *St. Louis Post-Dispatch*

Among the many factors which have developed commerce and industry and stimulated all the forces of progress during the first half century, none has played a part so radical and essential as electricity. Hardly a single nerve or fibre of that complex body which we call society, that has not thrilled and vibrated with its influence. It has strengthened the bonds of international amity; it has quickened all the methods of trade and lent ten-fold precision and celerity to the innumerable agencies by which it works; it has breathed new vitality into the arts and sciences; it has even warmed and strengthened the social forces; and in a word one, may justly claim for it such a universe stimulus, as cannot be credited to any other purely physical agency in the world's history.[89]

> January 18, 1885, *New York Tribune*

I haven't named the baby yet.[90]

> On his discovery of etheric force. May 23, 1885, *Electrical Review*

Just think, electricity employed to cheat a poor hen out of the pleasure of maternity. Machine born chickens. What is home without a mother.[91]

> On incubators for hatching chickens. July 12, 1885, diary entry

It's hard to make electricity interesting to the general public anyhow.[92]

> September 19, 1885, *Western Newspaper Union*

I do claim—and can make good my claim—to be the inventor of the only means for making the incandescent light practical. Before me, everybody who had experimented in that direction, endeavored to employ conductors of low resistance. I took exactly the opposite course, working with conductors of high resistance. When I demonstrated that was the right way, they all suddenly discovered that that was just what they had been doing all along.[93]

> October 1, 1885, *San Francisco Chronicle*

I shall be governed by circumstances in my experiments, but it looks now as if we were only on the threshold of electrical knowledge. The next twenty years will see great strides.[94]

> February 2, 1886, *New Orleans Times-Democrat*

But this is the point I have been working on for years, to convert heat directly into electricity without the intervention of boilers, steam and all that. What an enormous amount of expense could be saved if this could be done. Think of putting something into the heat of that natural gas fire and making electricity out of it. It can be done. I feel it in my bones, and just now I have a suspicion that I am on the right track, but it is a pesky problem—one that can be worked out only in time.[95]

June 12, 1889, *Pittsburgh Dispatch*

The great development in electricity will be, I am firmly convinced, in discovering a more economical process of producing it.[96]

September 1, 1889, *Levant Herald*

The steam-engines will be abolished, and that day is not far off.[97]

September 1, 1889, *Levant Herald*

They say I am prejudiced, but if I had anything to say I would abolish the alternating current.[98]

Edison promoted direct current, not George Westinghouse's alternating current. October 14, 1889, *New York Sun*

I never believed in overhead [electric] wires in larger cities and never put up any.[99]

October 20, 1889, *New York World*

I have always consistently opposed high-tension and alternating systems of electric lighting . . . not only on account of danger, but because of their general unreliability and unsuitability for any general system of distribution.[100]

November 1889, *North American Review*

Electrical science is in embryo now. New points are discovered and new knowledge developed every day. We are doing and undoing constantly. Electricity is undoubtedly destined to be a great blessing to mankind; one of the greatest, if not absolutely the greatest natural force in the universe. Its wonders cannot be conceived nor its possibilities estimated by the mind of man today.[101]

February 16, 1891, unnamed newspaper

I left electricity because there are too many in it. It offers one no inducements. . . . There is no end to the possibilities of electricity, however.[102]

September 10, 1893, *Dallas Morning News*

But electricity is an evasive, subtle thing.[103]

November 22, 1896, *Philadelphia Press*

[S]urgery, optics and astronomy [will be operated by electricity], but greater minds than mine must dwell on this particular branch of electrical usage.[104]

September 10, 1893, *Dallas Morning News*

Why we don't even know what electricity is yet. How can we say that we've reached the limit of a force whose very nature we are ignorant of?[105]

January 12, 1908, *New York Times*

The vacum [*sic*] house cleaner is a great gift to the home and a boon to health.[106]

January 19, 1911, *Wellsboro (Pa.) Gazette*

All cooking should be done over an electric range.[107]

March 1913, *Good Housekeeping*

If buses are desirable for intercity traffic, the electric one is the only practicable one. It is noiseless, odorless, and can be stopped and started quicker than the gasoline vehicle, and is also more economic in operation.[108]

November 30, 1913, *New York Times*

I have never claimed to have invented electricity—that is a campaign lie—nail it![109]

Circa 1914

When we learn how to store electricity, we will cease being apes ourselves; until then we are tailless harangue-outangs.[110]

Circa 1914

I am getting to be an old man and I am afraid it will remain for others to give industry this new method [of creating electricity from coal]. But it's a certainty, that's the important thing, and no man living can estimate how vastly it will affect the commercial use of electricity in the future.[111]

June 6, 1914, *New York Times*

I don't know much about electricity—nobody does. We know only one millionth of all there is to be known about it.[112]

June 6, 1914, *New York Times*

The development of electricity as applied in the homes, the cleaners, the cookers, the washers, and the many other useful things is a great thing for women. It lightens labor in a way that years ago was not even dreamed of.[113]

October 2, 1916, *New York Times*

Electricity will do practically all of the manual work about the home. Just as it has largely supplanted the broom and dustpan, and even the carpet sweeper, it will be applied to the hundreds of other littler drudgeries in the house and in the yard.[114]

October 12, 1912, *Good Housekeeping*

Electricity will not only, as now, wash the clothes when turned on in a laundry and plugged into one of dozens of existent patent washers, but will gather them and iron them without the use of the little manual labor even now required.[115]

October 12, 1912, *Good Housekeeping*

The housewife's work, in days to come, will amount to little more than superintendence, not of Norah, fresh from Ireland, or Gretchen, fresh from Germany, but of simplified electrical appliances.[116]

October 12, 1912, *Good Housekeeping*

Electricity in farming is one of our coming developments.[117]

May 21, 1915, *Huntington Long Islander*

But the cities will soon see universal transmission of electrical power. Belts in factories will be done away with.[118]

December 2, 1916, *Collier's Weekly*

Electricity will be so cheap that it won't pay to use any other form of power.[119]

December 2, 1916, *Collier's Weekly*

[F]or the Pearl Street station was the greatest adventure in my life. It was akin to venturing on an uncharted sea.[120]

On the first central power processing plant in the United States, which first began generating electricity on September 4, 1882. September 12, 1922, *New York Times*

I am proud of the electrical industry, of its vision, courage and devotion to the public service, and I feel every American feels the same way about it.[121]

June 7, 1929, *New York Times*

[Electricity's] uses are unlimited. We haven't begun yet. Why we don't even know what it is. It's like light. We had a theory, but they found in practice that there are too many grave exceptions to that theory. It must be wrong. That's how it is with electricity. I don't see how we can be at the end of our discoveries in it when we don't even know, haven't even a suspicion, as to what it is.[122]

January 1931, *Review of Reviews*

On Motion Pictures

In 1892, Edison worked with photographer W.K.L. Dickson to invent a motion picture camera and a viewing device called the kinetoscope. They produced short films at Edison's New Jersey laboratory in a rotating movie studio called the Black Maria.

Edison quickly realized the entertainment value of films. Going to see silent films was one of Edison's great amusements. Although he was deaf, he could easily follow the action. He complained vehemently when sound pictures replaced silent films.

I am experimenting upon an instrument which does for the eye what the phonograph does for the ear. Which is the recording and reproduction of things in motion.[123]

October 8, 1888, technical notes

I make forty-six photographs a second on a moving sheet and by exhibiting this sheet moving at the same speed the scene is reproduced.[124]

May 9, 1891, *Brooklyn Eagle*

The kinetograph. What does that mean? The first half of the word means "motion" and the other half write. That is, the portrayal of motion. This instrument or the result is a combination of photography and phonography. By means of it I shall be able to reproduce operas, prize-fights, or a drama—anything which human beings enact that may be photographed or heard.[125]

May 14, 1891, *Chicago Tribune*

[A] man can sit in his own parlor and see depicted upon a curtain the forms of players in opera upon a distant stage, and to hear the voices of the singers.[126]

May 20, 1891, *Electrical Engineer*

I hope to be able by the invention [of the kinetograph] throw upon a canvas a perfect picture of anybody, and reproduce his words. Thus, should Patti be signing somewhere, this invention will put her full length picture upon the canvas so perfectly as to enable one to distinguishes every feature and expression—.[127]

June 11, 1891, *Quincy (Ill.) Daily Journal*

It was very hard to get the exact grimaces of the face or the clear workings of a man's fingers playing the piano, but we perfected it at last.[128]

September 10, 1893, *Dallas Morning News*

I have constructed a little instrument I call the kinetograph with a nickel slot attachment + some 25 have been made but I am very doubtful if there is any Commercial feature in it + fear that they will not Earn their Cost. These Zootropic devices are of too sentimental a character to get the public to invest in.[129]

Edison underestimated the popularity of kinetoscope parlors. February 21, 1894, letter to Eadweard Muybridge

This has been largely a work of sentiment on my part. I do not believe there is much money in it. But I believe it is in the interest of science and history. A great man will never die if his pictures and speeches are saved.[130]

March 15, 1894, *Quincy (Ill.) Daily Herald*

Small towns whose yearly taxes would not pay for three performances of the Metropolitan Opera company, can see and hear the greatest stars in the world for 10 cents. And it will pay because of the volume of business.[131]

June 18, 1904, *Quincy (Ill.) Daily Whig*

We want democracy in our amusements. It is safe to say that only one out of every fifty persons in the United States has any real right to spend the price asked for a theater ticket. What chance has the workingman for amusements whose income is from \$2 to \$3 a day? No chance at all, except at motion pictures.[132]

June 18, 1904, *Quincy (Ill.) Daily Whig*

Actors will have to leave the legitimate stage to work for the "movies" in order to get any money. This is all the better for them. They can live in one place all year round and barnstorming will cease automatically when no one wants to pay several times the amount of the movies' show for some inferior production of a successful play.[133]

June 18, 1904, *Quincy (Ill.) Daily Whig*

As for the phonograph, taking it in connection with the kinetoscope, I believe that it will be perfected to such an extent in another fifty years that people in New York will be able to attend an entire theatrical performance, or listen to an opera from beginning to end, where there is not an actor or a singer present—and yet every gesture, every syllable, every note, will be there with the most perfect illusion that art could demand.[134]

May 19, 1907, *New York Times*

The speaking picture is already perfected.[135]

August 2, 1910, letter to Hawenstein

We'll be ready for moving-picture shows in a couple of months, but I am not satisfied with that. I want to give grand opera, I want to have people in far stranded towns able to hear and see John Drew. And I want to have "Teddy" [Roosevelt] addressing a meeting.[136]

August 27, 1910, *New York Times*

I'd like to see every last school book thrown out of the schools, and they'll do it some time. They'll do all the teaching by moving pictures. Every bit of it. That machine is especially for schools.[137]

January 3, 1912, *New York Times*

[I want] to make it possible for the poorest families in Squeedunk to see the same operas and plays that are produced in New York City for an admission price of 5 cents.[138]

January 4, 1913, *New York Times*

I believe that its greatest use, for the present and for a considerable time to come, will be for music. By this I mean opera, musical plays, and kindred entertainment. I have always wanted to bring the great music of the world within the range of the people.[139]

March 1913, *Munsey's Magazine*

The talking motion picture will not supplant the regular silent picture.[140]

March 1913, *Munsey's Magazine*

As a matter of fact, the only kind of amusement which seems to be in jeopardy as a result of the introduction of [talking motion pictures] is the cheap vaudeville. The elimination of most of this will be a benefit, instead of a loss.[141]

March 1913, *Munsey's Magazine*

The educational value of the moving picture is, and will be, enormous. . . . Through these mediums the great masses of the people can have the advantages of the rich man.[142]

July 12, 1913, *New York Times*

All delusions will be perfect, and probably the actual color will be produced.[143]

Edison prediction of color films. July 12, 1913, *New York Times*

I am going to erect a studio here to perfect the kinetophone [talking movie] to the limit. We are the only ones who can do it. I want . . . to show the theatrical people that scientific people can beat them at their own game and produce things that will open their eyes.[144]

Circa 1914

I told the people when the kinetophone was first put on the market that sooner or later they would be able to see and hear opera by the best artists for a nickel. The workingman has popularized the "movie," and now we are going to give the poor man and his family something more for a nickel.[145]

November 9, 1914, *New York Times*

[B]ut the additions and changes [of other inventors] were merely detail improvements on my prior and basic invention, namely, the Kinetograph, or Recording Machine, under which I claim to be the inventor of the modern motion picture.[146]

June 9, 1921, *New York Times*

The public does not want "talking movies."[147]

February 12, 1922, *New York Times*

I believe, as I have always believed that you control the most powerful instrument in the world for good or evil. . . . Remember that you are servants of the public, and never let the desire for money or power prevent you from giving the public the best work of which you are capable.[148]

Edison's advice to the motion picture industry. February 16, 1924, *New York Times*

Whatever part I have played in [the development of the motion picture industry] was mainly along mechanical lines. The far more important development of the motion picture [is] as a medium for artistic efforts and as an educational factor.[149]

February 16, 1924, *New York Times*

I enjoyed Harry Carry and the vaudeville very much.[150]

Edison after seeing a film clip of baseball announcer, Harry Carry. February 16, 1926, *Hendry County (Fla.) News*

Americans require a restful quiet in the moving picture theater and for them talking from the lips of the figures on the screen destroys the illusion. Devices for the projecting the film actor's speech can be perfected, but the idea is not practical. The stage is the place for the spoken word. The reactions of the American public up to now indicated the movies will not supersede it.[151]

May 21, 1926, *New York Times*

You ask about the new talking moving picture? It is not new. It is as old as you are nearly. I recall my first attempts on the subject some 15 years ago. We took the voice on a phonograph record and arranged a talking machine so that it could be operated from the projection room of the theater. The phonograph was placed in front of the screen and it worked fine.[152]

March 7, 1927, *St. Petersburg Times*

I sweated blood over that damned thing.[153]

Of his motion picture camera.
December 20, 1927, *New York Times*

Talking is no substitute for good acting we have had in the silent pictures.[154]

August 1, 1929, *New York Times*

The talkies have spoiled everything for me. There isn't any more good acting on the screen. My, my, how I should life to see Mary Pickford or Clara Bow in one of those good old fashioned pictures. They concentrate on the voice now; they've forgotten how to act. I can sense it because I am deaf.[155]

January 21, 1930, *Fort Myers (Fla.) Press*

Let's see now—what's the name of it? Oh, yes, I remember—*The Birth of a Nation*, that great picture Griffith made. But who cares?[156]

On his favorite movie, the 1915 silent film by D. W. Griffith. February 1930, *American Magazine*

I congratulate you and your members of the association for working out a code for production of mobbing picture. . . . Your foresight will, I believe, not only insure to this universal medium of expression the continued patronage of the vast audience the motion picture has today, but will insure for it the respect and support of coming generations.[157]

On the Motion Picture Production Code of 1930, which set moral standards for the film industry. April 2, 1930, *New York Times*

I see they are trying out a large size film again. I tried that thirty years ago but it was not good as the film kept tearing up and my Hebrew friends thought the process too expensive. I wanted forty pictures per second and they wanted fifteen. I don't see how they stand expense of colored films.[158]

April 11, 1930, *Fort Myers (Fla.) Press*

I don't like these talking pictures. I can't hear a word they say. Something will have to be done for the entertainment of two million deaf persons like myself. Take this "It" girl. I used to like her, but now she's talking too and that spoils the fun for me.[159]

April 11, 1930, *Fort Myers (Fla.) Press*

On Ore Milling and Separation

During the 1890s, Edison invested millions of dollars into a project to create high-grade ores for steel mills. The venture was an abysmal failure, bringing him to the verge of personal and financial ruin.

> Yes: I have taken up the mining business. We have a great lot of big machinery for concentrating ore down east. It will either work or "bust."[160]

> September 10, 1893, *Dallas Morning News*

> I'm going to do something now so different and so much bigger than anything I've ever done before people will forget that my name was ever connected with anything electrical.[161]

> Circa 1890s

> Yes, I sold the stock and transferred it, as I actually needed the money. My Wall street friends think I cannot make another success, and that I am a back number, hence I cannot raise even $10000 from them, but I am going to show them that they are very much mistaken; I am full of vinegar yet, although I have had to suffer from the neglect of an absent minded Providence in this scheme.[162]

> Despite his "vinegar," Edison was unable to raise additional funds for his failing enterprise. August 6, 1897, letter to Richard Rogers Bowker

> We're making a Yosemite of our own here. We will soon have one of the biggest artificial canyons in the world.[163]

> No matter how deep Edison dug, he didn't find success in iron ore. November 1897, *McClure's Magazine*

On Cement and Cement Houses

While his iron ore mining enterprise failed, Edison realized he could make money selling waste sand to cement manufacturers. During the

1890s, Edison started the Edison Portland Cement Company, an enterprise that helped offset earlier losses. In 1906, Edison announced a plan to manufacture cement homes to provide inexpensive housing for workers. The few houses that were built proved unpopular.

Next Summer I will build within twelve hours a three-story house on a lot, 25 by 45 feet. It will cost only $1000, and will be built on the basis of its ownership by the $1.50 a day laborer who works in it. I have a model of the first house that is to be built. It will be built during the span of twelve hours and will include plumbing, heating apparatus, and everything that means of comfort to-day and beauty in architecture.[164]

October 19, 1907, *New York Times*

The economic value of this rests, for one instance, in that the house will never be in need of repair. The roof and the floors will be of concrete; the concrete will be made on the very site; there will be no fire insurance, as another instance of saving value; the man who owns the house can let his children hack at it with hatchets and axes and lose nothing but the hatchets and axes.[165]

October 19, 1907, *New York Times*

But I'll do it! I'll do it! I'll build those houses by the mile, and they won't cost the workingmen who live in them more than $6.40 a month outside of trolley fares. Perhaps I am giving them too much. Maybe the houses are too big, too roomy. The poor fellows who have been used to being cooped up in tenement house rooms won't know what to do with themselves in a house such as I'll give 'em to live in.[166]

October 1909, unnamed newspaper

If I succeed, as I feel certain I shall, the cement house will be my greatest invention. It will take from the city slums everybody who is worth taking.[167]

December 3, 1909, *Huntington Long Islander*

The use of cement for building concrete bridges, sewers and subway walls has increased wonderfully and will go forward more rapidly by the use of steel models for this work. They are my own invention.[168]

January 19, 1911, *Wellsboro (Pa.) Gazette*

I am going to have concrete furniture that will make it possible for the laboring man to put furniture in his home more artistic and more durable than is now to be found in the most palatial residence in Paris or along the Rhine.[169]

December 15, 1911, *Huntington Long Islander*

On the Storage Battery

Early in his career, Edison experimented with storage batteries. By the 1890s, he became convinced that if he could make a battery powerful and light enough, electric cars would become viable. He made great progress, especially with his iron-nickel battery, but before he could achieve success, the internal combustion engine became dominant. Edison's batteries were commercially successful as power sources for train signals, mining lamps and submarines.

The storage battery is, in my opinion, a catch-penny, a sensation, a mechanism for swindling by stock companies. . . . The storage battery is one of those peculiar things which appeal to the imagination, and no more perfect thing could be desired by stock swindlers than that very self-same thing.[170]

Comment made before he entered the battery business.
January 28, 1883, *Boston Herald*

I have, after three years of hard work, solved the problem of an electrical storage battery which can be used for long distance work and which will wear three or four automobiles out before it will succumb itself.[171]

May 29, 1902, *New York Times*

All the fellows said it could not be done, but I've solved the problem. I could not believe that nature possessed such a paucity of material for electric storage batteries that lead was the only substance we could use for that purpose.... [T]he only thing left for me to do was to perfect such cells so as to make them of economical use.[172]

July 29, 1905, *New York Times*

[The storage battery] will mean the elimination of the horse and the clearing of traffic congestion in New York and other cities.[173]

October 19, 1907, *New York Times*

The storage battery is now an accomplished fact.[174]

June 27, 1909, *Oakland (Calif.) Tribune*

[With the success of the battery,] the commercial value of the gasoline motor will then disappear. Vehicles charged with the new battery will be about as noiseless as it will be practicable to make any rapidly moving thing.[175]

June 27, 1909, *Oakland (Calif.) Tribune*

I don't think nature would be so unkind as to withhold the secret of a good storage battery if a real earnest hunt for it is made. I am going to hunt.[176]

Circa 1910–19

The light storage battery, however, will make it possible to build a light electric automobile which can carry a great deal of power and go long distances without being recharged. That is the sole mission of such a battery, and it will not be long before we will have light electric automobiles that everyone can afford and anybody can handle.[177]

June 6, 1914, *New York Times*

On Rubber Research

As a U.S. Naval Consulting Board advisor during World War I, Edison learned how much of the America depended on natural rubber to support the war effort. Following the war, with the support of Henry Ford and Harvey Firestone, Edison launched into a campaign to find a domestic source of rubber to be used in the event of war. His search continued until his death.

Florida will manufacture rubber yet.[178]

April 7, 1925, *Fort Myers (Fla.) Press*

Americans must awake to the necessity of doing something to relieve the grip now held by foreign interests on a commodity so important to our welfare and prosperity.[179]

April 7, 1925, *Fort Myers (Fla.) Press*

Henry Ford is a sort of partner of mine in this business, and we're going to work together on the experiment. I hope that I will be able to drive the first Ford equipped with tires made from the domestic rubber out of the shops before so very long.[180]

February 27, 1927, *New York Times*

My whole idea behind this experiment is to produce a crop that will prove a boon to the southern farmer. I want nothing out of it in a financial way. The south must have a crop that will take the place of cotton, if the south is ever to come into a period of prosperity.[181]

March 18, 1927, *Venice (Fla.) News*

I realize that one of the greatest needs of the United States today is an American-grown rubber of commercial value. I am convinced it can be had and am going to do my bit to see it through. [182]

March 20, 1927, *New York Times*

[T]hey are sometimes as bad as humans to handle.[183]

On rubber plants. July 27, 1927, *New York Times*

I am not working to cheapen rubber. . . . I believe enough rubber can be grown in the U.S. to pull us through [in case of war]. The price is not serious in such a case.[184]

August 1, 1927, *Time*

We can't compete commercially with the tropics in the production of rubber.[185]

November 26, 1927, *Literary Digest*

We must find something which will produce enough rubber within a year after the beginning of war, to replace the year's supply which we normally have on hand; something which won't be occupying valuable land meantime, or tying up capital, or requiring a continuous expenditure of money without any return.[186]

November 26, 1927, *Literary Digest*

The United States requires and independent rubber supply, easily accessible. We all hope that we shall never see another war. But suppose we do, and our rubber supply is far overseas, in foreign hands? Modern armies—future armies—will travel on rubber. Every need of our times demands rubber. So I am trying to assure a domestic supply of war rubber for the United States—if the time should come when it is needed. Yes, that is my greatest problem now.[187]

August 12, 1928, *New York Times*

I believe those states bordering on the Gulf of Mexico can grow plant rubber with profit to the farmer in case of war prices, but it might be possible in the future to grow rubber and compete with the tropics.[188]

February 11, 1929, *Tampa (Fla.) Tribune*

I would like to correct the impression that I am working on synthetic rubber by stating that it is real rubber. I aim to produce only in an emergency such as a war.[189]

February 17, 1920, *New York Times*

Give me five more years and the United States will have a rubber crop which can be utilized in less than twelve months' time.[190]

March 18, 1930, *New York Times*

I have just made a great discovery in this giant goldenrod plant. I hope to cross-breed it with a variety containing a high percentage of latex to produce an emergency rubber supply for the United States which farmers can grow and harvest in six months.[191]

April 12, 1930, *New York Times*

Maybe I will have to do a little Burbanking with my plants.[192]

Referencing the work of his friend, the American botanist Luther Burbank.
April 12, 1930, *New York Times*

I want to get something the farmers can raise for a cash crop. There's something wrong, the farmer doesn't seem to make much money. I notice they import all their food down here [in Florida].[193]

April 13, 1930, *New York Times*

Let me say for your information, that the pollen of goldenrod is carried entirely by insects. . . . I am informed that no cases of pollen fever are known.[194]

> Responding to a campaign to eliminate goldenrod.
> September 26, 1930, *New York Times*

I don't think the Moscow report is true. I don't believe one can get good rubber from oil. I would even go so far as to say oil rubber is a fake.[195]

> May 8, 1931, *New York Times*

The ingredients [for synthetic rubber] cost more than the rubber which makes the experiments impractical. The great German dye trust has experimented with synthetic rubber and has taken out many patents but none of them is practical.[196]

> May 8, 1931, *Fort Myers (Fla.) Press*

I believe it can be done—and I'm going to try to do it.[197]

> Edison was convinced he could find a domestic source for rubber
> for use in wartime. Circa late 1920s or early 1930s

On Inventions of Others
and the Machine Age

Edison believed electric cars would eventually supersede gasoline-powered vehicles. In 1910, he and his friend Colonel E. M. Bailey powered this Bailey Electric vehicle with an Edison battery. *Courtesy of the Thomas Edison National Historical Park, 14.625.11.*

When it came to the innovations of other inventors, Edison was either completely supportive or extremely critical. If he had a connection to the industrial application of an innovation, he generally promoted it. This was the case with electric trains and automobiles. He disparaged inventions that he feared would compete with his own. Though his company eventually produced radios, he criticized the industry because he rightly believed radio would interfere with phonograph sales. Though he was in his eighties when television was pioneered, he felt threatened by the new technology, decades before it would be in everyday use.

On the Typewriter

This typewriter proved a difficult thing to make commercial. The alignment of the letters was awful. . . . The typewriter I got into commercial shape is now known as the Remington.[1]

Circa 1880s

I made the first dozen typewriters, and it took me seven years to convince the public they wanted them and then another three years to sell them.[2]

October 18, 1923, *Boston Daily Globe*

On Airplanes

A flying machine? Oh, yes, I'm going to do the best I can toward solving that ancient problem.[3]

June 29, 1888, *New York Sun*

If I am able to construct the kind of machine they want I shall have practically solved the long-mooted question of the possibility of aerial navigation.[4]

June 29, 1888, *New York Sun*

Almost all persons when they think of aerial navigation imagine the necessity of rising to a great height. But why do this? Why not go along the road at an elevation of about ten feet? Of course, when necessary we could rise higher, but, as a rule a few feet above the ground would answer all the purpose of aerial navigation.[5]

June 29, 1888, *New York Sun*

I believe this [aerial navigation] will be the popular mode of travel in the future.[6]

June 29, 1888, *New York Sun*

I'm awfully afraid [navigation through the air] isn't [possible] unless you can get up an engine of about fifty horse-power out of aluminum, say, to weigh about forty pounds.[7]

February 11, 1888, *Chicago Mail*

I would construct actual ships of the air—yachts, schooners, and brigatines—which would tack and gibe and sail before the wind. My idea is that the lifting power for these air ships should be gas stored in the sales. . . . I am no flying machine crank, but this is a theory which I am surprised has not occurred to those who are devoting serious thought and large expenditure to the solution of this problem.[8]

December 25, 1895, *Times of India*

When an airship is made it will not be in the form of a balloon. It will be a mechanical contrivance, which will be raised by means of a very powerful motor, which must be made of very light weight. . . . I am not, however, figuring on inventing an airship. I prefer to devote my time to objects which have some commercial value. At the best, airships would only be toys.[9]

May 11, 1897, *Arkansas Democrat*

In the present state of sciences, there are no known facts by which one could predict any commercial future for aerial navigation.[10]

August 11, 1902, *Brooklyn Daily Eagle*

If you start building engines in the sky, you'll go crazy. There's plenty to be invented within three feet of the ground. No need going to the moon. An invention is no good unless it's commercial and people are willing to pay for it. There's no money in sky engines, see?[11]

Circa 1903, quoted in September 1932, *Harper's Magazine*

The time has not come for the production of an airship of use commercially; capable of making regular trips from a given place to a given place. One will never be built until a new motive power is produced.[12]

April 1904, *Outing*

Oh, yes, undoubtedly we shall [fly through the air]; it's bound to come. It won't be the aeroplane, however, and it won't be the dirigible balloon.[13]

October 11, 1908, *New York Times*

The aeroplane is a remarkable experiment, but it comes as a theory, controlled by the man who has that theory, and it is not yet adjusted to universal uses. But I firmly believe that some day we shall know how to fly; it's only a matter of inventing a compact engine with sufficient power. It will be done.[14]

October 11, 1908, *New York Times*

The aeroplane of the Wright brothers depends too much on the personal equation. Place some other man in that aeroplane and it would not work.[15]

October 15, 1908, *Fort Myers (Fla.) Press*

I am firmly convinced that the time is near at hand when it will be possible to sail through the air as easily and as safely as we now go by land or sea.[16]

October 15, 1908, *Fort Myers (Fla.) Press*

No, I can't see where the great benefit to humanity, to the world, is coming from flying through the air. . . . Flying is fine and beautiful and sensational, but I'd rather perfect my cement house for the dollar-a-day, or the dollar-an-a-half-a-day man, than fly from here to San Francisco and back.[17]

October 1909, unknown newspaper

Oh, of course I've been interested in what [the Wright Brothers and Glenn Hammond Curtiss] are doing. But they have a heap to learn yet. They will have to get the secret from the birds before they really can hope to fly.[18]

October 1909, unknown newspaper

Every morning I get a stack of letters a foot high from aeroplane cranks who are worrying their heads off because I have neglected to manifest an interest in aviation.[19]

December 1, 1910, *New York Times*

I admit that I have a little patent along aeroplane lines, but please don't publish anything about it, for really I have too much to do to become interested in the navigation of the air. It is a simple little thing that I sent along to Washington with some other patents a long time ago.[20]

December 1, 1910, *New York Times*

I believe aerial navigation will become practical.[21]

January 19, 1911, *Wellsboro (Pa.) Gazette*

I never cared to go up in the air.[22]

February 12, 1913, *New York Times*

I am trying to get a battery of extremely light weight, and some day aeroplanes may accomplish the feat of the bee.[23]

June 4, 1914, *New York Times*

It has been said that the light storage battery will make possible the operation of aeroplanes by electricity. That is impossible. Aeroplanes will never be operated by electricity.[24]

June 6, 1914, *New York Times*

I don't know anything about airplanes and haven't taken any interest in aviation. I shall wait for a helicopter, if I ever do go up. I am of the earth, earthy.[25]

February 16, 1926, *Fort Myers (Fla.) Tropical News*

Whether the airplane and flying will have a comparable general effect [to societal changes made by radio and the automobile] I doubt. Children will not get accustomed to flight as they have become accustomed to automobiling. Many years must elapse, I think, before airplanes will be so developed that they can come into general use as motor-cars have. The present types of flying machines have their utility, but only in the hands of experts.[26]

January 1927, *Forum*

Stunts, which always follow pioneering of new things.[27]

On transatlantic flights. August 13, 1927, *New York Times*

Take no interest in airplanes until they're further perfected.[28]

Advice to Henry Ford. January 12, 1928, *New York Times*

[I] might try some flying with an old-timer who would not stunt.[29]

September 19, 1930, *New York Times*

Well, you've got them so now that they will do anything but chew tobacco.[30]

On the autogiro, a rotary winged aircraft.
September 22, 1930, *New York Times*

They probably can never be so universal as cars, but now they are only in their infancy.[31]

January 1931, *Review of Reviews*

On Radio

It may be done, but how are we going to know whether a man or a chimpanzee receives our message?[32]

Regarding the possibility of radio transmissions to Mars. February 12, 1920, *New York Times*

I don't think the radio will ever replace the phonograph.[33]

July 19, 1922, *New York Times*

The vacuum tube is one of the things I am most interested in. This plitron tube should lead to a greater advance in radio. It doesn't look to me as if you could transmit power with it, but may be you can under certain conditions. It opens another big field.[34]

October 19, 1922, *New York Times*

In three years [radio] will be such a cutthroat business that nobody will make any money . . . you'll get busted if you get into it.[35]

Advice given to sons Charles and Theodore Edison, whose venture into radio was, indeed, too late. Circa late 1920s.

You'll never take static out of the air while these great plants function. You can't stop a rainstorm with an umbrella you know.[36]

May 22, 1925, *New York Times*

Why, I don't know what to say. This is the first time I ever spoke into one of these things. Good night.[37]

> Edison's first radio address. May 20, 1926, *New York Times*

The radio is a big and new thing but after the novelty has worn off the phonograph will reclaim its own.[38]

> September 23, 1926, *New York Times*

Electricity in its various manifestations, the steam-engine and railroad, and to an even greater degree the internal combustion engine and its child, the automobile, have had a great developing effect upon the minds of youth. Radio now serves a similar purpose.[39]

> January 1927, *Forum*

Radio is good for current events, and every family that can afford one should use it, but as for music, it is distorted and not enjoyable. The phonograph is coming back as fast.[40]

> February 12, 1927, *New York Times*

Despite the fact that the radio is far from a stage of perfection and is still in the infancy class, it is a mighty good thing for those who like it. It is beneficial to the young people because it is constructive and gives them something to think and read about. It also tends to keep the young folks at home at night—a mighty hard thing to do in these modern times.[41]

> March 7, 1927, *St. Petersburg (Fla.) Times*

Radio is a mighty good thing for those who like it.[42]

> June 16, 1928, *New York Times*

I wish I could invite all of you to have some birthday cake, but unfortunately we can't eat by radio—just yet. I'll have to work on that problem.[43]

> February 11, 1929, *Tampa (Fla.) Tribune*

As I sit here in my laboratory at Orange, N.J., talking to you, my friends of the National Electrical Light Association, at San Francisco, and to you, my friends at the World Power Conference, assembled in Berlin, I rejoice in the wonderful advance that has been made in the art of electrical communication.[44]

June 19, 1930, *New York Times*

Radio, at the present time, is a bit too delicate . . . I think it would be better to devise something that is less involved.[45]

November 26, 1930, *New York Times*

There isn't ten percent of the interest in radio that there was last year. It's a highly complicated machine in the hands of people who know nothing about it.[46]

October 4, 1931, *Time*

No dealers have made any money out of it. It isn't a commercial machine because it is too complicated. Reports from 4,000 Edison dealers who have handled radios show that they are rapidly abandoning it.[47]

October 4, 1931, *Time*

It's awful—I don't see how they can listen to it.[48]

October 4, 1931, *Time*

On Automobiles

[T]he making of a practical and economic motor is merely a matter of detail. . . . I should say that by 1890 at the latest we shall see [electric automobiles] running noiselessly and swiftly in every large city, doing the work of thousands of horses without noise, smoke or dust and at less expense.[49]

December 22, 1886, *Brooklyn Eagle*

Talking of horseless vehicles, by the way, suggests to my mind that the horse is doomed.[50]

November 27, 1895, *Electrical Review*

Ten years from now you will be able to buy a horseless vehicle for what you would have to pay to-day for a wagon and a pair of horses. The money spent in the keeping of the horses will be saved, and the danger to life will be much reduced.[51]

October 10, 1895, *Philadelphia Bulletin*

As it looks at present, it would seem more likely that [horseless carriages] will be run by gasolene or naphtha motor of some kind. It is quite possible, however, that an electrical storage battery will be discovered which will prove more economical.[52]

October 10, 1895, *Philadelphia Bulletin*. (Naphtha is a petroleum product.)

I have solved the automobile problem. I can make an automobile that will go so fast a man cannot sit in it. The speed of storage battery machines is unlimited.[53]

May 30, 1902, *Rochester (N.Y.) Times*

We have put the horse out of business.[54]

May 29, 1902, *New York World*

The electric carriage of the near future will, in my opinion, not only supersede other types of automobiles, but it will be built and run on such practical lines that accidents will soon become things of the past.[55]

June 27, 1902, *Brooklyn Daily Eagle*

The electric carriage will be practically noiseless and easily stopped in an emergency. Above all, it will need no irresponsible chauffeur.[56]

July 1902, *North American Review*

In fifteen years from now the horse will be a curiosity; we shall be paying 50 cents to look at him in side shows.[57]

October 21, 1906, *New York Times*

I am having a touring automobile built on the lines of the gasoline car, but fitted with one of my batteries. . . . With one charging the battery will take it under the most unfavorable conditions 200 miles or, under favorable conditions 125 miles, with four people, at a speed of thirty miles an hour. . . . This will practically do away with breakdowns, and will mean that every man can be his own chauffer.[58]

February 11, 1907, *New York Times*

There is absolutely no reason why horses should be allowed within the city limits, for, between the gasoline and electric car, no room is left for them.[59]

June 4, 1910, *South Jersey Republican*

"Horseless carriages" we used to call automobiles. And all of us have seen crowds gathered around them on the street, looking at them with wonder. The automobile has been one of the things which have made the city grow so rapidly. . . . We have only barely begun really to investigate this problem of traffic. It has caught us unawares, as things always do.[60]

December 1926, *Forum*

Marvelous, wonderful! I don't see how Henry can do it at such a price.[61]

On Henry Ford's new Model A automobile.
December 20, 1927, *New York Times*

I'll keep it till it rusts away.[62]

Referring to his old model T Ford.
December 20, 1927, *New York Times*

On Electric Trains

There is no doubt that railroads will be run by this electricity before very long.[63]

April 25, 1880, *Denver Tribune*

I believe that within thirty years nearly all railways will discard steam locomotives and adopt electric motors.[64]

August 11, 1902, *Brooklyn Daily Eagle*

On Television

[Television is] possible, but of very little general value. It's a stunt.[65]

February 12, 1927, *New York Times*

It will be hardly practical for General use.[66]

1929 interview.

Locomotives are pretty well developed, but you wouldn't want to buy one and have it in your house, would you? Television is like that.[67]

December 24, 1930, *New York Times*

On Listening Devices

I could fix a machine in the wall, and by resonations any conversation in a room could be recorded. Political secrets and the machinations of Wall Street pools might be brought to light, and the account charged to the devil. Kind parents could lie in bed and hear all the spooney courtship of their daughters and lovers.[68]

March 16, 1878, *Scientific American Supplement*

On Radar

Thus far we have converted sound into light and light into sound. There is no reason for not being able to solve the artificial eye [to see through fog].[69]

October 3, 1930, *New York Times*

On Machines and the Machine Age

Without machinery society would drift into the condition of master and slave.[70]

November 5, 1887, *Scientific American*

The wealth of the modern world has been made by labor-saving machinery; but no matter how fast it may be increased or how often it may be multiplied there will always be plenty of work for all, for the workmen set loose by the invention of a new labor-saving machine soon find employment in some other field of usefulness. Wealth is the product of labor, and the machine that saves the latter also saves the former, and adds to the general sum of wealth.[71]

1890 interview

This is the machine age; wherever man's power or horse power can be eliminated, speed, accuracy, and economy are the result. Much as machinery does for us to-day, I confidently believe that it is going to be called on to do more and more. Eventually, nearly everything in this world will be got down to a mechanical basis. That will mean that we can live easier and cheaper.[72]

May 15, 1910, *New York Times*

But so far as an Automatic Age is concerned, I have no hesitancy in saying that it's coming. No piece of machinery manufactured is more than 10 per cent perfect. As the years go on this will be improved upon tremendously; more automatic machines will be devised, and the articles of comfort and luxury will be produced in enormous numbers at such small cost that all classes will be able to enjoy the benefits of them.[73]

May 15, 1910, *New York Times*

Machinery is the salvation of the American manufacturer, and will result in the United States leading the world commercially in a few years.[74]

January 11, 1914, *New York Times*

Men are more efficient than they were fifty years ago. We have more machinery now, and some day all our work will be done by machinery. Then we'll be more efficient still. The men will be paid high wages and will simply direct the machines. We'll even have automatic machinery make the machines.[75]

February 12, 1920, *New York Times*

Everything in the world should be done by machinery and measurements.[76]

July 4, 1926, *New York Times*

The machine has been the human being's most effective means of escape from human bondage.[77]

October 1926, *Forum*

Not through fewer, but through more machines, not through simpler, but through more complex machines, will men find avenues that lead into lives of greater opportunity and happiness.[78]

October 1926, *Forum*

We must substitute motors for muscles in a thousand new ways. A human brain is greatly hampered in its usefulness if it has only two hands of a man to do its bidding. There are machines each of which can do the work of a multitude of hands when directed by one brain. That's efficiency.[79]

Therefore no man should rail against machine-power. It is application of good fertilizer to industry.[80]

We have scarcely seen the start of the mechanical age, and after it is under way we shall discover that it is all such a mental age as never has been known before.[81]

While slave labor was available, the brains of men in general were not stimulated to the creation of machinery. This was more disastrous in its general effects than was realized by the majority, even of those opposed to slavery. It meant that human beings all along the line, not only the enslaved but the enslavers, could not be released by machinery for efforts better and more elevating.[82]

There is no common-sense in the cry that machine work is monotonous.[83]

Human slavery will not have been fully abolished until every task now accomplished by human hands is turned out by some machine.[84]

On the Sciences

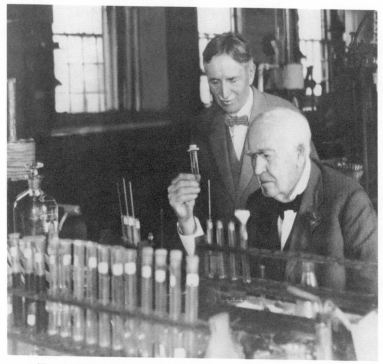

Thomas Edison shows a specimen of natural, domestically produced rubber to Harvey Firestone at his Fort Myers, Florida, laboratory on March 15, 1931. *Courtesy of the Thomas Edison National Historical Park, 14.400.70.*

Edison insisted that he was not a pure scientist, one who made discoveries for the sake of science alone. He regarded science as a tool, one of many he used in the pursuit of useful inventions. A true empiricist, he believed everything should be learned from personal experience, not from theory or scientific laws.

Edison's thoughts on science were greatly influenced by Charles Darwin. Edison admired the English naturalist whose revolutionary ideas of evolution and natural selection shook the scientific world. In 1877, the inventor wrote Darwin offering to send insect samples.[1] Darwin did not reply.

On Science and Nature

I have freely laid myself open to criticism by presuming to believe in the capacity of Nature to supply a new form of energy, which presumption rests upon experiment, it is fair that my critics should also back up their assertions by experiment, and give me an equal chance as a critic.[2]

February 12, 1876, *Scientific American*

[E]vidently Darwin has it right. [Flowers] make themselves pretty to attract the insect world who are the transportation agents of their pollen, pollen freight via Bee line.[3]

July 12, 1885, diary entry

I do not believe that matter is inert, acted upon by an outside force. To me it seems that every atom is possessed of a certain amount of primitive intelligence. Look at the thousand ways in which atoms of hydrogen combine with those of other elements, forming the most diverse substances. Do you mean to say that they do this without intelligence? When they get together in certain forms they make animals of the lower orders. Finally they combine in man, who represents the total intelligence of all atoms.[4]

July 16, 1885, *Salt Lake City Democrat*

The intelligence of man is, I take it, the sum of the intelligences of the atoms of which he is composed. Every atom has an intelligent power of selection and is always striving to get into harmonious relations with other atoms. The human body, I think, is maintained in its integrity by the intelligent persistence of its atoms, or rather by an agreement between the atoms so to persist. When the harmonious adjustment is destroyed the man dies, and the atoms seek other relations.[5]

November 8, 1891, *New York Herald*

Man, therefore, may be regarded in some sort as a microcosm of atoms agreeing to constitute his life as long as order and discipline can be maintained. But of course, there is disaffection, rebellion and anarchy, leading eventually to death, and through death to new forms of life. For life I regard as indestructible. That is, if matter is indestructible.[6]

November 8, 1891, *New York Herald*

I believe there are only two things in the universe—matter and energy. Matter I can understand to be intelligent, for man himself I regard as so much matter. Energy I know can take various forms and manifest itself in different ways. I can understand also that it works not only upon, but through matter. What this matter is, what this energy is, I do not know.[7]

November 8, 1891, *New York Herald*

I do not regard myself as a pure scientist, as so many persons have insisted that I am. I do not search for the laws of nature, and have made no great discoveries of such laws. I do not study science as Newton and Kepler and Faraday and Henry studied it, simply for the purpose of learning truth. I am only a professional inventor. My studies and experiments have been conducted entirely with the object of inventing that which will have commercial utility. I suppose I might be called a scientific inventor, although really there is no distinction.[8]

Edison didn't see himself in the same league as Sir Isaac Newton, Johannes Kepler, Michael Faraday, and Joseph Henry.
July 8, 1893, *Scientific American*

The thing we call nature seems very cruel at times.[9]
December 1, 1898, letter to his wife, Mina

What I want now is a chance to get out in the woods and see the birds and flowers. I like to study them, and the rocks and ferns and other things in the woods; it rests me.[10]
August 4, 1905, *New York Times*

I have always found [nature] ready for any emergency, and based on this confidence that she has never betrayed, I communed diligently with her.[11]
October 21, 1906, *New York Times*

But science works slowly, even though it does discover the marvelous, the unlooked-for.[12]
May 19, 1907, *New York Times*

During my forty years of experiment and observation I have come across some things which were intensely interesting from a scientific point of view. These things however, I could not investigate, since I limited myself to commercial possibilities.

Now I shall take them up, or at least some of them, and work purely for the sake of scientific knowledge; that is, after I have finished with the things I have under way.[13]
May 19, 1907, *New York Times*

Everything, anything, is possible; the world is a vast storehouse of undiscovered energy.[14]

October 11, 1908, *New York Times*

There is a great distinction, however between the scientific experiment that accomplishes its end and the practical adaptation of it to humanity at large. We read of wonderful things being done experimentally, but whether they can be accomplished practically is another matter.[15]

October 11, 1908, *New York Times*

There is always a technical investigation of a new idea in science that is reliable and can be trusted.[16]

October 11, 1908, *New York Times*

The indications of scientific discovery are so amazing and the corelation of all its various forms of progress are so intimate that we just begin to find out how feeble we really are to cope with them. Look at bacteriology, what wonderful advancement there is in it.[17]

October 11, 1908, *New York Times*

But careful, exact, scientific investigation will reveal new things, and accident will reveal others. Great forces, material forces, undoubtedly exist, under our very noses, of which we know at present absolutely nothing.[18]

October 2, 1910, *New York Times*

The earth, the air, the sea, and above all, space, contain all sorts of things of which we now know absolutely nothing. There is a fascinating realm of speculation there, and speculations, sometimes, is a dangerous thing. It will lead other honest folks astray.[19]

October 2, 1910, *New York Times*

They talk about the danger of working with chemicals, but chemicals are nowhere near as dangerous as bacteria.[20]

February 1917, *New York Sun*

I believe that life, like matter, is indestructible. There has always been a certain amount of life on this world and there will always be the same amount. You cannot create life; you cannot destroy life; you cannot multiply life.[21]

October 30, 1920, *Scientific American*

I am interested in botany and believe that plant breeders should receive encouragement in the form of federal protection.[22]

May 30, 1930, *Fort Myers (Fla.) Press*

I am not I—I am not an individual—I am an aggregate of cells, as for instance, New York City is an aggregate of individuals.[23]

April 1931, *Golden Book Magazine*

At the time I experimented on the incandescent lamp I did not understand Ohm's law. Moreover, I do not want to understand Ohm's law. It would prevent me from experimenting.[24]

On the law describing the relationship between power, voltage, current, and resistance. Circa 1870s

On Scientists

They are a pleasant set of fellows, these scientific men; just chock full of fun as they can be. They don't care for good clothes though.[25]

April 19, 1878, *Washington Post*

Anything that is not a commercial success, of course, I won't bother with. The scientific men abroad were greatly surprised that I was not more of a scientist, in the higher sense of the phrase. They could not understand that I am between the scientific man and the public.[26]

October 7, 1889, New York Herald

There is as much difference between an inventor and a scientist as there is between an explorer and a geographer. Of course inventors may be scientists. And explorers may write geographies, but they seldom do. The inventor discovers things and then the scientist steps in and tells or tries to tell what it is that has been discovered. The telephone is an invention. Its principle was discovered. Scientists are still endeavoring to tell how it works. We all know it works—that is all an inventor cares to know; but a scientist wants to know why and how it works.[27]

May 13, 1891, Chicago Globe

No one can ever be a great scientist who is not as much up-to-date on the questions of the day as he is on developments in his own specialty.[28]

August 1, 1930, New York Times

That is the way the scientist has to work. He must teach himself to observe things that the ordinary person would pass by without notice.[29]

January 1931, Review of Reviews

On Chemistry

I think freckles on the skin are due to some salt of Iron, sunlight brings them out by reducing them from high to low state of oxidation. Perhaps with a powerful magnet applied for some time and then with the proper chemicals, these mudholes of beauty might be removed.[30]

Playful musing from his July 12, 1885, diary entry

I believe there is one primordial element to which all the elements we know at present are finally reducible. I believe that the discovery of this primordial element is within the possibilities of science.[31]

November 29, 1896, *New York Herald*

[I]t is a thing which should certainly be handled with the greatest caution.[32]

Statement following damage to his own eye and the death of an assistant from radium exposure. July 6, 1905, *Fort Myers (Fla.) Press*

The biggest value to the world has come from chemical discovery, if we set aside the work of the medical men. It has been a very fruitful period in chemistry.[33]

October 11, 1914, *New York Times*

I have always been more interested in chemistry than physics, but I got into electricity and stuck there for a long time because there were certain things to be accomplished in that field. Oddly enough it was the war that gave me the chance I had been looking for to putter with chemicals.[34]

February 1917, *New York Sun*

It is possible to make synthetic milk, and it would probably be more pure than the milk we now have. I see great advances just ahead in the field of chemistry. There are enormous opportunities.[35]

February 12, 1921, *New York Times*

On Chemists

Trouble with these damn graduate Chemists, they think they know everything. I can't tell them anything.[36]

Circa 1920s

On Alternative Energy

When I was on shipboard coming over [from Europe] I used to sit on the deck by the hour and watch the waves. It made me positively savage to think of all that power going to waste. But we'll chain it up one of these days along with Niagara Falls and the winds. That will be the electric millennium.[37]

September 1, 1889, *Levant Herald*

Niagara [Falls] is the greatest storage battery in the world.[38]

November 9, 1889, *Brooklyn Daily Eagle*

So long as the sun shines, man will be able to develop power in abundance, no matter whether there are coal mines or not, and when its rays have been quenched power will no longer be needed. It is from the sun in fact that we get all our power now, for coal is only stored sunshine and the rays that fall upon the earth's surface to-day are as full of power as ever they were.[39]

November 22, 1896, *Philadelphia Press*

I know of no good reason whatever why we should not get our steam and electric power direct from the earth's internal fires. . . . Nature makes steam for herself.[40]

November 22, 1896, *Philadelphia Press*

Natural resources are simple if we will only take advantage of them. Men say that we shall be out of fuel for heat and power production in a comparatively short time, just because they foresee the possible exhaustion of the coal supply. But there need be no alarm, even in behalf of the future generations. It is true that, in time, the available coal will all be gone, providing its burning is continued. But while that is being done, Nature will be making more fuel, if men will only encourage her a little, and, as a business, this encouragement will be quite as profitable as most occupations.[41]

January 1, 1897, *Denver Rocky Mountain News*

What will happen [when the country runs out of coal]? Unless science takes hold of this mighty problem and finds something, some force, that will run our engines and light and heat our houses, as a substitute for coal, it takes no prophet to foresee that our grandchildren will be forced to live in a world that is destitute of heat and light, except as these blessings are given to them by the sun. What is to be done?[42]

May 19, 1907, *New York Times*

We haven't half demonstrated the forces of water power yet as a universal energy in engineering.[43]

October 11, 1908, *New York Times*

No, the energy of the tides is not great enough to generate sufficient motive power. I don't believe that will work out.[44]

October 11, 1908, *New York Times*

Quite probably there is motive power in the light of the sun as it reaches the earth that may be utilized some day.[45]

October 11, 1908, *New York Times*

Among the many problems which await solution in the future, one of the most important is to get the full value out of fuel. This wastefulness of our present method of combustion is tremendous.[46]

January 14, 1910, *Seattle Star*

Some day some fellow will invent a way of concentrating and storing up sunshine to use instead of this old, absurd Prometheus scheme of fire. I'll do the trick myself if some one doesn't get at it.[47]

Circa 1914

There must surely come a time when heat and power will be stored in unlimited quantities in every community, all gathered by natural forces. Electricity ought to be as cheap as oxygen, for it cannot be destroyed.[48]

Circa 1914

Sunshine is spread out thin and so is electricity. Now the trick was, you see, to concentrate the juice and liberate it as you need it. The old-fashioned way inaugurated by Jove, of letting it off in a clap of thunder is dangerous, disconcerting and wasteful. It doesn't fetch up anywhere.[49]

Circa 1914

Sunshine is a form of energy, and the winds and the tides are manifestations of energy. Do we use them?

Oh, no; we burn up wood and coal, as renters burn up the front fence for fuel. We live like squatters, not as if we owned the property.[50]

Circa 1914

Power from the sun is not only possible, but we are already using it.[51]

September 21, 1924, *Boston Daily Globe*

Water power seems to have been adopted as the shibboleth of politics in this campaign. . . . Water power, then as now, will be quite inadequate to meet the demands for electrical power, and posterity will have to develop other substitutes.[52]

November 2, 1928, *New York Times*

[A] great deal more fuss is being made over hydro-electric power than its intrinsic value warrants. Water power is a political issue, not a business one. It can never at the best mean very much to us except as something to talk about.[53]

1929, *Mining and Metallurgy*

On Astronomy, the Universe and Life on Other Planets

I will try and call at your place and see how you peek at the almighty through a keyhole.[54]

August 8, 1877, letter to Henry Draper

Oh no; there would be no money in such an invention. I never bother with anything that doesn't mean dollars and cents. If I were convinced that upon discovering the first moon to Saturn, I could dispose of the article at a good round profit, I should leave no effort undone to find the missing planet.[55]

July 30, 1888, *Pittsburgh Times*

By the use of instruments every change could be recorded, and by the use of the telephone all sounds produced on the sun could be heard on our planet.[56]

September 7, 1890, *Quincy (Ill.) Daily Whig*

There are the most wonderful things going on in the sun's spots all the time. Didn't you ever see them? Why, they are beautiful. . . . Awful things happen up there. You can see them every day with my telescope.[57]

June 14, 1891, *Chicago Tribune*

I can hear them with this telephone. The next time there is any violent change in the sun's spots which disturbs the magnetic lines or earth I shall know it.[58]

June 14 1891, *Chicago Tribune*

There, there, you're getting over my head. My province goes as high as the top of Mount Everest. When you get above that you must consult others.[59]

On the possibility of communication with other planets
January 7, 1906, *New York Times*

Communication with other worlds has been suggested. I think we had better stick to this world and find out something about it before we call up our neighbors. They might make us ashamed of ourselves.[60]

January 28, 1910, *Decatur (Ill.) Review*

[W]e can't grasp [the universe as a complete whole]. We may be like cells in a great big body. Everything is held together by wonderful laws.[61]

July 1911, *Century Magazine*

When we consider that there is apparently no end to space, that every time we increase the power of our telescopes we see more unknown suns of gigantic size, then why should there not be the infinitely little?[62]

July 1911, *Century Magazine*

I believe that the force of energy we call life came from some other planet, or, at any rate, from somewhere in the great spaces beyond us. We know that life could not have been here when the earth was a molten mass. Later life was here. Was it created here or did it come here? I believe it came here, just as electricity comes from the sun.[63]

October 15, 1926, *New York Times*

I hear they have discovered a new planet. That's wonderful. The present state of knowledge is in infancy and man is only beginning to touch the vast realms of science. There is hope for civilization as long as man keeps experimenting and searching into the unknown.[64]

March 17, 1930, *Fort Myers (Fla.) Press*

On Work and Business

Edison even worked on his birthday. In this February 11, 1921, photograph,
the inventor punched a time clock at his West Orange, New Jersey, laboratory.
Courtesy of the Thomas Edison National Historical Park, 14.220.1.

Thomas Edison believed in the power of hard work and he hoped to inspire others with his quips on the subject. Statements like "Genius is ninety-nine percent perspiration and one percent inspiration" went through many versions while he experimented with the best way to express himself.

Edison's love of work did not coincide with a love of money. Dollars were not an end unto themselves, but merely a means to continue his experiments and inventing. Edison opposed the gold standard, which he felt unfairly restricted the flow of currency. During the turbulent times of multiple recessions and the Great Depression, he always encouraged people to persevere.

On Work

I need more money. I am going to do things and I must have more money. There is no reason why I cannot get a regular job and work during the time I am not studying.[1]

Negotiation with his parents for a job when he was twelve.
Circa 1860s

Genius is all bosh. Clean hard work is what does the business.[2]
August 29, 1878, *New York Sun*

I work nights in order to escape from visitors. It is very nice and still here at nights! I fled out to this uninhabited spot so as to be alone, ... when I would see a lot of heads coming over the hill from the depot—amiable and delightful people, ministers, teachers, scholars, farmers, doctors, who wanted to know, you know, and those excellent people would just devour two straight hours of my time and pay for it with expressions of admirations.[3]
December 28, 1878, *New York Graphic*

Rest! Why, I have come down here [to Florida] to work harder, if anything. I will tell you how I rest; I am working on at least six or seven ideas. When I get tired of one I switch off onto another and alternate to such an extent that I have a constant succession of new and pleasurable efforts.[4]

March 28, 1887, *New York World*

Never look at the clock.[5]

October 2, 1890, *Quincy (Ill.) Daily Whig*

That is my idea—to work on at what best pleases me, to let the object be great enough, and when that is done with to begin with something else.[6]

July 26, 1891, *New York Journal*

Work that interests one is a delight.[7]

July 26, 1891, *New York Journal*

I have got so much to do and life is so short, that I have got to hustle.[8]

July 1893, *Review of Reviews*

There are just two things a man should do: Obtain an education . . . and never mind the clock. The last is an axiom he should always have in his mind. He may miss many social engagements, but it is a sure road to success.[9]

December 31, 1894, *Ottumwa (Iowa) Courier*

What counts in the world is the man who produces, not the man who talks. I found out a long time ago that if you talked about a thing it wasn't remembered, but if you produced it was remembered.[10]

May 22, 1896, *New York Journal*

Two per cent is genius and 98 per cent is hard work.[11]

> On his definition of genius. April 1898, *Review of Reviews*

Genius is not inspired. Inspiration is perspiration.[12]

> April 1898, *Review of Reviews*

I scarcely get any sleep as everything has to be attended to by me. . . . Had I an intelligent assistant I could have come but while I am trying to obtain such a man I have not yet succeeded. . . . [I]t will be impossible to find a man.[13]

> December 1, 1898, letter to his wife, Mina

Hell! there *ain't* no rules around here! We are tryin' to accomplish somep'n![14]

> Circa 1903, quoted in September 1932, *Harper's Magazine*

Then again a lot of people think I have done things because of some "genius" that I've got. That too is not true. Any other bright-minded fellow can accomplish just as much if he will stick like hell and remember that nothing that's any good works by itself.[15]

> Circa 1903, quoted in September 1932, *Harper's Magazine*

Genius is one per cent inspiration, ninety-nine per cent perspiration. Yes, sir, it's mostly *hard work*.[16]

> Circa 1903, quoted in September 1932, *Harper's Magazine*

All things come to those who hustle while they wait.[17]

> July 9, 1904, *American Eagle*

Genius is perspiration.[18]

> Circa 1907

Agreeable work never hurt any one, and I am no exception to the rule.[19]

> February 12, 1911, *New York Times*

After a while I tired of this work [of farming]. Hoeing corn in a hot sun is unattractive, and I did not wonder that boys had left the farm for the city.[20]

Circa 1911

I think the time has just arrive when the menial phases of existence may be said to be upon the verge of disappearing.[21]

October 12, 1912, *Good Housekeeping*

Some men might get sick and tired of work, but . . . I'm tired of being idle. It's eating and sleeping and walking around. If this satisfies any able-bodied, active-minded man, some one ought to put him up as the woman suffrage candidate for President.[22]

April 6, 1914, *New York Times*

There's no better or more healthful vacation imaginable than hard work and lots of it; the only trouble is that most people don't know it. They've never tried to scheme.[23]

June 6, 1914, *New York Times*

Don't talk—act.[24]

November 1914, *System*

For most of my life I refused to work at any problem unless its solution seemed capable of being put to commercial use. I looked forward to the time when I could fiddle around with things I had caught a glimpse of here and there and which would give me personal satisfaction.[25]

February 1917, *New York Sun*

You know we are used to working here at high pressure. It's the only way to work and everybody likes it.[26]

February 25, 1919, *Edison Herald*

My ambition is to lay out a line of work that will keep my Laboratories busy for the next hundred years.[27]

February 25, 1919, *Edison Herald*

I'm glad that the eight-hour day had not been invented when I was a young man. . . . This country would not amount to as much as it does if the young men of fifty years ago had been afraid that they might earn more than they were paid. There were some shirkers in those days, to be sure, but they didn't boast of it. The shirker tried to conceal or excuse his shiftlessness and lack of ambitions.

I am not against the eight-hour day or any other thing that protects labor from exploitation at the hands of ruthless employers, but it makes me sad to see young Americans shackle their abilities by blindly conforming to rules which force the industrious man to keep in step with the shirker.[28]

February 11, 1920, *New York Times*

Hard work won't hurt anybody who likes it.[29]

February 12, 1920, *New York Times*

What is genius? Why, genius is simply hard work, stick-to-it-iveness and common sense.[30]

July 10, 1920, *Fort Myers (Fla.) Press*

There's an old saying, "If at first you don't succeed, try, try again." But most of us don't try again. We try something new, something that seems easier.[31]

July 10, 1920, *Fort Myers (Fla.) Press*

Every man has some forte, something he can do better than he can do anything else. Many men, however, never find the job they are best fitted for. And often this is because they do not *think* enough. Too many men drift lazily into any job, suited or unsuited for them;

and when they don't get along well they blame everybody and everything except themselves.[32]

January 1921, American Magazine

When the doctors bring in the oxygen tanks to keep me going I'll quit. Not before.[33]

February 12, 1921, Dallas Morning News

Nothing is impossible. We merely don't yet know how to do it.[34]

Advice to a fellow inventor. January 1922, Current Opinion

It goes to show that if you want something bad enough and stick to it, you will get it.[35]

October 19, 1922, New York Times

It is not always necessary, perhaps not always desirable, to be a specialist in a subject in order to make suggestions related to it which start useful angles of research. We specialists are likely to get into ruts of our specialties out of which it is difficult to progress.[36]

October 7, 1923, New York Times

The time will come when full automatic machinery will be so largely introduced that production will not require a man's working more than four hours a day. That may not be a good thing. Idleness is rather objectionable to the ordinary type of man. But from the standpoint of the old man it will be a good thing because then old men need never work. The young man can work and support the family.[37]

October 18, 1923, New York Times

I've been working two shifts most of my life. Lots of other men work two shifts too, but [they] devote the other one to poker.[38]

February 12, 1926, Fort Myers (Fla.) Tropical News

Anything which tends to slow work down is waste.[39]

October 1926, *Forum*

There cannot be over-production of anything which men and women want, . . . Talk of over-production is a bugaboo.[40]

October 1926, *Forum*

I think work is the world's greatest fun.[41]

January 1927, *Forum*

A few days before the funeral.[42]

On when he planned to retire. February 12, 1927, *New York Times*

If you can't think a thing out yourself, get as many other people as you can to thinking on the subject. Somebody may find some facts that have eluded you and through them come to the solution. Who thinks a matter out is of no importance whatsoever. The important thing is that the problem should be solved.[43]

February 27, 1927, *New York Times*

I am not a genius. Any success that I have had in life is due to hard work. Success is 98 per cent hard work and sticking at the job until it is completed.[44]

February 11, 1928, *Fort Myers (Fla.) Press*

I have plenty of work to do and that keeps me young.[45]

February 8, 1929, *New York Times*

Brains are never a substitute for hard work.[46]

July 31, 1930, *New York Times*

[T]here is no substitute for hard work.[47]

July 31, 1930 *New York Times*

My philosophy on life: Work. Bringing out the secrets of nature and applying them for the happiness of man. Looking on the bright side of everything.[48]

April 1931, *Golden Book Magazine*

Let a young man get a job and work so hard at it that he has no time to fall into temptation.[49]

April 1931, *Golden Book Magazine*

I tackle but one job at a time.[50]

May 9, 1931, *New York Times*

When I don't understand work like this I get two men to work at it independently. If they agree, maybe it is all right; if they don't agree, I get a third man.[51]

January 15, 1932, *Science*

Didn't I tell you right along, that you'd git it? I've been telling you all the time that *all* you got to do is stick to it and work like hell and you'd get it in the end. . . . He hasn't got a damn thing. But that's the way to talk![52]

Encouraging an employee. September 1932, *Harper's Magazine*

Ford, ever since the first cell, it has always been dog eat dog, hasn't it?[53]

Comment to Henry Ford, quoted
in October 1934, *American Magazine*

On Business

[G]et everything in *Black* and *White* which is the only possible Manner of doing business.[54]

July 24, 1871, letter to his father

[A] man cannot sell what isn't existing.[55]

October 12, 1878, letter to Ebenezer Baker Welch

My business is thinking.[56]

December 5, 1878, New York World

I cannot entertain the idea of buying him out. I would much prefer fighting it out.[57]

March 18, 1879, letter to George H. Bliss
regarding his electric pen and mimeograph endeavors

I paid no attention to my business affairs until within two years, when I found that everybody else was growing rich out of me.[58]

February 24, 1881, Cincinnati Enquirer

What are you so excited about? Everybody steals [ideas] in commerce and industry. I've stolen a lot myself. But I knew how to steal. They don't know how to steal—that's all that's the matter with them.[59]

Circa 1903, quoted in September 1932, Harper's Magazine

No machine will ever be a success until it has a commercial value.[60]

April 1904, Outing

I was a business man for half a century, and now I am merely having a good time.[61]

February 12, 1911, New York Times

The trouble is that the American manufacturer can not go into the proposition deliberately enough. With him it is a matter of skinning the big idea and skinning it as quickly as possible.[62]

June 1, 1912, Literary Digest

American manufacturers are so busy with the big ideas that all the other ideas may be conveyed to the back burner.[63]

June 1, 1912, *Literary Digest*

The trusts are all right provided they can be regulated. What we want is protection for the smaller fellows, so that nothing can be bought below the cost of production. If you can get that, you will have plenty of competition all right, and the trust problem will be solved.[64]

October 7, 1912, *New York Times*

If you have five lines of business, any two of them will carry you through a bad period; but if you have only one or two kinds and they both go bad, then you are in the soup.[65]

Circa 1920s

On Competition

We must all expect competition; if not from one person, then from another.[66]

February 8, 1890, letter to Henry Villard

There seems to be a law in commercial things as in nature. If one attempts to obtain more profit than general average he is immediately punished by competitions.[67]

April 7, 1891, letter to William Dennis Marks

On Employees and Labor

I have always done everything to help every one of the [employees]; I have always been glad they were getting wealthy; the more they made the better it pleased me.[68]

November 23, 1888, letter to Sigmund Bergmann

Yes, [my employees] have the energy necessary to stand the strain of night work and they know that if I am successful that I don't keep it all for myself.[69]

1888 interview

Machinery is settling the labor question and in favor of the laborer, who is every day becoming worthier of his hire. The multiplication of machinery in the last fifty years has doubled wages, while reducing the cost of living one-half. When motive power is still further cheapened, the laborer will be master of his own destiny, and the labor question will cease to exist.[70]

1890 interview

Why shouldn't business men use their brains a little to help out the hard working man with a family who is doing the best he can with his limited intelligence. Just as much money will be made and it will be able to look any man in the face.[71]

On a profit-sharing and pension plan. December 4, 1910, letter to N. F. Brady

I hire a man to take charge of a branch of my factories and I say to him, "I'll give you two months to make good and if you don't make good I'm through with you."[72]

October 7, 1912, *New York Times*

This great [profit-sharing] scheme of Mr. Ford's will do a world of good. When we use machines instead of humans and have a single apparatus to do the work of 250 men, then the employees will enjoy real benefits. This is already true in the Ford factory in Detroit. It is a case where scientific management has rolled up enormous profits, because an article can be very cheaply manufactured.[73]

January 11, 1914, *New York Times*

The time is passing when human beings will be used as motors. We are to-day putting brains into machinery, and are replacing by machinery the energies of thousands of humans with only a few men to see to it that the apparatus keeps working. If other concerns were to set about to study the question of efficiency and reduce operation to the minimum cost, then employes would profit.[74]

January 11, 1914, *New York Times*

The business men of this country must see to it that employment is provided for our war workers and returning soldiers. We have shown our service stars and worn our Liberty Loan buttons with pride. Let us take equal pride in doing our share to make employment for the men who have worked and fought to win the war.[75]

November 24, 1918, *New York Times*

The employer who is not square with his employes, or the employe who is not square with his employer, is going to be out of step with the times.[76]

June 28, 1919, *New York Times*

The time is coming when the unjust employer and the disloyal employe will share equal odium in the esteem of society at large.[77]

June 28, 1919, *New York Times*

Of course, I realize that the leaders of labor unions have their political problems and they must appeal to the collective intelligence of their followers, which is lower than the average individual intelligence of the same men.[78]

February 11, 1920, *New York Times*

I wonder if the time will ever come when the unions, generally, will teach their members how to be better workmen, and train the ablest and the most ambitious to become bosses and employers. If that time ever does arrive, trade unionism will be one of the world's greatest forces in social progress, and I think there will be a much better understanding between capital and labor.[79]

February 11, 1920, New York Times

As soon as I see a scheme is not good, I discard it.[80]

February 12, 1923, Boston Herald

I have experimented with advertising. You can't tell about the results. But they're all doing it.[81]

November 16, 1923, New York Times

If labor everywhere would strike against the use of men as animals instead of protesting against their use as human beings, it would show superior wisdom.[82]

October 1926, Forum

Certainly, why not give the laborer a good wage as long as the business he works for is making money.[83]

June 11, 1930, New York Times

On Economics and Money

I have enough money to last ten days.[84]

May 8, 1869, letter to Ebenezer Baker Welch

I kept no books. I had two hooks. All the bills and accounts I owed I jabbed on one hook, and memoranda of all owed to myself I put on the other. When some of the bills fell due . . . I gave a note. When the notes were due a messenger came around from the bank with the note and a protest pinned to it for one dollar and twenty-five cents. Then I would go to New York and get an advance or pay the note if

I had the money. This method of giving notes for my accounts and having all notes posted I kept up for over two years, yet my credit was fine.[85]

> Edison's earliest accounting system. Circa 1870s

Plans for paying much from nothing.[86]

> Title of an August 15, 1875, business plan

Can you pay one of the smallest of my bills tomorrow If you can't it won't work extraordinary hardship to me, but if you could I think under the benign influence of the comely greenbacks this beautiful world of ours would inhance in beauty.[87]

> November 11, 1875, request for payment of a bill

In regard to money matters, should you get any for me at any time Cable it over as that is a commodity I can always find use for.[88]

> November 11, 1879, letter to Theodore Puskas

Haven't rec'd a dam cent from Europe yet.[89]

> On European investment in the electric light and power systems. March 26, 1880, marginalia on letter from George H. Bliss

The Lord only knows where I am to get the shekels—Laboratory is going to be an awful pull on me.[90]

> On operating costs of the West Orange, New Jersey, facility. July 6, 1887, marginalia on a letter from Edward Hibberd Johnson

I have been under a desperate strain for money for 22 years.[91]

> February 8, 1890, letter to Henry Villard

Considered purely as inventions, [my inventions] have cost me more than I have ever received from them. . . . However, you must not think from this that I have not made money, but I have made it as a manufacturer and not as an inventor.[92]

> 1890 interview

Well, it's all gone, but we had a hell of a good time spending it.[93]

> On learning that his General Electric stock would have been
> worth over $4 million had he not sold it. Circa 1902

It's one thing, for instance, to be sure, and another thing to be—Wall Street sure![94]

> October 21, 1906, *New York Times*

If I should loan money to all that ask me it would burst the Bank of England.[95]

> June 2, 1909, letter to A. Dalgleish

Now, I'll say this much about [money]—at least I'll say I'm not going to take any of it with me or leave much behind; I'm having an awfully good time blowing it in my own way, as I blow it as fast as I want to get my work done.[96]

> January 3, 1912, *New York Times*

Money? Why all the money I make on an invention goes for furthering my experiments. I do not seek money.[97]

> June 18, 1904, *Quincy (Ill.) Daily Whig*

Luxury is a relative term. What is luxury for one man is almost a necessity to another. No matter what is said or done, the increased earning power of the American people is going to result in the increased purchase of luxuries, and the urge to possess luxuries will do more to speed up production than all the prize contests, bonus plans, and proclamations that can be devised. The laziest and most non-productive man in the world is the man whose wants are the simplest. The fellow who has a family that wants luxuries and is endeavoring to gratify them is the man who is usually working the hardest and producing the most.[98]

> June 8, 1918, *New York Times*

I don't believe there is any such thing as Money Power. There is the power of money.[99]

July 16, 1922, *New York Times*

When a bank sells its credit for so much per cent, that isn't interest. That's a charge for a certain service. But when a man puts his wealth in bonds, ceases to produce anything and lives abroad on his income—that's interest.[100]

July 16, 1922, *New York Times*

Why shouldn't a bank make 15 per cent. or more? I make more if I can. A bank takes risks. It has to gamble.[101]

July 16, 1922, *New York Times*

Money has got to be self-limiting, in proportion to the amount of actual wealth produced.[102]

July 16, 1922, *New York Times*

In all the books on banking and economics I read how stupid and disastrous it was for the Government to have done this or that in a crisis. I never find out from them what the government should have done.[103]

July 16, 1922, *New York Times*

Agriculture and manufacturing cannot be financed by the same method. Their needs are too dissimilar. The farmer has one turnover. Business has many.[104]

July 16, 1922, *New York Times*

We ought to do something about the farmer. It's a moral obligation. He doesn't know anything about figures. He gets skinned.[105]

July 16, 1922, *New York Times*

There is no free lunch.[106]

February 22, 1929, *Fort Myers (Fla.) Press*

Bear this in mind. The demand for things made by the manufacturers is unlimited. People want automobiles, radios and all sorts of things. They want more things all the time but the stomach is the measure of the farmer's output. Seems a pity, that the farmers' prosperity should be bounded by what can fill this little space, [indicating his stomach] two or three quarts. When that is filled we have nor more use for the farmer. The stomach's capacity gluts his market.[107]

July 16, 1922, *New York Times*

On Monetary Policy

I think the best dollar could be made out of compressed wheat. You take a bushel of wheat and squeeze the water out of it and then compress it into a hard cake the size of a silver dollar and stamp the government mark upon it.[108]

October 7, 1891, *Rolla (Mo.) New Era*

Gold is a relic of Julius Caesar and interest is an invention of Satan. Gold is intrinsically of less utility than most metals. The probable reason why it is retained as the basis of money is that it is easy to control. . . . It is the control of money that is the root of all evil.[109]

December 6, 1921, *New York Times*

Money ought to be plentiful and gold is not plentiful. It would be plentiful if it were mined in as large quantities as it could be, but an artificial scarcity is maintained by those who use gold to monopolize money. That's one way to do it—make it so plentiful that it drowns its fictitious value and drowns the superstition of people along with it.[110]

December 6, 1921, *New York Times*

Gold and money are separate things, you see. Gold is the trick mechanism by which you can control money.[111]

December 6, 1921, New York Times

It seems absurd to me that all our values should be based on boxes of metal in any treasury. It is an absurdity, but everyone has been educated to believe that absurdity is common sense.[112]

January 1, 1922, Mentor

I want to cast the variable out of money.[113]

July 16, 1922, New York Times

I've been thinking on the subject [of money] steadily for several months. Maybe I'm in a rut.[114]

July 16, 1922, New York Times

Any man who has been ten years in banking is unable to see a new thing clearly. He's in a rut.[115]

July 16, 1922, New York Times

You'd be surprised to know how many people are out-and-out Greenbackers—think the Government should just print money as it's wanted.[116]

July 16, 1922, New York Times

This gold money is not good enough. It's a fiction.[117]

July 16, 1922, New York Times

I wouldn't issue money on land. Land isn't worth anything. It's what you get from land.[118]

July 16, 1922, New York Times

All new things about money and banking, all the great reforms, come from outside.[119]

July 16, 1922, New York Times

While the gold miner can bring in his commodity and get full value, any attempt of the farmer to attain parity is met by a glut and a lowering of the price of his commodity, which is equal, if not superior, in value.[120]

July 16, 1922, New York Times

Let's make money itself absolutely sound as the first step. Then the credit problem can be taken up. This is a vast problem. I can't do anything with it in my mind—not yet.[121]

July 22, 1922, New York Times

I seek to keep the currency always the same value. Therefore, prices will always be due to the supply and demand and to nothing else.[122]

July 23, 1922, New York Times

What is really wanted is a single currency based entirely on mortgage loans with twice the value of the par of the bank note behind it. . . . Somebody will some day evolve a plan, so I thought I would at least make a stab at it.[123]

July 23, 1922, New York Times

I believe that all the principal banks of Europe take government warehouse receipts in lieu of gold, and so why would not a plan of currency based on the farm products themselves be valid? There the goods are graded and weighed. Of course gold is a handy thing, and bankers can ship and transport it easily. But actual goods are even better than gold.[124]

June 18, 1929, New York Times

On Depressions

There are those who fear a business depression. The surest way to bring on a depression of business is to nurture fears and act hesitatingly.[125]

November 24, 1918, New York Times

There is no doubt that economic conditions in our country are somewhat upset, but they are not so seriously disarranged that we cannot remedy them by grit, determination and hard work.[126]

September 29, 1921, New York Times

Don't call it a panic. It is nothing but a period of depression, and nothing to worry over, provided we set ourselves resolutely to the task of overcoming it. These periods of depression come in recurring cycles. They are nothing new. The point to be driven home is that the country always recovers from them and goes forward with greater strides than ever before. We will get over this one too.[127]

September 29, 1921, New York Times

These periods of depression are caused by a faulty adjustment of our economic machine, or by it being thrown out of gear by some unusual force, such as war. The machine is all right; it will work properly as soon as the obstruction is removed.[128]

September 29, 1921, New York Times

The psychology of fear is the prime cause of the present depression. The people have been frightened out of good times, unnecessarily so, because our country and its economic conditions are fundamentally sound, and being sound they will finally triumph.[129]

September 29, 1921, New York Times

Of course we cannot expect the flush times, the big wages and big profits that we enjoyed during the war.[130]

September 29, 1921, New York Times

We must get back to normal living and spending, forget our fears, our extravagances and our niggardliness, and live as if it were ordinary times. During the war America lost its head. Money was so plentiful, such high prices could be obtained for commodities, jobs paying such big wages so easily could be secured, that we fairly wallowed in extravagance. Then came the reaction, and we went to the other extreme.[131]

September 29, 1921, *New York Times*

Good times are coming, and like the traffic block, everybody will whip up a bit to make up for lost time.[132]

September 29, 1921, *New York Times*

Stability! That's what we want. There's no gain from instability except for the speculators—and what happens to them? When I had charge of the Wall Street tickers and indicators in the time of Jay Gould and Black Friday I saw what happened to them. If one had a stroke of apoplexy he might die rich.[133]

Edison worked for the American financier and robber baron
Jay Gould during the 1869 "Black Friday" Panic. July 16, 1922, *New York Times*

We are bound to have these depressions, no matter how perfect our financial standings. Men are natural born gamblers and will always overdo things.[134]

July 31, 1930, *New York Times*

We need something like this, to show us how lucky we are. I believe the depression has served to demonstrate to the American people that they can only be really happy when helping others.[135]

January 21, 1931, *Fort Myers (Fla.) Press*

Why should I rush and say anything as to when the depression will end? These other fellows are rushing in. I don't think I'll do it. I've passed through six of these depressions now and I've got sense enough not to make too many predictions.[136]

January 21, 1931, *Fort Myers (Fla.) Press*

At present my income has nearly disappeared on account of the depression in business.[137]

January 1932, *Modern Mechanics and Inventions*

On Success

If you want to succeed, get some enemies.[138]

April 1898, *Ladies' Home Journal*

Intelligence, imagination and the will to work are the important characteristics necessary for success.[139]

October 7, 1927, *New York Times*

On Failure

These stories about my failure have had the effect to thin out the crowd of visitors who usually come to see me, which to me is a blessing in disguise. I have prayed for an earthquake or something of the sort to keep some of them away.[140]

April 11, 1879, *New York Graphic*

Spilled milk don't interest me. I have spilled lots of it, and while I have always felt it for days, it is quickly forgotten.[141]

1911, personal correspondence

Although I am over 67 years old I'll start all over again tomorrow. I am pretty well burned out tonight, but tomorrow there will be a mobilization here and the debris will be cleared away, if it is cooled sufficiently, and I will go right to work to reconstruct the plant.[142]

Comment following the devastating fire at his experimental plant in West Orange, New Jersey. December 10, 1914, *New York Times*

I have tried a million schemes that will not work—I know everything that is no good.[143]

Circa 1916

We sometimes learn a lot from our failures if we have put into the
effort the best thought and work we are capable of.[144]

January 1921, *American Magazine*

I am always disappointed until [a] problem is solved. Not more than
one out of 20 of the details work at first.[145]

February 12, 1930, *Fort Myers (Fla.) Press*

There are fifty failures to one success—more than that. It is all because of our ignorance. And it is often the side issue, not the thing
that a man is working on, that is important.[146]

January 1931, *Review of Reviews*

On Religion

Portrait of Edison, circa 1915.
Courtesy of the Thomas Edison National Historical Park, 14.130.137.

Edison's religious beliefs were influenced by the British-born radical and American Revolutionary Thomas Paine, author of *The Age of Reason*. Both Paine and Edison were suspicious of the political and social power exerted by organized religion. During their lifetimes, both men were erroneously called atheists. For the most part, Edison believed in a divine creator, but he struggled with questions of how human beings related to the Almighty.

Séances, Ouija boards, and mind reading were popular pastimes in the nineteenth century. Edison's natural curiosity extended to supernatural subjects, causing him to wonder if mind reading and telekinesis could be extensions of human evolution. He once played a practical joke on the press (see chapter 8), claiming to have created a machine to speak with the dead.

On Religion

My conscience seems to be oblivious of sunday. It must be incrusted with a sort of irreligious tartar. If I was not so deaf I might go to church and get it taken off or at least loosened.[1]

July 12, 1885, diary entry

The existence of such a God, in my mind, can almost be proved from chemistry.[2]

July 16, 1885, *Salt Lake City Democrat*

One of the first things I do when I reach heaven is to ascertain what flies are made for.[3]

July 20, 1885, diary entry

Satan is the scarecrow of the religious cornfield.[4]

July 20, 1885, diary entry

What a wonderfully small idea mankind has of the almighty. My impression is that he has made unchangeable laws to govern this

and billions of other worlds and that he has forgotten even the existence of this little mote of ours ages ago. Why can't man follow up
and practice the teachings of his own conscience, mind his business,
and not obtrude his purposely created finite mind in affairs that will
be attended to without any volunteered advice.[5]

July 21, 1885, diary entry

I am an optimist by nature, and believe that good prevails, but I have
never had time to bother my mind about creeds, dogmas and the
like.[6]

1890 interview

Most assuredly I do [believe in God]. Nature and science both af-
firm His existence, and where the layman believes the man of science knows.[7]

1890 interview

President McKinley in his Thanksgiving proclamation thanked
God for our victory over Spain but . . . the *New York World* calls
attention to the fact that the same god gave yellow fever and to be
consistent McKinley should have thanked him for that also. Thus
we see terrible contradictions everywhere about the mystery of life.[8]

December 1, 1898, letter to his wife, Mina

Why, after years of watching the processes of nature, I can no more
doubt the existence of an intelligence that is running things than I
do the existence of myself.[9]

July 9, 1900, *Cincinnati Enquirer*

"Y-e-s, [lightning rods] might be of use on churches. It does look
as if Providence were a trifle absent-minded at times.[10]

July 13, 1902, *Brooklyn Daily Eagle*

People call me a great inventor. *I'm* no inventor worth talkin' about.
When I think that I can't build even the damnedest kind of a fool

who could think and speak some darn fool thing of his own, then I know that I am just a hell of an inventor. *That's* [motioning upward] the *real* Inventor![11]

> Circa 1903, quoted in September 1932, *Harper's Magazine*

If you and I can't find the solution, then let's honestly admit that you and I are damn fools, but why blame it on the Lord and say *He* created somep'n impossible—a problem that's got no solution?[12]

> Circa 1903, quoted in September 1932, *Harper's Magazine*

No man can build a machine after the structure of a bird that will fly as a bird flies. The Creator alone did that. He built the bird wonderfully.[13]

> April 1904, *Outing*

Mercy? Kindness? Love? I don't see 'em. Nature is what we know. We do not know the gods of the religions. And nature is not kind, or merciful, or loving. If God made me—the fabled God of the three qualities of which I spoke: mercy, kindness, love—He also made the fish I catch and eat. And where do His mercy, kindness, and love for that fish come in?

No; nature made us—nature did it all—not the gods of the religions and nature did it mercilessly; she has no thought for mercy or against it. She did it impersonally, what we call cruelly. Nature seems to be a very undesirable member of society.[14]

> October 2, 1910, *New York Times*

They say I am an atheist. Well, I am not, never have been, never said I was. Those people who have called me one have not read what I said. I believe in a Supreme Intelligence, but I have grave doubts whether the good folk of the earth are going to be aroused from their graves to go to some beautiful shining place aloft. Don't see it, can't understand it, and neither can these ministers of fashionable churches. They don't even say what they think. Often they don't even think. It's all business with them.[15]

December 1, 1910, New York Times

Science cannot reach any other conclusion that there is a great intelligence manifested everywhere.[16]

July 1911, Century Magazine

I believe in the existence of a Supreme Intelligence pervading the Universe.[17]

June 24, 1916, letter to Joseph Metagon

There is a great directing head of things and people—a Supreme Being who looks after the destines of the world. I have faith in a Supreme Being.[18]

August 11, 1923, New York Times

My brain is incapable of conceiving of such a thing as a soul. I may be in error, and man may have a soul, but I simply do not believe it. What a soul may be is beyond my understanding.[19]

1924, Hearst's International Magazine

The headmaster who balances that food knows his business.[20]

Commenting on God's creation of the perfect food, milk. August 20, 1924,
Boston Daily Globe

All this talk about fundamentalism will die out in a few years because there is nothing to it. We have got to have truth and in spite of all the furor over Mr. Bryan, his ideas were obsolete long ago. There is more truth to be found in nature than in the Bible, for nature never lies. The chief trouble with religion is that it is being exploited too much. There is visible evidence for an absolute Being all around us.[21]

Reaction to William Jennings Bryan and the Scopes Trial,
which pitted creationism against Darwin's theory of evolution.
February 12, 1926, Fort Myers (Fla.) Tropical News

The Soul apparently is not something to be analyzed by chemists or weighed in scales, or photographed, or recorded by any instruments whatever.[22]

November 1926, *Forum*

I believe Christianity will continue to produce the world's best leadership; the Christian nations are the wisest nations and one proof of their wisdom is the acceptance of Christianity; therefore it seems to be the fact that I am a full subscriber to the moral code of Christ, as to all true moral codes.[23]

November 1926, *Forum*

Somehow I cannot be impressed by the idea that merely spoken prayers are likely to be answered, but I am absolutely sure that lived prayers are certain to be answered.[24]

November 1926, *Forum*

[P]reachers in the pulpits of our churches are very likely to mistake hair-splitting for teaching. Arguments on theological points are not, I think, of great value to the mentally and spiritually distressed and just how they can save the souls of men from sin I never have been able to understand. I may be dull.[25]

November 1926, *Forum*

In science only one thing counts and that is basic truth. Perhaps some day we shall find that science and religion do not differ in this matter.[26]

November 1926, *Forum*

There are sermons in all the beauties and wonders of the natural world around us. There is a mighty sermon in the thunderstorm, but one as mighty in the wildflower. The Book of Nature never lies; and in it may be found lessons concerning almost every fact of life, death, and perhaps, immortality.[27]

November 1926, *Forum*

I am not so deeply certain of the value of Mohammed's teachings because he achieved eminence by means of war. . . . That warlike detail of his teachings robbed it of its loveliness and Mohammedanism is not really beautiful as Christianity and Buddhism are, Christianity, I think being the most beautiful of human conceptions.[28]

November 1926, *Forum*

Nature can teach us more about God Almighty in a day than all the text-books of the theological seminaries can teach us in ten years.[29]

November 1926, *Forum*

An educational church might save the world.[30]

November 1926, *Forum*

The laboratories of the colleges and universities, the research departments of the great industrial concerns are places where the word of God is revealed and worshipped even though some of the worshippers know not that they are uncovering it and bowing down before it.[31]

November 1926, *Forum*

Some of the existing so-called religious creeds remind me of certain other savage theories. . . . We establish many rules and consider them inspired, when, in the light of actual knowledge, they are no more inspired than the rule of the wild head-hunter who cannot get a really nice girl to marry him unless he gives to her two human heads.[32]

November 1926, *Forum*

The greatest error ever made in the name of religion has been that of those who have made morality an ugly thing, oppressive, restrictive and repellent in the mind of those who have gone to them to learn. Morality is always beautiful.[33]

November 1926, *Forum*

I would not deny a supreme Intelligence. Heaven forbid that I should diminish by a shade of one degree, let alone destroy, the faith or hope of any man or woman. The thing which I urge on religious teachers is to pile up the evidence and make it the sort of evidence which no fool skeptic can demolish.[34]

November 1926, *Forum*

The creeds have come to an end and religion is beginning.[35]

November 1926, *Forum*

[The word of God] has no meaning to me, but I believe there is a superior intelligence pervading the universe.[36]

February 12, 1927, *New York Times*

The trouble with all those men [clergy members] is that they make no effort to get data on which to base conclusions. If we went at the study of electricity in that way we should get nowhere with it.[37]

February 27, 1927, *New York Times*

People are drifting away from superstition and bunk; increase in scientific knowledge is responsible.[38]

February 12, 1928, *New York Times*

The existence of a supreme intelligence can be proved.[39]

July 30, 1928, *New York Times*

I do not pose as a preacher; but let me tell you that there is a God. He will not let us advance much further materially until we catch up spiritually.[40]

1929, unnamed newspaper

I believe in an Eternal Reason that pervades the universe and co-ordinates all things.[41]

August 2, 1930, *New York Times*

I know this world is ruled by infinite intelligence. It required infinite intelligence to create it, and it requires infinite intelligence to keep it on its course. Everything that surrounds us—everything that exists—proves that there are infinite laws behind it.[42]

January 1932, *Review of Reviews*

On the Supernatural

[I] Think mind reading contrary to commons sense, wise provision of the Bon Dieu that we cannot read each others minds twould stop civilization and everybody would take to the Woods. In fifty or hundred thousand centuries when mankind have become perfect by evolution then perhaps this sense would be developed with safety to the state.[43]

July 16, 1885, diary entry. ("Bon Dieu" is French for "Good Lord.")

We experimented on hypnotism by placing a man's head in an immense magnetic plane, but it didn't work. We tried telepathy, too, but without success.[44]

November 3, 1893, *Albany (N.Y.) Telegram*

The psychic forces? The supernatural? Merely words for perfectly natural things which, as yet, we do not understand.[45]

October 2, 1910, *New York Times*

Well, [mind reading] only indicates to me the race's future possibilities. What the abnormal man of now can do, the normal man of coming days may very likely do.[46]

November 13, 1910, *New York Times*

I cannot conceive of such a thing as a spirit. Imagine something which has no weight, no material form, no mass; in a word, imagine nothing. I cannot be a party to the belief that spirits exist and can be seen under certain circumstances, and can be made to tilt tables and rap, and do other things of a similar unimportant nature. The whole thing is so absurd.[47]

October 30, 1920, *Scientific American*

I have been thinking for some time of a machine or apparatus which could be operated by personalities which have passed on to another existence or sphere. Now follow me carefully; I don't claim that our personalities pass on to another existence or sphere. I don't claim anything because I don't know anything about the subject. For that matter, no human being knows. But I do claim that it is possible to construct an apparatus which will be so delicate that if there are personalities in another existence or sphere who wish to get in touch with us in this existence or sphere, this apparatus will at least give them a better opportunity to express themselves than the tilting tables and raps on ouija boards and mediums and the other crude methods now purported to be the only means of communication.[48]

On his supposed machine to communicate with the dead. October 30, 1920, *Scientific American*

Why should personalities in another existence or sphere waste their time working a little triangular piece of wood over a board with certain lettering on it? Why should such personalities play pranks with a table? The whole business seems so childish to me.[49]

October 30, 1920, *Scientific American*

I don't know what the word "spiritual" means. I am not interested in matters of the spirit.[50]

February 12, 1922, *New York Times*

I don't believe in spirits. That's all rainbow business. Everybody seems to have misunderstood me.[51]

February 12, 1922, *New York Times*

The natural is so much bigger than we can understand that it does seem worth while to try to find the supernatural. Of course there's no such thing. Whatever is, is natural. But there are many things we do not know which if we knew would startle us.[52]

February 27, 1927, *New York Times*

On Death, Dying, and Immortality

[T]here seems nothing else to do than to bow to the laws that govern all.[53]

December 1, 1898, letter to his wife, Mina, on the death of her sister

No, all this talk of an existence for us, as individuals, beyond the grave is wrong. It is born of our tenacity of love—our desire to go on living—our dread of coming to an end as individuals. I do not dread it, though. Personally I cannot see any use of a future life.[54]

October 2, 1910, *New York Times*

There is no more reason to believe that any human brain will be immortal than there is to think that one of my phonograph cylinders will be immortal.[55]

October 2, 1910, *New York Times*

There is nothing in such cases that would either prove or disprove the existence of life after death.[56]

October 2, 1910, *New York Times*

They tell me I am heading straight for Hades. Maybe I am, but I'll take my chances with the fashionable minister, and if there is such a spot as heaven I'll bet I get there first.[57]

December 1, 1910, *New York Times*

[W]hat we call death is simply the departure of the entities from our bodies. . . . While the life entities live forever, thus giving us the eternal life which many of us hope for, this means little to you and me if, when we come to that stage known as death, our personality simply breaks up into separate units which soon combine with others to form new structures.[58]

October 30, 1920, *Scientific American*

If people would occupy themselves with other things there would be no cause to run toward immorality.[59]

February 12, 1921, *New York Times*

The soul after death takes flight, but in what form and manner is unknown. We know that the soul does exist after death. . . . I have not found it possible to demonstrate the existence of the life beyond the grave, and I can not say that men, including the beloved President Harding, live after death.[60]

August 11, 1923, *New York Times*

When the entity deserts the body, the body is like a ship without a rudder—deserted, motionless and dead. It is mere clay, as all orthodox Christians believe. I still believe in the religion of our Lord and Master.[61]

August 11, 1923, *New York Times*

When life ceases in the human body its communities of these entities leave it, but remain living, intelligent. Whether they keep together in a swarm or separate and go in different directions, where they go, whether or not they resume, through the conception of other humans, their former tasks or take up other tasks or none, are speculations not involved in the hypothesis.[62]

October 7, 1923, *New York Times*

[A]s I do not believe that the human being has a soul—unless you want to call these entities a soul—not that a human being has a conscious individual life after death in any form, spiritual or physical.[63]

October 7, 1923, *New York Times*

At present the Soul's immortality is one of those things in which man instinctively believes, but about which there is no proof when it is regarded from a strictly practical standpoint.[64]

November 1926, Forum

To-day the preponderance of probability very greatly favors belief in the immortality of the intelligence, or soul, of man.[65]

November 1926, Forum

[P]erpetual youth and virtual immortality on this earth would seem to me to be most undesirable. When the time comes, normal human beings do not desire abnormal extension of the earthly life-period.[66]

January 1927, Forum

I am convinced that at the end of that which we call life this subconscious desire for something new is very great, and in many instances influential, no matter how the conscious mind, trained by instinct and long habit to cling to this existence, may struggle to combat it. New scenes, new occupations, new emotions, new successes—these all normal human beings strive for during this life. When they have had all of these that they can get out of it they must turn for change to whatever may come beyond.[67]

January 1927, Forum

I have stated many times, but no one understands, that man is not the unit of life, that he is as dead as granite, that the unit consists of swarms of billions of highly organized entities which live in the cells. I believe at times when a man dies this swarm deserts the body—goes out into space, but keeps on, enters into another or last cycle of life, and is immortal.[68]

February 12, 1927, New York Times

I proposed that, to get some reasonable data, every known fact in favor of immortality should be put in one column and every fact against immortality should be put in an opposite column. Then in time we might find in summing up that there were 56 per cent in favor and 44 per cent against. That would give a hope; as it is now we have no data.[69]

February 12, 1927, *New York Times*

There is a small percentage of all the things we know about nature that favors immortality. We should get more data.[70]

February 12, 1927, *New York Times*

Experimenting, if there are any facilities.[71]

On how he would spend his time in a possible afterlife. February 11, 1928, *Fort Myers (Fla.) Press*

[After death, a man's] personality has a chance of surviving, perhaps enter a new cycle, but still is on earth.[72]

July 30, 1928, *New York Times*

A man on his deathbed would be in such a weakened condition that he couldn't have any worth-while ideas.[73]

August 2, 1930, *New York Times*

I am working on the theory that our present personality exists after what we call life leaves our present material bodies.[74]

April 1931, *Golden Book Magazine*

Well, if there is a hereafter, it doesn't matter, and if there isn't a hereafter, it doesn't matter either. I've lived all my life and done my best.[75]

Conversation related by Edison's physician just days before Edison's death. October 18, 1931, *New York Times*

On Politics and Government

President Herbert Hoover and Thomas Edison in Michigan on
October 21, 1929, for the Light's Golden Jubilee. The event honored
Edison on the fiftieth anniversary of his invention of the electric light.
Courtesy of the Thomas Edison National Historical Park, 14.140.97.

Thomas Edison was an adherent to the tenets of Progressivism, a social and political movement based on a belief in progress and the improvement in humankind in an evolutionary sense. Edison's views were Progressive in the areas of education, women's suffrage, his support for Prohibition, and his advocacy for the professionalization and centralization of government. He did not support the movement's efforts to regulate industry and aid unions, or its views on welfare.

Though Edison opposed warfare, he readily supported his nation when World War I was declared. He served on the U.S. Naval Consulting Board, an organization established to solicit inventions for the armed forces. As a true Progressive, Edison hoped that once the world had experienced the true horrors of armed conflict, there would be no more wars. As a realist, he feared nations would not learn this lesson. He also correctly predicted that new technology would make modern warfare more deadly and destructive than ever before.

On Politics and Government

I was never interviewed on politics in my life; never made a political speech and, to tell you the truth, I don't believe any newspaper man ever thought I knew enough about politics to think it worth his while to ask me for my opinions.[1]

November 4, 1892, *New York Advertiser*

As for myself, looking at the state of affairs people have brought on themselves, I think they have formed themselves into a grand national lunatic asylum.[2]

August 5, 1893, unnamed newspaper

I am a Progressive. I believe in experimentation. Children should be taught at the age of 8 years that progress is life. You can't have progress without changes, without experimentation. The public doesn't seem to know what 8-year children [*sic*] ought to know.[3]

October 7, 1912, New York Times

We need experimentation in our Government.[4]

October 7, 1912, New York Times

You don't find me hiring any man on a four-year contract and putting him in charge of a department where he has the chance of a lifetime to ruin me. A man's tenure of office should cease five minutes after his usefulness ceases.[5]

October 7, 1912, New York Times

I don't believe in Government ownership at all, but if we must have it in some departments, the Government should never undertake to operate these departments. I do think that the Post Office Department is operated inefficiently on the whole. It could simply be done with less money.[6]

October 7, 1912, New York Times

What we need is a man who knows that bunch in Washington and who can make them behave.[7]

October 25, 1912, Suffolk County (N.Y.) News

Real Americans must drop parties and get down to big fundamental principles.[8]

September 4, 1916, New York Times

Times are too serious to talk in terms of Republicanism or Democracy. Parties are all right. Reckon we've got to have them with our system of government. But when it's America that's at stake, men have got to vote as Americans and not as Democrats or Republicans.[9]

September 10, 1916, New York Times

Well, if it were not for the interference of the Government with the railroads, they would be all electrified by now.[10]

December 2, 1916, *Collier's Weekly*

I think the League of Nations will be all right. It may not work out perfectly, but it is better than nothing.[11]

June 22, 1919, *New York Times*

A new order of things is emerging from the events of the last five years. Whatever may intervene, the ultimate result is going to approach more closely a square deal—for labor, for capital, for the merchant, for the farmer, for every one.[12]

June 28, 1919, *New York Times*

The square deal is fatal to radicalism. There can be no social revolution in the United States or Canada for the very simple reason that our Government and the Canadian Government are founded on the idea of giving everybody a fair show.[13]

June 28, 1919, *New York Times*

There are many promises made by Presidential candidates that are soon forgotten when they reach the White House.[14]

May 12, 1920, *New York Times*

Democracy is inefficient. You can't get the best man.[15]

June 20, 1920, *New York Times*

The time has arrived for some understanding among the nations which won the war. A League of Nations document with proper safeguards to protect American interests would be the proper thing. You know you must learn to creep before you walk. No matter how small the effort may appear to be, the League seems to be able to creep.[16]

June 20, 1920, *New York Times*

There are 10,000 politicians all over this country who are playing the newspapers for suckers. They get thousands and thousands of columns printed about themselves. . . . The papers all seem to fall for it.[17]

February 13, 1923, *New York Times*

I'm not in politics. I leave that for the politicians.[18]

August 20, 1924, *Boston Daily Globe*

If we could as completely eliminate politics from the management of our American cities, turning it over to real experts, we would have tax-rates which would seem ridiculously low, when compared to those which we charge ourselves today.[19]

December 1926, *Forum*

When American cities go at the problems of their management as intelligently as big business goes after the problems of its management most of those problems automatically will vanish.[20]

December 1926, *Forum*

Government management is fatal to success. The Government should regulate, not manage, private business in its relations with the public.[21]

October 22, 1927, *New York Times*

If the people of our great commercial nation fail to obtain Hoover to manage their business for them they will show a pretty low state of intelligence.[22]

August 14, 1928, *New York Times*

There is far more danger in a public monopoly than there is in a private monopoly for when the government goes into business it can always shift its losses to the taxpayers.[23]

June 28, 1929, *Davis County (Utah) Clipper*

One of the highest duties of the President is to keep the government out of business. That is his biggest job, and I should include in that job the clearing out of the bureaucracies which are growing up in Washington and becoming a wasteful nuisance.[24]

December 31, 1929, *New York Times*

Pay more attention to engineers than politicians.[25]

February 12, 1930, *Fort Myers (Fla.) Press*

Self-government is the essence of democracy.[26]

April 2, 1930, *New York Times*

The United States Government is the most inefficient big business organization in operation today. . . . The government is the worst managed business in the United States.[27]

June 11, 1930, *New York Times*

Am not in favor of any kind of dole.[28]

February 12, 1931, *New York Times*

Reason, Justice and Equity never had weight enough on the face of the earth to govern the councils of men.[29]

April 1931, *Golden Book Magazine*

Property in common has never been successful. . . . The Russian plan would never work out in this country. To begin with you never could get the American people under the control to the extent that the Russians have been controlled. It is impossible.[30]

May 8, 1931, *Fort Myers (Fla.) Press*

On Specific Candidates for Office

[President Taft is a] [f]ine man, but unable to cope with that bunch at Washington. They put it all over him.[31]

October 7, 1912, *New York Times*

[Theodore] Roosevelt? He's a dominating personality. He knows men better than [Taft and Governor Wilson]. He's capable of handling the bunch he will have to contend with when he gets to be President. I haven't seen in all my career that he has ever failed to make good and that he hasn't practiced what he's preached and that he hasn't succeeded in carrying out his contentions.[32]

October 7, 1912, *New York Times*

I've read Roosevelt's books and speeches, too. Yes, Sir. I became convinced, and I am convinced now, that he's a solid fellow who can meet any situation.[33]

October 7, 1912, *New York Times*

I haven't seen in all the career of [Theodore] Roosevelt that he hasn't made good and practised what he preached.[34]

October 11, 1912, *Suffolk County (N.Y.) News*

I think President Wilson has made himself clear as to his attitude toward business. To date I think he has done very well.[35]

January 3, 1915, *New York Times*

[Theodore] Roosevelt would win easily if there were not so many sheep in the world who won't think.[36]

May 21, 1915, *Huntington Long Islander*

Roosevelt was my choice. He had had experience, and is one of the best Americans. But the machine-controlled Republican Party would not have him. Therefore I am for Woodrow Wilson.[37]

September 10, 1916, *New York Times*

Shucks. I say that I'm for Woodrow Wilson. I say it because I feel that it's up to every man in times like these to take a position. But, pshaw! It's just my opinion.[38]

September 10, 1916, *New York Times*

We know what Wilson has done and what he will do, but I hope he will go more into preparedness. He has done enough humane things; now give us some war machinery and policemen to protect ourselves.[39]

November 7, 1916, *New York Times*

I am for Hoover for President. Engineers are good propositions for the Presidency. I recall an engineer in American history who made good. That was George Washington.[40]

May 12, 1920, *New York Times*

President Harding's a good old fellow, isn't he?[41]

August 12, 1922, *New York Times*

[Calvin Coolidge is] a mighty smart man and the country is fortunate in finding a man like him for the White House job. He'll be elected, I think, if he doesn't get the oration habit.[42]

August 20, 1924, *Boston Daily Globe*

One of the great troubles with our politicians is that they talk too much and work too little. [William Jennings] Bryan is a good example of that.[43]

August 20, 1924, *Boston Daily Globe*

Mr. Coolidge is a pretty good representative of the average American citizen and I believe that a great majority of them like him for his simplicity and democracy. They know he is honest. They are convinced that he will not wink at graft in or out of the White House.[44]

August 20, 1924, *Boston Daily Globe*

Al Smith will never make it. Being a Catholic or Protestant has no effect on a President discharging his official duties. But Smith is all Tammany and will never make it.[45]

Tammany Hall was an organization founded in New York City to influence government and elections that became known for graft and corruption under ward bosses like William M. Tweed. May 5, 1927, *New York Times*

If the people of the United States fail to elect Herbert Hoover as the next president they can be classed as a bunch of saps.[46]

January 28, 1929, *Time*

I think [the election of Hoover] will give us an engineer to manage our affairs.[47]

June 14, 1928, *New York Times*

That's what I like about Hoover. He listens and works while the other fellow talks.[48]

January 18, 1929, *Fort Myers (Fla.) Press*

I can't understand [Senator Dwight W. Morrow]. He knows nothing of the business and industrial world. He has been cooped up in an office away from the working man.[49]

December 9, 1930, *New York Times*

On Tariffs

I am a thorough believer in a Protective Tariff. I believe in every man looking out for himself and taking care of his own interests, and I believe in every community of men doing the same thing.[50]

November 4, 1892, *New York Advertiser*

The tariff is a political bluff.[51]

October 7, 1912, *New York Times*

[I]t is high time that American industries have protection against foreign competition.[52]

February 17, 1929, *Fort Myers (Fla.) Press*

The [Smoot-Hawley] tariff bill will bring about greater agricultural development, especially in the South, where the farmer competes with cheap labor in tropical countries.[53]

May 30, 1930, *New York Times*

On Drink, Temperance, and Prohibition

Though I have no conscientious scruples against the use of spirituous liquors, I don't care much for them, and drink them very little.[54]

November 17, 1889, *New York World*

Why, you take these fellows who never drink at all and you'll see 'em with pale, sallow complexions and abnormally broad shoulders, and they invariably die of consumption.[55]

November 17, 1889, *New York World*

Spirituous liquors I use very moderately, but I am fond of an occasional glass of beer or champagne, and am not a total abstinence man either in theory or practice.[56]

1890 interview

[A]nd all took *whiskey* instead of lemonade except your loving + devoted partner.[57]

September 1901, letter to his wife, Mina

Do you think they have any champagne left?[58]

> While avoiding guests at a dinner party, Edison gave his young
> daughter Madeleine, son Charles, and their cousins champagne.
> His wife was not pleased. Madeleine Edison oral history

I want to tell you that one of the greatest things to-day is this temperance movement. If it keeps on spreading, as it gives promise of doing, it's going to bring about a wonderful change in this country. There's nothing that means more to the future of this country.[59]

January 12, 1908, *New York Times*

Society will have to stop this whiskey business, which is like throwing sand in the bearings of a steam engine.[60]

January 14, 1910, *Seattle Star*

The war against stimulants is a fine, big human sign. The temperance movement's advance ought to be a subject for general congratulation; last Winter's crusade in New York for better regulation of habit-forming drugs was mighty worthy work; presently we shall be cutting out tobacco, tea, and coffee, and we all shall be better for it.[61]

October 11, 1914, *New York Times*

Man isn't perfect yet and you cannot take alcohol away from him all at once.[62]

February 12, 1916, *New York Times*

There are some booze-fighters who are brilliant men. If I know a man is a booze-fighter I can handle him. I don't like boozers, but in the past I have had a few men of that kind who could get results. Of course, you must be careful about the work you give them, but once in a while you will find a booze-fighter who is a good man—while it lasts.[63]

March 9, 1918, *Literary Digest*

We don't need that stuff.[64]

February 12, 1920, *New York Times*

Drinking whisky is a rotten habit, just like opium, cocaine and too much eating. Everybody ought to help to protect themselves against the sale of whiskey. Even the drunkards should help and they would if they had plain common sense.[65]

August 13, 1921, *New York Times*

If it is enforced for another 20 years [Prohibition] will be all right. For the children of today are the important consideration, and the dry laws will keep them from ever knowing whiskey. It is useless to try and change the people who are used to drinking.[66]

February 12, 1926, *Fort Myers (Fla.) Tropical News*

I am [a total abstainer]. I have a better use for my head.[67]

November 29, 1929, *Huntington Long Islander*

I still feel prohibition is the greatest experiment to benefit man.[68]

March 6, 1930, *New York Times*

I cannot understand this talk of repeal. Those men who advocate it have not had the experiences I have had in dealing with men.[69]

December 9, 1930, *New York Times*

On pay days, before prohibition, hundreds of pale-faced women, shabbily dressed, some with faded shawls around their heads, appeared at our factory at West Orange. They were waiting to get some of their husbands' money before he got to a saloon. Within a year after the amendment, not a single woman appeared. Surely we Americans do not want a return of this state of affairs.[70]

December 18, 1930, *New York Times*

[Boys and girls] certainly cannot develop on alcohol and other narcotics.[71]

December 18, 1930, Fort Myers (Fla.) Press

Prohibition is eternally correct. And even if the 18th Amendment is lost, the people will battle for it.[72]

December 22, 1930, Time

On War

Of course, if we should have a war with Spain, that would stimulate inventors and make many startling applications of electricity. But we won't have a war, eh?[73]

January 1, 1897, New York World

War is a dreadful thing + life itself is one of the great mysteries of the Universe. I am sorry it all has happened. There is no use saying anything as words of sympathy are too common place.[74]

Comment to his wife who had lost her brother during the Spanish-
American War. July 1898, note to his wife, Mina

How utterly absurd this military nonsense is! ... As we approached Italy and Austria from Switzerland we found each pass elaborately fortified; even with its surrounding country littered and defaced by barbed-wire entanglements. . . . Medieval nonsense! Relics of the past! It seemed incredible that all the warlike readiness of these abutting nations, prosperous, profoundly peaceful, progressive in all other things, should be manifestations of the same human beings who had been accomplishing all the extraordinary peaceful wonders we had seen.[75]

October 29, 1911, New York Times

The silliness of warfare! Science will put a stop to it someday. Philanthropists have failed to. Science can and will.[76]

October 29, 1911, *New York Times*

Are we ready for general peace? No. We are still not so far from the chimpanzee. The navy is an insurance policy for which the merchants must pay a premium.[77]

December 6, 1911, *New York Times*

Why should the American people be compelled to pay for the maintenance of an army in Mexico to protect the properties of a few men who got concessions and went in there for their own profit. This dollar diplomacy will soon be a thing of the past. Governments are not supported by the many to protect the few, and the sooner some of the few realize it the better.[78]

January 19, 1914, *New York Times*

We are conquering the enemies of life at a great rate. Our increase of the life-rate more than makes up for the decrease in the birth-rate . . . but war still helps to keep the population down.[79]

October 11, 1914, *New York Times*

This war is a catastrophe, but it isn't going to change the basic facts of life.[80]

October 11, 1914, *New York Times*

This war had to come. The tower of armament had to reach its apex, a point at which it had to stop. It reached it and it stopped. When it stopped the war came. Of course, it is a world disaster, but if it results in the general disarmament it will be an evil out of which great good will emerge. It will take the world a long time to recover from the evils of the war, but the whole disaster would be far more than offset by the advantages of a general disarmament.

After the war an era of general and rapid advance will begin.

Instead of turning toward military development the world's mental energies will be devoted to invention, engineering, and productive labor. I firmly believe that in a few years after the war we shall see the greatest constructive era that the world has ever known.[81]

October 11, 1914, *New York Times*

Making things which kill men is against my fibre. I would rather make people laugh. I leave that death-dealing work to my friends, the Maxim brothers.[82]

Hiram and Hudson Maxim manufactured weapons for the
U.S. military, including the machine gun.
October 26, 1914, *New York Times*

This war had to come. You can't blame anybody in particular. Those military gangs in Europe piled up armament until something had to break. It has to come, and it will be epoch-making. And its end will see the boundaries of Europe drawn around racial lines.[83]

October 26, 1914, *New York Times*

The war may not mean the end of kingdoms, but it will mean the ending of autocratic government. Democracy is spreading in Europe, and this will do more to bring it about than anything else could. You may talk about your orderly direction of government under such authority and how happy the people are, but I would rather live in a corrupt American city, where there is a lot of hesitation about legislation, than one of your orderly German cities, where a man must perform every act according to a code of laws set down and guarded jealously by armed hands.[84]

October 26, 1914, *New York Times*

The present war has taught the world that killing men in war is a scientific proposition.[85]

January 3, 1915, *New York Times*

There have been wars that have lasted thirty years, but those days are past. Killing men is a different matter today, and I believe the present struggle will not end for at least two years, although I hope it may end sooner than any of us expects.[86]

> January 3, 1915, *New York Times*

It has surprised me to see how the Americans have become weak-kneed over this war. They seem to be stricken with a sort of commercial paralysis. They want to get out and do something and now is the opportune time.[87]

> January 3, 1915, *New York Times*

If I could be reasonably sure of complete annihilation or absolute safety, I would go. The probability of "passing out" does not worry me, but I do draw the line on becoming an invalid or a cripple—a burden to myself and family for the remainder of my days.[88]

> Response when asked if he would volunteer for the navy
> in the event of war. April 18, 1915, *New York Times*

Going into war is the very last thing we should think of at present, as the President has said. . . . There is in my heart a feeling of the deepest horror over the destruction of the Lusitania. But if Germany agrees not to attack American ships with her submarines, I think we should be satisfied for the present, believing, as I do, of course, that she promptly will make such financial reparations for the destruction of American life as is possible. This must not be construed as meaning that I think money can condone such a crime, however.

. . . Then, if Germany does not keep her word and in the future show some regard for American rights we can find some way in which to retaliate.[89]

> Response to the sinking of the RMS *Lusitania*, which was
> torpedoed by a German U-boat off the coast of Ireland, killing
> all 1,959 people aboard. May 22, 1915, *New York Times*

I cannot take very seriously the stories that the German population is in imminent danger of starvation, and therefore, I am not
as deeply impressed as I might be by Germany's protests that the
blockade maintained by the Allies is destroying many innocent lives
of noncombatants through denying them food. And even were this
true starvation is a more humane method of warfare than asphyxiat-
ing bombs.[90]

May 22, 1915, *New York Times*

I have said that it is impossible for me to forgive the Lusitania horror. I hope something in the nature of palliation for it may lie in the
discovery of the fact that it really was the work of an irresponsible
naval officer.[91]

May 22, 1915, *New York Times*

I cannot imagine anything which Germany could do which would
make [war] an advisable or admirable course.[92]

May 22, 1915, *New York Times*

How could we help by going into the war? We haven't any troops,
we haven't any ammunition, we are an unorganized mob. I cannot
believe that Germany even seriously fears our entrance.[93]

May 22, 1915, *New York Times*

We don't want to fight and we won't have to fight, unless we go out
and look for a fight. The fact remains that I believe we ought to be
ready for it.[94]

May 22, 1915, *New York Times*

Incidentally the new methods [of warfare] offer an opportunity to
democracy such as it never had before. They have eliminated the
fortress and the secret movements of large armies and have made
trench fighting the most effective method. In that one addition to
military tactics it is fair to assume that the aeroplane has given to

the United States what amounts to an addition of two or three million soldiers.[95]

May 22, 1915, *New York Times*

I believe that the developments of the European war have proved beyond the shadow of a doubt the uselessness of large standing armies.[96]

May 30, 1915, *New York Times*

If any foreign power should seriously consider an attack upon this country a hundred men of special training quickly would be at work here upon new means of repelling the invaders. I would be at it, myself. There would be no lack of the spirit of determination or the spirit of self-sacrifice. Of these two qualities was the "Spirit of '76" made up. It is still latent here.[97]

May 30, 1915, *New York Times*

Germany was ready for war after the old idea of readiness, but her army never got to Paris. She was overready. She was so overready that she was nervous. Her trigger-fingers became jumpy. It was an attack of hysteria, due to overreadiness, which plunged Europe into war.[98]

May 30, 1915, *New York Times*

Another thing which has been proved is that no engine of destruction or defense can be so effective that the ingenuity of desperate men cannot devise something which will offset it. Germany's new field guns, the secret of which had been so carefully kept, were the sensation of the first weeks of the war, yet France matched them before it was too late.[99]

May 30, 1915, *New York Times*

I consider it a reasonable certainty that some day we shall have a war; and I consider it a probability that when that day comes we shall find ourselves unprepared to meet it. I believe it to be the duty of every American patriot to do what he can to see that this does not occur, but I do not believe that the events of recent months in Europe have shown their methods of preparation to be the right one.[100]

May 30, 1915, *New York Times*

Modern warfare is more a matter of machines than men.[101]

May 30, 1915, *New York Times*

There is practically no military sentiment in the United States, nor ever has been, but we have proved ourselves to be among the world's most powerful fighters whenever we have had to fight.[102]

May 30, 1915, *New York Times*

I am the last man who would be willing to suggest parsimony in expenditure upon coast and harbor defense. We should have more guns than we have now at all our harbors and they should be better guns, of long range than any ship can carry.[103]

May 30, 1915, *New York Times*

In trench fighting, with our unlimited supply of the most intelligent and independently thinking individual fighters in the world, we would be invincible.[104]

May 30, 1915, *New York Times*

[T]he Government should maintain a great research laboratory, jointly under military and naval and civilian control. In this could be developed the continually increasing possibilities of great guns, the minutiae of new explosives, all the technique of military and naval progression, without any vast expense.[105]

May 30, 1915, *New York Times*

The European war has served to draw attention to the fact that many American ideas and inventions have been allowed to slip by, and if this matter is put off until the war is over there is danger of it being forgotten.[106]

July 13, 1915, New York Times

The soldier of the future will not be a saber-bearing, blood-thirsty savage. He will be a machinist. The war of the future, that is, if the United States engages in it, will be a war in which machines, not soldiers, fight. For that reason we can gamble safely on a volunteer army provided we have a great quantity of officers trained and ready for service in forty-eight hours to lead and drill the new men.[107]

October 16, 1915, New York Times

I am down on military establishments. A standing army is not worth anything unless it is on a war footing, which is absurd.[108]

October 16, 1915, New York Times

Ideas! Well, bless your heart, I should say we have. . . . You also would be surprised to know the sources of the ideas. Bank Presidents sent them, messenger boys send them. I am reminded to say this by the fact that two of the best ideas we have had sent in to us touching upon offensive warfare have come, one from a bank President and another from a young messenger boy who has not yet cast his first vote.[109]

On suggestions made to the U.S. Naval Consulting Board, which Edison joined in 1915. October 16, 1915, New York Times

Tell them that the preparation for war is not military war, but should be done by shrewd business men in and economical way. Machines should be invented to save the waste in men.[110]

October 16, 1915, New York Times

The day of universal peace is a long, long way off. There's got to be a great deal more war, and it's going to be more destructive every year.

Science is going to make war a terrible thing—too terrible to contemplate. Pretty soon we can be mowing men down by the thousands—or even millions—almost by pressing a button. The slaughter will be so terrible that the machinery itself will virtually have to do the fighting.... A man is only one man, after all. A machine can be easily as good as twenty men. Then one man, using it, is as good as twenty men. He should be at least that good if he is American.[111]

November 6, 1915, *New York Times*

We must never become a military nation in the old sense of the term.[112]

November 6, 1915, *New York Times*

Since this [U.S. Naval Consulting] board was organized it has accomplished many good things, and they are pretty new, too, and will be very valuable.[113]

February 10, 1916, *New York Times*

There need be no fear that I will be as unsecretive [*sic*] as others, and divulge this all-important matter.[114]

March 9, 1916, *New York Times*

This talk about the United States being despised is nonsense. Neutrality is a mighty trying policy, but back of it are international law, the right of humanity and the future of civilization.[115]

September 4, 1916, *New York Times*

I am no pacifist. I believe that there are times when a nation has to fight. But war for the sake of war, or war for purposes of conquest, is horrible and unthinkable.[116]

September 10, 1916, *New York Times*

This war has broken into the progress of scientific discovery in general, but it will go on very rapidly as soon as the war is over.[117]

December 2, 1916, *Collier's Weekly*

We're setting up a good laboratory, and as soon as it is ready to work in I've got a lot of stunts I want to try for Uncle Sammy.[118]

Of his work as a naval consultant. December 2, 1916, *Collier's Weekly*

I want it understood that my aim in working on military problems is solely to help protect the country from attack. I wouldn't want a single hour in the interest of any plan for the aggression on the part of the United States against any other country.[119]

December 2, 1916, *Collier's Weekly*

I am in favor of compulsory military education. I know that if our twelve million young men were in good training and were educated *somewhat* in military matters, they would not be shot down like sheep.[120]

December 2, 1916, *Collier's Weekly*

How much is it worth to you to be an American citizen? How much are you willing to pay for the privilege of living under the Stars and Stripes? The fathers of some of you fought to save the Union; the great-grandfathers of a few of you fought to make this a free nation. Some of you came to America in order that your children and your children's children might have a fair chance at the battle of life. They are saying in Germany that the hearts of the American People are not in this war. Traitors to this country are secretly working to that end. Most of you here tonight are ineligible to military service, but it is within your power to help refute the slander that has been put on American patriotism. I do not believe we have become a decadent race in the last fifty years. I believe we are ready to make every sacrifice we are called upon to make.[121]

May 25, 1917, *New York Times*

These are strenuous days, with the fate of civilization hanging in the balance.[122]

June 8, 1918, *New York Times*

We are in this war, and we must see it through to a conclusion that justifies the sacrifices we have made. I do not say that Germany must be crushed. It may be that her deluded people will strike the scales from her eyes and overthrow the powers that have plunged the world into war.[123]

June 8, 1918, New York Times

We must not put our own selfish interests about the interests of the nation. We must give and we must do to the full limit of our respective abilities, in order that the war may be won in the shortest possible time.[124]

June 8, 1918, New York Times

We must win the war. We must provide all the arms, ammunitions, ordinance, airplanes, and equipment that can be transported to Europe, and we must build ships as rapidly as possible. We must make all the other goods that we can possibly make. We must keep on creating new wealth. We must keep our manufacturing organization in good running order. We must continue to go after foreign trade, and we must prepare ourselves for the intense competition for foreign markets that will come after the war.[125]

June 8, 1918, New York Times

[War is] [m]an's foolishness, that's all you can make out of it, man is a damn fool.[126]

August 28, 1918, New York Times

Yours for the Fourth Liberty Loan.[127]

Slogan coined by Edison for the Liberty Loan Committee.
September 18, 1918, New York Times

But I am absolutely opposed to letting them come over here.[128]

Predicting a future war with Japan, Edison believing Japan would become militaristic as a result of population growth.
February 10, 1921, New York Times

The only dynamite that works in this country is the dynamite of a sound idea.[129]

December 6, 1921, New York Times

Future wars are going to be waged almost exclusively with airplanes, submarines and gas. Battleships will not count for much. Guns are very spectacular instruments for killing—they make a great noise, and explosive shells blow great holes in the earth—but guns do not carry destruction over a broad area.[130]

A single charge of such gas as chemists now know how to make is sufficiently deadly to kill every man, woman and child in an equivalent to five or six city blocks.[131]

December 21, 1921, Wellsboro (Pa.) Gazette

We should experiment with the most deadly gasses and the biggest guns. Not that we will ever make use of them, but so that we may be prepared in case some other nation, through rascality, should attack us. I want all nations to be prepared so that it will be so terrible that the game will be up.[132]

February 12, 1922, St. Louis Globe-Democrat

I made about forty-five inventions during the war, all perfectly good ones, and they pigeon-holed every one of them. The Naval officers resented any interference by civilians. Those fellows are a close[d] corporation.[133]

On his war work for the U.S. Naval Consulting Board.
February 13, 1923, New York World

All the nations have had a terrible example in the World War, but memory is short. The sooner the World Court is established the better. But it must have something behind it to enforce its decrees; otherwise it will be useless.... [I]t might prevent war altogether, or, at least prevent them from becoming of great magnitude.[134]

February 12, 1925, New York Times

If wars are ever done away with, their cessation will not be due to sentimental arguments, but to the fact that science and invention may make war so dangerous to everyone concerned that the sheer patriotism of educated people in all nations, plus their common sense, will be universally against this stupid war-idea.[135]

January 1927, *Forum*

Don't make any mistake about that war; it will come. We may run along for a good many years without it, but sooner or later the nations of Europe will combine against the United States.[136]

November 26, 1927, *Literary Digest*

We will probably always have wars, for we go along with no change in our habits. It would be necessary to change human nature first.[137]

September 28, 1928, *New York Times*

There may be another war if people don't quiet down and be more sensible.[138]

April 1931, *Golden Book Magazine*

On the Press

Edison often cupped his ear in order to hear better.
Courtesy of the Thomas Edison National Historical Park, 022505007.

During Edison's lifetime, increasing literacy rates combined with the rise of the telegraph revolutionized news dissemination. Newspapers and magazines proliferated, and journalism assumed a new role in society. Because he sold and briefly published his own newspaper as a youth, Edison knew what reporters wanted.

Edison wasn't called the "Wizard of Menlo Park" solely for his inventions. His charm and wit drew reporters to him, and their stories brought him fame, free advertising, and investors. He was also a prankster who played practical jokes on a press all too willing to believe Edison capable of anything.

I lost the telephone patent in Germany through indulgence to the newspapers. . . . It is from no purely selfish motive that I keep my secret from the public. I have no wish to do it, but it is necessary for my own protection.[1]

October 20, 1878, *New York Sun*

Have I been too ready to talk about my schemes and projects? It is possible. But I like to talk about a thing I am interested in.[2]

December 28, 1878, *New York Graphic*

I know very well that my way of telling of every step I take is not strictly scientific; it is not the method of a reticent man, always asking himself what is prudent. I get letters from Europe urging me to fight reporters off. . . . But I have begun by taking the public into my confidence and I don't propose to keep anything I know, or propose to do, if I can help it.[3]

December 28, 1878, *New York Graphic*

I won't say a word to a newspaper man. Some of the newspaper men have so misconceived and misrepresented everything I have done with regard to the electric light that I am not going to give them any more information. They can rummage around here and draw their own conclusions.[4]

August 30, 1879, *New York World*

Now if [a rival's claims] hadn't gotten into the papers and explained his system, I wouldn't probably have received the necessary information to gain the suit with. Since then I have thought it best to let others do the talking for newspapers.[5]

September 8, 1885, *Lancaster (Pa.) New Era*

I like newspaper men and am always willing to do anything I can for them, so come and sit down.[6]

October 10, 1895, *Philadelphia Bulletin*

I don't mind being interviewed. I am used to it. It don't hurt me and I know the newspaper men must have something to give their readers.[7]

February 1896, *Norwalk (Ohio) Reflector*

I wish to protest through the *[New York] Sun* the many articles appearing in the sensational papers of New York from time to time, purporting to be interviews with me. About the colorful inventions and discoveries made or to be made by myself. Scarcely a single one is authentic. . . . I especially desire it to be known, if you will permit me, that I have nothing to do with an article advertised to appear in one of the papers about Mars.[8]

January 11, 1898, *New York Sun*

[P]ublish . . . a fact now and then.[9]

Response to being asked what the press needed to do.
February 24, 1901, *Dallas Morning News*

But what is it you want me to say?[10]

January 7, 1906, *New York Times*

It would give me all the pleasure imaginable to make an announcement every day in the year, but it is mere foolishness to express hopes when all [the] world wants or is concerned in are results.[11]

January 7, 1906, *New York Times*

To the Fourth Estate—through *The New York Times*—tell the truth.[12]

October 19, 1907, *New York Times*

I take three newspapers, and I read them, and I don't believe all they say, either.[13]

October 7, 1912 *New York Times*

Of course, I know that nothing is more interesting to the public than a good lie.[14]

Circa 1916

If a newspaper man is to be any good he must have imagination.[15]

February 13, 1923, *New York Times*

I think every newspaper ought to have a scientific reporter to go around to the research laboratories and see what they are doing.[16]

February 13, 1923, *New York Times*

Another thing you could do with the newspapers is to cut out a lot of trash. There is too much scandal trash in the papers, and the readers are losing interest.[17]

June 16, 1929, *New York Times*

[L]et me go home and have a little peace.[18]

June 16, 1929, *New York Times*

Practical Jokes Played on the Press

In ten years my machines will be used to provide the tables of the civilized world. Meat will be no longer killed and vegetables no longer grown, except by savages, for my methods will be so much cheaper.[19]

On his April Fool's Day hoax of 1878. May 23, 1878, *Pittsburgh Dispatch*

[The] April-first hoax concerning my alleged food machine has brought in a flood of letters from all parts of the country. It was very ingenious.[20]

May 10, 1878, letter to the *New York Graphic*

The gullibility of the South American may be appreciated when it is known that soon after the shirt story met their eyes the Brazilians began to send me drafts and checks for shirts.[21]

Remarking on his satirical story about inventing shirts made of thin sheets of gelatin that could be worn for a day, then peeled off and discarded. August 25, 1886, *New York Sun*

That man came to see me on one of the coldest days in the year. His nose was blue and his teeth were chattering. I really had nothing to tell him, but I hated to disappoint him, so I thought up this story about communicating with spirits, but it was all a joke.[22]

On his claim to a gullible reporter that he had a machine to communicate with the dead. October 12, 1926, *New York Times*

On the Law

Portrait of Edison. *Courtesy of the Thomas Edison
National Historical Park, 022605010.*

Edison believed in the value of a police force as a means of maintaining a safe and well-ordered society. When it came to the enforcement of patents, the inventor felt the system was entirely ineffective, failing to protect inventors and rewarding infringers.

His opinions on capital punishment reveal his pragmatic nature. Though personally opposed to execution, he was more than willing to develop and promote the electric chair as a quick and painless means of putting criminals to death. Further, he used such executions as a marketing tool. To illustrate that AC, or alternating current, promoted by George Westinghouse, was more dangerous than his own DC, or direct current, he filmed public executions of animals, including Topsy, a Coney Island elephant.

On the Legal System

[T]he contract was handed to me. I signed without reading it.[1]

Circa 1870s

I will stick to my contracts with [representatives in Europe, even] if I never make a dollar.[2]

November 14, 1879, letter to George G. Ward

I think we should be satisfied . . . onerous contracts are decidedly unsafe.[3]

April 3, 1880, letter to George Edward Gouraud

A lawsuit is the suicide of time.[4]

July 13, 1885, diary entry

The man who framed the law making American patents expire when the prior foreign patents expires was a Himalayan jackass.[5]

March 29, 1893, *Quincy (Ill.) Daily Herald*

Curious business, this law business, isn't it?[6]

> December 5, 1902, *New York Times*

Business matters are distasteful to me. When the lawyers say sign, I sign.[7]

> December 5, 1902, *New York Herald*

I'd rather do almost any kind of a day's work than be a witness [at a trial].[8]

> December 5, 1902, *New York Herald*

There is no justice in law. It has resolved itself into technicalities and formulas. A case will be thrown out of one court and carried to another, it will be sent back on writs and advanced on argument, and bandied back and forth more for the exercise of legal practice than for the attainment of justice. Where an important case might be settled in a short time by the use of common sense, it is prolonged for years through the technicality of jurisprudence, the whole course of which defeats the object sought.[9]

> September 13, 1913, *Literary Digest*

All good lawyers know how to break wills and contracts.[10]

> Circa 1916

On Patents

If prior publication [of an invention] is of no use, what protection has any scientific man[?][11]

> October 7, 1878, letter to William Fletcher Barrett

[S]uch a rule [limiting protections for inventors and forcing them to pay more] in the past might have embarrassed and discouraged the inventor who had got hold of the clue to the secret of nature, have delayed for a hundred years the beneficial use by mankind of inventions which are now indispensable to modern life and commerce.[12]

> February 17, 1879, letter to Benjamin Franklin Butler

They have infringed my lamps, but I am not surprised at that. I wonder that all the companies have not stolen the lamp. When you get anything like this perfected you have infringers on every side of you.[13]

> February 24, 1881, *Cincinnati Enquirer*

Within the last few years I have become extremely skeptical as to the value of any patent, and so long as our patent law remains in its present iniquitous shape, I shall try to do without patents.[14]

> January 1888, *New York Post*

I have lost all faith in patent judges + everything relating to patents + don't care if the whole system was squelched.[15]

> July 2, 1888, marginalia on a letter from the National
> Electrical Light Association and Arthur Steuart

Every one is infringed. After a thing is perfected and commercially introduced so as to show there is money in it half a dozen parties start to infringe it.[16]

> 1888 interview

The Edison Company have [*sic*] never stolen or infringed a patent yet, and never will if I can prevent it.[17]

> June 18, 1890, letter to Samuel Insull

Our present patent laws, which, as interpreted by the courts, encourage perjury and put a premium on fraud, are worse than a farce, and I would have been a gainer if I had never taken out a patent.[18]

> 1890 interview

No sooner does an inventor make known some important mechanical discovery by applying for a patent, than a pirate comes along and steals it. Years pass before the case comes to trial, and in the meantime the practice of the courts gives the pirate the benefit of the doubt. Many patents are decided in the inventor's favor only when the patent is about to expire, and has therefore become almost worthless. This is all wrong.[19]

1890 interview

The patent laws are made for the protection of the inventor, but they operate to his disadvantage if any one has capital enough to steal his inventions.[20]

July 26, 1891, *New York Journal*

By the way, I would like to correct an idea that seems to be pretty generally held that I make my money out of patents. That is not a fact. I make my money out of manufactures, not out of patents, although the processes may be founded upon discoveries which I have patented.[21]

July 26, 1891, *New York Journal*

I have taken out 700 patents but I have never had one minute's protection.[22]

November 9, 1891, *New York Journal*

[S]o far as the patents themselves go, I have stood an actual loss in experimenting and in lawsuits of $600,000. I should have been better off if I had not taken out any patents.[23]

March 18, 1892, *Cranbury (N.J.) Press*

[I have] 600 [patents] and in not one of them have I been sustained by the courts. I have spent thousands of dollars in endeavoring to maintain a right to my own inventions, but until the laws on that subject are radically changed there can be no incentive to any inventor dependent on his inventions for sustenance to give the world the benefit of his work.[24]

April 22, 1892, unnamed newspaper

Our patent system puts a premium on rascality.[25]

May 18, 1895, unnamed newspaper

One of the biggest inventions, for which patents were asked years ago, has just been declared mine by law. Meantime other men have been and are using it and are deriving the financial benefit, all on account of the workings of the patent system. Of course, I can sue them, but it will be a long time before I do anything. In short, there is comparatively little reward for the inventor of the important machine.[26]

December 26, 1897, *St. Louis Star*

If you have a good idea, go ahead and invent a way to use it and keep your process secret.[27]

Circa 1916

You patent a thing and the other fellow starts even with you. Keep it to yourself and you have the machinery going before the other fellow is awake. Patents may protect some things, and still others they only advertise.[28]

Circa 1916

The new plant-patent bill will be a great boon to agriculture and plant development. . . . As a rule the plant breeder is a poor man, with no opportunity for material reward. Now he has a grubstake.[29]

On the Plant Patent Act of 1930. May 30, 1930, *New York Times*

But it is a miserable system we have in this country that menaces a poor man starting out to invent something. I know of several inventors who are poor. Their ideas would have made them millionaires. But they were kept poor by the pirates who were allowed to usurp their rights in courts.[30]

January 1932, *Modern Mechanics and Inventions*

On Police and Law Enforcement

[W]ith the aid of the police, civilization so rapidly advances.[31]

July 13, 1885, diary entry

I have never had time, not even five minutes, to be tempted to do anything against the moral law, civil law, or any law whatever. If I were to hazard a guess as to what young people should do to avoid temptation, it would be to get a job and work at it so hard that temptation would not exist for them.[32]

January 1917, *New York Mail*

We believe ourselves to be highly civilized, but if we took the police out of New York City half the population would be in panic-stricken flight within two days. If I were asked to make a definition of civilization I might say something of this sort: Civilization is a lot of people in one place—plus a policeman.[33]

December 6, 1924, *Collier's Weekly*

But that policeman must be a scientific product, not a hit or miss affair.[34]

December 1926, *Forum*

What is civilization but the restriction of personal liberty for the improvement of mankind?[35]

September 28, 1928, *New York Times*

On Capital Punishment and the Electric Chair

[A]lthough I would join heartily in an effort to totally abolish capital punishment, . . . it is the duty of the [government] to adopt the most humane method available for the purpose of disposing of criminals under the sentence of death.

The best appliance in this connection is to my mind the one which will perform its work in the shortest space of time, and inflict the least amount of suffering to its victim. This I believe can be accomplished by the use of Electricity and the most suitable apparatus for the purpose . . . principally in this country by Mr. Geo. Westinghouse.[36]

December 19, 1887, letter to A. P. Southwick

There is no reason why there should be any failure in an execution by means of electricity.[37]

November 4, 1888, *New York Sun*

I do not approve of any execution. I think that the killing of a human being is an act of foolish barbarity. It is childish—unworthy of a developed intelligence. Society must protect itself, but it is not driven to any such means except by its own refusal to be wise. I believe in the confinement of criminals. There are some that should be restrained all their lives, but killing them destroys the last hope of making them useful. I would have them work, but not in such a way as to conflict with the laborers of the factories. I would like to see them trained to the labors of making statues from designs and other works or ornamentation for the beautifying of public buildings perhaps. Let the prisoners be put into the quarries, or something of that sort. It seems to me that there are enough ways to make the criminal useful without infringing upon the rights of honest laborers. No; I am not in favor of executions, but if they are to take place electricity will do the work, and it is more certain and perhaps a little more civilized than a rope.[38]

November 4, 1888, *New York Sun*

We killed a dog here yesterday.... So far as the unfortunate animal's death was concerned, the experiment was a success.[39]

November 4, 1888, *New York Sun*

That's a good idea. The man will be killed with a current of the proper number of volts in the tenth of a second. There won't be time for the sense-bearing nerves to telegraph the news that he is hurt to his brain before he will be dead from the shock. And it will be so lightning like quick that the criminal can't suffer much.[40]

November 4, 1888, *Brooklyn Citizen*

The Westinghouse engines and not mine were considered best adapted to the speedy extermination of criminals.[41]

May 23, 1889, *Pittsburgh Post*

I have come to the conclusion that there is no doubt that 1,000 volts will cause instantaneous and painless death.[42]

July 23, 1889, *Brooklyn Daily Eagle*

No, the action of the electricity is too rapid for a man to be conscious of it.[43]

August 8, 1895, *Buffalo Times*

Society is rich enough to confine [prisoners] for life. Killing them is a relic of our barbaric past. The pardoning power should be severely restricted.[44]

1929 interview

On the United States

Edison represented the U.S. Naval Consulting Board in the New York City
Preparedness Parade on June 16, 1916. *Courtesy of the Thomas Edison
National Historical Park, 25.300.10.*

Many of Edison's comments about the United States and other nations were influenced by his visits to Europe in 1873, 1889, and 1911. His keen observations of militarism in Europe were often uncannily predictive of World War I.

The inventor also commented about particular places within the United States. His homes in New Jersey and Florida helped him to escape the pressures of society's expectations.

On the United States

[A]nd what I saw [in Europe] convinced me that American is still the greatest of them all.[1]

> October 8, 1911, *New York Times*

I found no country on the other side [of the Atlantic] which could compare with this one, found no people so intelligent, so honest, so companionable as our own.[2]

> October 22, 1911, *New York Times*

We neglect the magnificent opportunities our country offers us with startling carelessness.[3]

> October 22, 1911, *New York Times*

I don't know whether American life is really as enervating as they are fond of calling it, but I feel sure that life in the average small European town is stagnating, dulling, deadening to energy and ambition. If we have too much excitement, they have too little.[4]

> October 22, 1911, *New York Times*

There is only one place in the world where women really have either opportunity or that peculiar consideration which their sex, its limitations, and its unavoidable responsibilities entitle them, and that place is this country. In the United States, no matter what our critics, foreign or domestic, say to the contrary, the Paradise of womankind is located. Our women are the finest in the world, mentally and physically, and we have treated them and do treat them better than women ever have been treated elsewhere.[5]

October 29, 1911, *New York Times*

We are more chivalrous with women, we are more hospitable, we are, in the best sense of the word, far more polite than any of the European peoples whom I came in contact with.[6]

October 29, 1911, *New York Times*

[W]hat I saw made me ashamed for my own United States, I am afraid. The workingmen of New York City are not housed as are these Berliners. What a contrast to the dreadful tenements which disgrace and deface New York's crowded districts![7]

October 29, 1911, *New York Times*

Americans, when traveling in Europe, too often wear a chip upon their shoulders.[8]

October 29, 1911, *New York Times*

I guess I am a patriot. Nothing seemed as good to me in Europe as the same thing here, in the long run, although I recognized innumerable detailed superiorities.[9]

October 29, 1911, *New York Times*

I am a patriotic American, I believe, but some of this patriotism is false pride. I think we could stand a little humiliation and the expense of remaining away from war.[10]

February 12, 1914, *New York Times*

We are as clever at mechanics, whether they be those of war or peace, as any people of the world. We gave the world the ironclad war vessel as the result of one emergency. We gave the world the submarine. Our Wright brothers perfected the aeroplane.[11]

May 30, 1915, *New York Times*

Always we have done new things or done old things in a new way, and frequently they have been better things and better ways than Europe has developed.[12]

May 30, 1915, *New York Times*

America is the greatest machine country in the world, and its people are the greatest machinists. They can, moreover, invent machinery faster and have it more efficient than any other two countries.[13]

October 16, 1915, *New York Times*

This nation has agreed to save democracy from despotism, and at no matter what cost it must carry out its contract. The nation is not a third person—it is ourselves. The nation's obligation is our obligation, and each of us should work harder than we ever worked before, in order to better discharge his share of the obligation which the nation has assumed.[14]

July 15, 1917, *New York Times*

Our boys made good in France. The word American has a new meaning in Europe. Our soldiers have made it with courage, generosity, self-restraint and modesty. We are proud of the North Americans who risked their lives for the liberty of the world. . . . The Great War will live vividly in the minds of Americans for the next hundred years.[15]

1918 radio address.

We, the people of the United States, by the grace of God free and independent, do not always seem to be, the same grace, free and intelligent. I suppose, however, that we are doing as well as anybody.[16]

October 1926, *Forum*

What the country needs now is the practical skilled engineer, who is capable of doing everything. In three or four centuries when the country is settled and commercialism is diminished, there will be time for the literary men.[17]

April 1931, *Golden Book Magazine*

Be courageous! I have lived a long time. I have seen history repeat itself again and again. I have seen many depressions in business. Always America has emerged from these, stronger and more prosperous. Be as brave as your fathers were before you. Have faith! Go forward![18]

June 11, 1931, *Fort Myers (Fla.) News-Press*

On Places within the United States

ON NEW YORK CITY

I never go to New York if I can help it. I would not go if I were to be paid $500 a trip.[19]

February 1917, *New York Sun*

The electric sign is pretty good. Broadway would not be so nice looking without it. That's what makes Broadway. But I haven't seen Broadway more than half a dozen times. I feel like a countryman because I get over here so infrequently.[20]

November 16, 1923, *New York Times*

ON NEW JERSEY AND MENLO PARK, WEST ORANGE, AND GLENMONT

[Menlo Park is] the prettiest spot in New Jersey.[21]

Circa 1870s

But when I entered I was paralyzed. To think that it was possible to buy a place like this, which a man with taste for art and a talent for decoration had put ten years of enthusiastic study and effort into—too enthusiastic in fact—the idea fairly turned my head and I snapped it up. It is a great deal too nice for me, but it isn't half nice enough for my little wife here.[22]

> Edison's reaction to Glenmont, the West Orange, New Jersey, home when he first saw it in 1885

ON FLORIDA, SOUTHWEST FLORIDA, AND FORT MYERS

The air here is perfect; the weather, as you see, is beautiful, and the days are a constant succession of blue skies and warm sunshine, and to all this I owe my rapidly returned health.[23]

> March 1887, *New York World Magazine*

Why this will be the finest thing that ever happened to lovely Fort Myers. Beyond doubt you have the finest place in the country and if you build this sea wall, inside of a few years this section will not be large enough to hold the tourists that will be scrambling to get here every winter. Yes, sir, by all means build the sea wall.[24]

> He later changed his views upon learning that the seawall would obstruct his view and put an end to his privacy.
> April 2, 1908, *Fort Myers (Fla.) Press*

There is only one Fort Myers in the United States, and there are 90,000,000 people who are going to find it out.[25]

> The population of the United States was 90 million at the time. The statement became the motto for the community. March 25, 1914, *Fort Myers (Fla.) Press*

There are over one hundred million people in the United States, but only one Fort Myers, the flower city of Tropical Florida.[26]

> Edison updated the slogan as population increased, but it never caught on. The locals considered 90 million enough and kept the original quote as their motto. May 3, 1923, *Fort Myers (Fla.) Press*

The Land of Perpetual Spring.[27]

April 24, 1916, *Fort Myers (Fla.) Press*

Southwest Florida is one of the best places in the world to spend the winter and Fort Myers is the best spot in Southwest Florida.[28]

February 12, 1926, *Fort Myers (Fla.) Tropical News*

There are millions of people up north in the cold who are going to learn about Florida. Let them sell all the land they want but they can't buy our place.[29]

May 29, 1926, *Fort Myers (Fla.) Palm Leaf*

Florida is about as near to heaven as any man can get.[30]

March 17, 1930, *Fort Myers (Fla.) Press*

Florida can't live off the tourists. Must produce more from the soil.[31]

March 17, 1930, *Fort Myers (Fla.) Press*

It feels like living again to be back home in Fort Myers.[32]

January 22, 1931, *Fort Myers (Fla.) Press*

On Other Nations and Their Populations

Edison was visited by a delegation from the Japanese Chamber of Commerce in October 1909. *Courtesy of the Thomas Edison National Historical Park, 14.820.16.*

Edison harbored prejudices against a number of ethnic groups. He feared Sicilians, thought Mexicans were lazy, and was alternately repulsed and fascinated by the business acumen of Jews. These views were influenced by contemporary pseudoscientific beliefs that separated humanity into a continuum of civilized and savage races. Unlike others of his generation, Edison did not believe racial groups were static in their development. He had faith that education and evolution would combine to enlighten all races eventually.

On Europe and Europeans

They are far more sensible in their expenditures. The average European who cannot afford that thing which happens, for one reason or another, to be abnormally high-priced, meets the situation simply by getting on without it. Thus the high price does not drive him into bankruptcy.[1]

October 22, 1911, *New York Times*

Both France and Germany drink too much alcohol.[2]

October 22, 1911, *New York Times*

I saw no drunkenness upon the Continent. They spread their alcohol over a long time and absorb it in a highly diluted form, but, while it does not madden them into sudden frenzies, it has its sad effects of quite as great importance. The Continent, as a whole, is not intoxicated but stupefied by alcohol, and I cannot see that the effect of this upon the human system, brain and body, is likely to be any better than that of quick drinking and more apparent drunkenness.[3]

October 22, 1911, *New York Times*

The Englishman manufactures bulk, the German works upon a little finer scale, and the Frenchman makes high-grade, high-art, and high-value goods.[4]

October 22, 1911, New York Times

In Europe drinking with the meals is universal among young and old, and this may to a large extent, if not entirely, offset America's bad cooking. Personally I would rather have bad cooking and no liquor than good cooking and a lot of alcohol.[5]

October 22, 1911, New York Times

But it is not to be denied that the Continental European farmer is an infinitely better, principally because an infinitely more careful and less wasteful farmer, than the average man who tills our soil. And everywhere he is being taught how best to better methods, decrease even his slight wastefulness, fertilize, save labor.[6]

October 29, 1911, New York Times

The French must guard what laurels they have won in days gone by with an exceeding care. I firmly believe the Germans have begun a war against them upon lines quite different from any past hostilities.[7]

October 29, 1911, New York Times

[I]t is the intention of the German people to make Berlin, in days to come and not so far away, what Paris used to be—the greatest pleasure city in the world. And they will do it. They will make Paris second-class.[8]

October 29, 1911, New York Times

The average American has a sense of being crowded over there [in Europe]. The population is too dense, and everything is tainted by the hand of man. One sees nothing wild in Europe. Even the trees are planted. This got on my nerves. The only wild things which I saw on the whole trip were two wild rabbits. One gets to feeling as if he would give anything to get back into a world which nature has made and man had no hand in. One longs intensely to see something wild.[9]

October 29, 1911, *New York Times*

We saw some very beautiful women when we were in Paris, but throughout France the women do not compare with ours. The Hungarian women are, some of them, very handsome, and there are handsome women in Vienna. There are not so many in Berlin. . . . I had previously believed, and now I am quite certain, that our women are the handsomest in all the world.

. . . The unparalleled beauty of our women is, very likely, due to our cross breeding. The laws of Mendel have a free chance here.[10]

October 29, 1911, *New York Times*

The French are not, I think, deteriorating, but they are not advancing. The Germans, on the other hand, are advancing very rapidly. The whole nation has awakened, sprung, as it were, out of its lethargy.[11]

October 29, 1911, *New York Times*

Germany has made the great mistake of believing Great Britain and France decadent nations. The Germans are a great people commercially, industrially, and agriculturally, but they have been brought up in the atmosphere of egotism. It is too bad that everything in the country has been subordinated to the military caste, and I think the sooner this system is ended, the better for the German people.[12]

January 3, 1915, *New York Times*

They treat me as if I were a kind of trade mark.[13]

May 26, 1916, *Cranbury (N.J.) Press*

I hope that when we do reference the brave boys who fell in France we shall not forget their brothers in arms who wore the uniforms of our allies. I believe that the national airs of France, Great Britain, Italy and Belgium should, for all time to come, be as familiar as our own *Star Spangled Banner.*[14]

1918 radio address

The Germans are miserably poor losers. The British are good losers.[15]

February 13, 1923, *New York Times*

On England and the English

English small towns are the prettiest in Europe.[16]

October 22, 1911, *New York Times*

The English are not an inventive people; they don't eat enough pie.[17]

April 1931, *Golden Book Magazine*

On France and the French

The French must be a very isolated people.[18]

February 10, 1878, letter to Theodore Puskas

Oh, they don't have inventors, in the American sense of the word, in Paris at all. . . . That is a profession which they seem to know nothing about over here.[19]

September 8, 1889, *New York World*

Take France, for instance. She is a republic, but something has gone wrong with her. She is no longer vital, as we are, if she ever was vital.[20]

October 22, 1911, *New York Times*

The cooking in France is far superior to ours, not only in the large cities, but in the smallest, meanest town. It has its effect upon the national health, the national temper, the national prosperity. Not only is it far more palatable than the cooking in this country, on the average, but it is far more sanitary.[21]

October 22, 1911, *New York Times*

An average French cook will take what an average American housewife would waste and make a good and wholesome meal out of it.[22]

October 22, 1911, *New York Times*

French cooking introduced here would prevent in a year's time at least a small proportion of our numerous divorce suits, and reduce our death rate.[23]

October 22, 1911, *New York Times*

There are not many newspapers in the French towns. The Frenchman does not seem to hanker after news, even after printed local news. I hadn't thought of that before. It's really a bad sign for France.[24]

October 22, 1911, *New York Times*

On Germany and the Germans

[The Germans] are turning out some up-to-date stuff, too. I noted progress everywhere but Germany is leading. I also noted that a lot of the machinery they are using was manufactured in America.[25]

October 8, 1911, *New York Times*

German small towns do not excel. Her little towns and villages are about as bad as those of France, but her manufacturing industries are pushing ahead much faster than ours are. That seems like a humiliating thing to say, but it is true undoubtedly. German manufacturing progress is remarkable. And the growth of her manufactures is constant and tremendous.[26]

October 22, 1911, *New York Times*

Germany is, indeed, up to date in all branches of mechanical and scientific advance. . . . She is the most scientific of all the nations although she is nowhere near us in applied science.

In some lines she is, however, preeminent. She stands alone in the chemical industries, but there, again, her chemical laboratories and factories are full of American machinery.[27]

October 22, 1911, *New York Times*

The Germans are the world's most persistent people. . . . It will take hard work and intelligent work in the United States to prevent them from outstripping us.[28]

October 22, 1911, *New York Times*

At German restaurants the general tendency toward overeating is a painful sight to witness, really. Americans, as a rule, I have observed, eat about twice as much as they need; Germans eat twice as much as Americans, which is four times as much as they need. The prosperity of the German nation is in spite of the most extraordinary overeating.[29]

October 22, 1911, *New York Times*

I became impressed with another thing—I believe I see the true inwardness of the Emperor's unwavering naval policy. No one wants war less than he; no one would do more to keep out of a war.[30]

October 22, 1911, *New York Times*

[Germany's] tremendous consumption of beer, wine, and high alcoholic ciders is appalling. It hurts her people mentally and physically and hurts the nation economically.[31]

October 22, 1911, *New York Times*

Berlin is truly wonderful.... They are doing great thing[s].[32]

October 29, 1911, *New York Times*

The German nation is most fortunate in the possession of its present Kaiser as a general factotum in its Government.... The description of him as the "War Lord" was mistaken. He is a man of peace, for peace means marks and florins on the right side of the ledger, while war means deficits and waste.... He'll never go to war if he can help it. He'll never go to war if war can possibly be avoided.[33]

October 29, 1911, *New York Times*

Germany prepared and trained for this war as a pugilist trains for a championship prizefight. She expected to deliver the knockout punch in the Fall of 1914. Her boasted far-sightedness proved to be gravely at fault. Today, after nearly four years of warfare, Germany is still trying vainly to land a knockout. Like a desperate pugilist, who feels his strength ebbing rapidly, and knows he can last but a few more rounds, the Hun is staking everything on the chance of landing a lucky punch.[34]

June 8, 1918, *New York Times*

Germany must be cured forever of the desire to wage war.[35]

June 8, 1918, *New York Times*

On the Irish

The Irish, you know, are good fighters.[36]

September 1932, *Harper's Magazine*

On the Jews

Do you want to know my definition of a successful invention? It is something that is so practical that a Polish Jew will buy it.[37]

July 1911, *Century Magazine*

The Jews are certainly a remarkable people, as strange to me in their isolation from all the rest of mankind, as those mysterious people called Gypsies.[38]

November 15, 1911, letter to Isaac Markens

The trouble with him is that he has been persecuted for centuries by ignorant, malignant bigots and forced into his present characteristics, and he acquired a sixth sense, which gives him an almost unerring judgement in trade affairs.[39]

November 15, 1911, letter to Isaac Markens

I believe that In [*sic*] America, where he is free, that in time he will cease to be so clannish and not carry to such extreemes [*sic*] his natural advantages.[40]

November 15, 1911, letter to Isaac Markens

Less of this [lag in the development of women's brains] is evident in the development of the Jewish than in that of any other race. The almost supernatural business instinct of the Jew may be, I think, attributed to the fact that the various persecutions of the race have forced it to develop all its strength—its strength of women as well as that of men. Women have, from the beginning, taken part in Jewish councils; Jewish women have shared, always, in the pursuits of Jewish men; especially have they been permitted to play their part in business management. The result is that the Jewish child receives commercial acumen not only from the father's but from the mother's side.[41]

October 12, 1912, *Good Housekeeping*

On Mexico and the Mexicans

Of course, the Latin Americans are a peculiar people, and fighting is second nature to them, but when they have been made to understand that life is not a mere fight, then Mexico will prosper.[42]

January 19, 1914, *New York Times*

[M]en, women, and children are inveterate smokers of cigarettes in the southern republic. That is why Mexicans as a race are not clear headed.[43]

May 11, 1914, *New York Times*

On Russia and the Soviet Union

The Reds have done pretty well, but they are cruel. And they are bucking human nature. Yes, perhaps they too can stimulate research, as private American industry does. But their experiment will end wrong, in my opinion. History says so. It is a peculiar thing that the common people are best off in that country which has the most millionaires. Yet they are always down on the millionaires. It doesn't seem right, and I cannot understand it.[44]

January 1931, *Review of Reviews*

On Sicilians

You can't trust [them]. . . . They'll stick a knife in your back.[45]

Circa 1929

On Switzerland and the Swiss

There are certain details of Swiss life that shocked me. There is less regard for women, there, then I have been accustomed to in my own country—so much less regard that I found the spectacle a bit appalling. I saw many women there, for instance, harnessed to plows, yoke-mates with cattle.[46]

October 22, 1911, *New York Times*

Switzerland is a republic, and I looked for progress there, but found very little.[47]

October 29, 1911, *New York Times*

On Gender, Humanity, and Youth

Edison views a demonstration of an Edison dictating machine on July 20, 1914.
Courtesy of the Thomas Edison National Historical Park, 14.650.1.

Edison has been called a misogynist. After all, he did say, "Direct thought is not at present an attribute of femininity." But this judgment neglects the larger context of his quotation, which goes on to say that he believed women lagged behind men intellectually, but not because of any inherent defect. Instead, the drudgery of women's work and their lack of education and vocational opportunities prevented them from evolving as an intellectual equal to men. He believed that his labor-saving devices, better education and the continued improvement of the human species as a result of evolution would elevate women. Still, Edison was no feminist. He came to support suffrage, but believed women's sphere should be limited to the home.

On Women

What is home without a mother?[1]

July 12, 1885, diary entry

[A] woman is a wonderful being, full of mystery and hard to manage.[2]

May 12, 1891, *Chicago Evening Post*

The time is not far distant when practically all of the work now done by women in her homekeeping, so painstakingly and laboriously, will be done better, more simply, without labor, by machine.[3]

August 11, 1908, *Dallas Morning News*

Not a word, not a word. I told you I would not mention the estimates [of what would happen in the future] except as to those I thought of the greatest value.[4]

Refusing to respond to a question on woman's suffrage.
January 3, 1912, *New York Times*

If women could only be made to realize that they would retain their girlish beauty of complexion and figure almost to the end of life, if they would eat less, a great part of our battle for right living would be won.[5]

April 13, 1912, *Health & Strength*

Many a woman's life in old days was shortened; many a woman's life in these days is being shortened, by her presence for long hours each day in an overheated atmosphere above a cook-stove. The application of electricity to domestic work will do away with this.[6]

October 1912, *Good Housekeeping*

Women do not take enough pains with their cooking.[7]

March 1913, *Good Housekeeping*

[Electricity] will develop woman to the point where she can think straight. Direct thought is not at present an attribute of femininity. In this woman is now centuries, ages, even epochs behind man. That it is true is not her fault, but her misfortune, and the misfortune of the race. Man must accept responsibility for it, for it has been through his superior strength that he has held his dominance over woman and delayed her growth.[8]

October 12, 1912, *Good Housekeeping*

Under these new influences [of electricity reducing the drudgery of women's work] woman's brain will change and achieve new capabilities, both of effort and accomplishment.[9]

October 12, 1912, *Good Housekeeping*

The exercise of women's brains will build for them new fibers, new involutions, and new folds. If women had had the same struggle for existence which has confronted men, they would have been physically as strong, as capable of mind. But in the past they were protected, or, if not protected, forced into drudgery. These days are the days of woman's start upon the race—her first fair start.[10]

October 12, 1912, *Good Housekeeping*

The brain of woman in the past has been, to an extent, an idle brain. She has been occupied with petty tasks which, while holding her attention closely, have not given her brain exercise; such thinking as she has had time for, she has very largely found unnecessary because the stronger sex has done it for her.[11]

October 12, 1912, *Good Housekeeping*

The evolution of the brain of the male human has been the most wonderful of all the various phenomena of nature. When, in the new era of emancipation from the thralldom of the everyday mechanical task, the brain of woman undergoes a similar development, then, and only then, will the race begin to reach its ultimate. Yes, the mental power of the child born in the future will be marvelous, for to it women will make a contribution as great as that of man.[12]

October 12, 1912, *Good Housekeeping*

There never was any need for woman's retardation. Man's selfishness, his lust for ownership, must be held responsible for it. He was not willing to make woman equal partner in his various activities, and so he held her back from an ability to fill an equal partnership.[13]

October 12, 1912, *Good Housekeeping*

The housewife of the future will be neither a slave to servants nor herself a drudge. She will give less attention to the home, because the home will need less; she will be rather a domestic engineer than a domestic laborer, with the greatest of all handmaidens, electricity, at her service.[14]

October 12, 1912, *Good Housekeeping*

What we want now is quality, not quantity. The woman of the future—the domestic engineer, not the domestic drudge—the wife, not the dependent; not alone the mother, but the teacher and developer, will help to bring this quality about.[15]

October 12, 1912, *Good Housekeeping*

If I had my way, no woman, no matter what her social station might be, would be exempt from the necessity of taking a course at a cooking school.[16]

March 1913, *Good Housekeeping*

[I]f women who set store on beauty would but realize that too much sleep and too much food are beauty wreckers they would see to it that their daughters started right. Many of them learn the truth by the time they are 50, but it is then too late to take advantage of it for themselves.[17]

October 11, 1914, *New York Times*

Every woman in this country is going to have the vote. [That women would neglect their homes is] Bosh! You haven't heard suffrage breaking up homes in the Western States, have you? I haven't.[18]

August 19, 1915, *Wellsboro (Pa.) Gazette*

Certainly I am in favor of giving women the right to vote.[19]

October 15, 1915, *Suffolk County (N.Y.) News*

The instincts of women are good and they will have their voice in government. They'll have their say.[20]

February 12, 1916, *New York Times*

I am a believer in the right of women to vote. When I see ignorant men voting, I think it is a shame that intelligent women like we see here today cannot vote. I am with you heart and soul. I believe in suffrage.[21]

October 2, 1916, *New York Times*

Hoover will carry through his program without interference or there will be trouble. Every woman that I have spoken to believes he is the right man for President.[22]

May 12, 1920, *New York Times*

I think on the whole this young flapper damsel, so often referred to is all right.[23]

February 11, 1924, *Boston Daily Globe*

I think the modern young women as a whole, are all right. Their actions are foolish but not serious.[24]

February 12, 1924, *New York Times*

You can't beat the women. They all want to find out about the future, and some of them believe it.[25]

Regarding his wife's conversation with a mystic at a fair.
February 12, 1930, *Fort Myers (Fla.) Press*

It is very difficult to make women believe anything that is so. Women as a class are inclined to be obstinate. They do not seem to want to get out of the beaten paths.[26]

April 1931, *Golden Book Magazine*

Ask me nothing about women. I do not understand them and don't try to.[27]

April 1931, *Golden Book Magazine*

On Men

If I get to love a man he dies right away.[28]

> Commenting on the unexpected deaths of several
> valued employees. April 23, 1878, *New York World*

I have always retained a soft spot in my heart for a Southern gentleman.[29]

> Circa 1910–19

Man is at present little, if any, more than half what he might be. The child may be considered the mean between his father and his mother—between the undeveloped female and the developed male. The male has had the full of mental exercise since society first organized; it has been denied the female.[30]

> October 12, 1912, *Good Housekeeping*

We need more men of imagination.[31]

> February 12, 1921, *New York Times*

Competent men are so scarce that there are not enough to go around.[32]

> October 22, 1927, *New York Times*

You ask me to give some advice for young men. What's the use of giving advice to young men when they won't take it?[33]

> February 11, 1928, *Fort Myers (Fla.) Press*

Capacity for leadership is born in a man.[34]

> February 11, 1929, *Tampa Tribune*

The man, who has reached the age of 36 is just about ready to discard the illusions built upon false theories, for which wrong instruction and usually ignorance previously have made him an easy mark.[35]

> September 8, 1929, *New York Times*

I like to see a man get mad sometimes and have some bad habits too. I don't like them when they're too good.[36]

> April 1931, *Golden Book Magazine*

On Marriage

Dot just read to me outlines of her proposed novel, the basis seems to be a marriage under duress. I told her that in case of a marriage to put in bucketful of misery. That would make it realistic.[37]

> July 12, 1885, diary entry regarding the literary endeavors
> of his daughter Marion, nicknamed "Dot"

Don't you know that the fixed Law of the Organic world requires one man for one woman and that all normal well balanced men never have the least desire to Contravene that law, its only the ill balanced degenerates + Conceited Egotist that does such things.[38]

> 1897–98, note to his wife, Mina

When women progress side by side with men, matrimony will become the perfect partnership. This perfect partnership will produce a childhood made up of individuals who would now be thought not only mental, but physical and moral prodigies.[39]

> October 12, 1912, *Good Housekeeping*

If you have decided it must be, then the sooner it is done the better. it can't be worse than life in front line trenches.[40]

> March 25, 1918, telegram sent to his son Charles
> upon learning he was to be married

It is not good for man—or woman either—to live alone. Of that I am sure.[41]

> January 1927, *Forum*

And one tendency of the times which I am inclined to think is bad is the apparently increasing avoidance of marriage or its postponement until an age when the adaptation of one individual of the couple involved to the other is difficult because habits have been fixed so firmly that their adjustment is a difficult or at least an annoying process. Obviously, therefore, it seems to me, early marriages should be encouraged.[42]

January 1927, *Forum*

On Humanity

We are only animals. We are coming out of the dog stage and getting a glimpse of our environment. We don't know—we just suspect a few things. Our practice of shooting one another in war is proof that we are animals. The make-up of our society is hideous.[43]

January 28, 1910, *Independent*

The spirit of inquiry is spreading among all classes. It has reached even the tramps.[44]

March 13, 1910, *New York Times*

There's so much talk nowadays about helping the poor man. Most of it results in nothing but talk.[45]

May 15, 1910, *New York Times*

But the will of man, that is the mystery.[46]

July 1911, *Century Magazine*

I tell you there is something wrong—deeply, sadly, fundamentally wrong with our social system when so many greedy men ride the backs of the men who are producers.[47]

January 3, 1912, *New York Times*

Humanity will have to live in double shifts, by and by, because the world will be so crowded; and it will have to sleep less.[48]

October 11, 1914, *New York Times*

Civilization's march means the march of artificial illumination adds to the hours of man's possible usefulness and interest, and because to the best men happiness means willingness to survive.[49]

October 11, 1914, *New York Times*

Humanity can adjust itself to almost any circumstances.[50]

October 11, 1914, *New York Times*

Whatever man likes he will have a tendency to overdo.[51]

October 11, 1914, *New York Times*

Humanity, however, doesn't think very far ahead. It is too fascinated by momentary things.[52]

December 1926, *Forum*

As man is now constituted it is impossible for him to be happy.[53]

October 7, 1927, *New York Times*

[Man's chief object in life should be] [t]o be as happy as possible—he apparently is a useless mechanism as far as I can see.[54]

July 30, 1928, *New York Times*

What is civilization but the restriction of personal liberty for the improvement of mankind?[55]

September 28, 1928, *New York Times*

I am not acquainted with anyone who is happy.[56]

February 11, 1929, *Tampa Tribune*

It must be remembered that there is no test—no suitable yardstick which can positively determine the relative value of one human being as compared to another. Life and human relationship are too complex, too involved to permit such determination.[57]

August 1, 1929, *New York Times*

We are very small, we humans. . . . Many times smaller [than an electron].[58]

April 1931, *Golden Book Magazine*

I believe the world is slowly getting better. The percentage of fine people is increasing. Man has not yet overcome his malignant environment, but men as animals will improve.[59]

January 1932, *Review of Reviews*

On Youth and Advice to Youth

[T]o-day's youngsters of both sexes are beginning to doubt the myths, miracle tales, ancient chronicles, and other imperfect and misleading legends which were once called "history" and were used by the shrewd, the unscrupulous, and the fanatical for the exploitation of the ignorant.[60]

January 1927, *Forum*

There is no justification for the view that the morals of modern youth are deteriorating. . . . [M]orals of modern youth are better than those of their fathers and grandfathers and much better than those of their remoter ancestors.[61]

January 1927, *Forum*

Why criticize our "flappers?" They're all right.[62]

January 1927, *Forum*

Most of us are so prone, as we grow older, to criticize youth for everything it does, forgetting how much worse we did when we were young.[63]

January 1927, *Forum*

It is not "unrest" in the bad sense in which the word is used which keeps young people moving, thinking doing. It is, however, the opposite of stagnation and that is a fine thing for the world.[64]

January 1927, *Forum*

What young people may be a century from now I do not care to predict, nor do I dare. They will be an improvement on the young people of the present.[65]

January 1927, *Forum*

Maturity often is more absurd than youth and very frequently is most unjust to youth.[66]

January 1927, *Forum*

When a boy around 15 or 16 is found trying all kinds of experiments he shows ambition and the will to work; this boy is safe for a good career.[67]

February 11, 1929, *Tampa Tribune*

Keep your heads clear and your feet on the ground.[68]

August 1, 1929, *New York Times*

On the Brain

Edison received an honorary doctor of science degree from Princeton on
June 15, 1915. *Courtesy of the Thomas Edison National Historical Park, 14.130.60.*

Edison believed human beings were at the beginning stages of intelligence. In the future, human evolution and education would create a high state of enlightenment.

The inventor's own experience colored his views of education. He had little formal learning, being homeschooled by his mother after a teacher called him "addled." Because he learned best by doing, he believed all children would. He saw motion pictures as a panacea for education.

Though Edison castigated universities and called a secondary education useless, all three children from his second marriage attended college. He also sponsored scholarship contests for the "brightest boy" in the nation. Chapter 12 contains his thoughts on the education of women.

On Thinking and Intelligence

I calculate that we know one-seventh-billionth of 1 per cent, about anything.[1]

> May 19, 1907, *New York Times*

Man is slow to understand, his five senses are not enough to gather all the meaning of experimental science.[2]

> October 11, 1908, *New York Times*

Well, there you are. We do not understand; we cannot understand. We are too finite to understand. The really big things we cannot grasp as yet. Our speculations are not even creditably intelligent. They cannot be intelligent till we have developed so that we can understand things better, grasp more. We cannot comprehend infinity, we can't comprehend space. We have found that out. We know it.[3]

> October 2, 1910, *New York Times*

[T]he human brain is capable of a very much higher development than it has reached as yet, and it has developed steadily. It indicates quite clearly that in time it will do things which now seem wholly impossible.[4]

November 13, 1910, *New York Times*

Well, there is another world—a world as real, but not, we now believe, of matter wholly—the mental world, which has its centre in the brain, which is itself, as I have said before, a mere meat mechanism. Why should there not be quite as great an evolution in this world as there has surely been in the material—meat world?[5]

November 13, 1910, *New York Times*

All kinds of ideas help to set the mind going. If a man has enough ideas to be an inventor, he can turn the same force in another direction, if he wishes to, and be a business man, an architect, or anything.[6]

July 1911, *Century Magazine*

The trouble is that we are animals and have only five senses to work with. Wonderful things are happening all around us all the time, and we have no means of grasping or understanding them. . . . If only we had another five senses—ah, then, perhaps we could soon make astounding discoveries.[7]

December 2, 1916, *Collier's Weekly*

Let us leave the cynics to their little pleasantries, and make our appeal to people who think.[8]

Circa 1916

One can let the imagination take such a grip that it becomes possible to imagine that things have actually occurred which have had no other foundation than in the person's imagination.[9]

October 1920, *American Magazine*

We don't know one millionth of one per cent about anything! . . . We are just emerging from the chimpanzee state mentally.[10]

October 1920, *American Magazine*

The brain can be developed just the same as the muscles can be developed, if one will only take the pains to train the mind to think.[11]

January 1921, *American Magazine*

Why do so many men never amount to anything? Because they don't *think!*[12]

January 1921, *American Magazine*

The brain that isn't used rusts.[13]

January 1921, *American Magazine*

[T]he brain that isn't used suffers atrophy.[14]

January 1921, *American Magazine*

The man who doesn't make up his mind to cultivate the habit of thinking misses the greatest pleasure in life. He not only misses the greatest pleasure, but he cannot make the most of himself.[15]

January 1921, *American Magazine*

All progress, all success, springs from thinking.[16]

January 1921, *American Magazine*

An opinion, to be of any value for immediate use, can only come from a brain containing a vast number of facts subject to call at any moment.[17]

June 26, 1921, *New York Times*

[O]nly 2 per cent. of the people think.[18]

December 6, 1921, *New York Times*

Thinking is a cumulative process.[19]

January 1927, *Forum*

The brain; if used has enormous capacity. People don't begin to suspect what the mind is capable of.[20]

December 24, 1930, *New York Times*

The capacity of the human brain is tremendous, but people put it to no use. They live sedentary mental lives.[21]

April 1931, *Golden Book Magazine*

On Education

I should like to see about a dozen professors sit down to a Banquet of Boiled Crow.[22]

Response to a professor's support for alternating current (AC), rather than his direct current (DC). October 27, 1889, marginalia on a letter from Henry Augustus Rowland to Edward Dean Adams

A man should thoroughly know what he has gone over before he can ever hope to be up to date, and no man can anticipate the future unless he is up to date.[23]

December 31, 1894, *Ottumwa (Iowa) Courier*

I think the practical method is the only way after all. Horace Greeley had a theory that self educated men were better than college graduates. I think he was right.[24]

December 31, 1894, *Ottumwa (Iowa) Courier*

[Education should begin] [t]he younger the better, in fact he cannot begin too young. The earlier the sense or instinct of scientific investigation is made part of his education the better for his aftersuccess. Our early habits duly crop out in our after life.[25]

December 31, 1894, *Ottumwa (Iowa) Courier*

Electricity as a science should be made one of the several studies in every school in the land. It should rank with spelling and arithmetic.[26]

January 13, 1901, *Dallas Morning News*

School? I've never been to school a day in my life! D'you think I would have amounted to anything if I had gone to school?[27]

Circa 1903, quoted in September 1932, *Harper's Magazine*
Edison seems to have entirely forgotten his brief
experience with formal education.

Why teach Latin? Latin is a dead language; the professor himself doesn't know how to order in Latin a sirloin steak with potatoes. Who the hell uses Latin outside the Catholic church? And *there* nobody understands it except the Pope, so even he can only use Latin when he is talkin' to himself.[28]

Circa 1903, quoted in September 1932, *Harper's Magazine*

[A]t about that age [twelve] a boy is interested in knowing how things are done, and you can build on that interest easily. It is hard to teach a man anything if he isn't interested in it. But if you can get him when he is, then everything you do to instruct him counts. His brain or recording department wants work and receives it with pleasure.[29]

July 1911, *Century Magazine*

There are great possibilities in starting the mind right with toys. Give them problems to work out that will make them think for themselves.[30]

July 1911, *Century Magazine*

They take too much time teaching things that don't count. Latin and Greek—what good are they? They say these train the mind. But I don't think they train the mind half so much as working out practical problems. Work is the best kind of school to train the mind. Books are good to show the theory of things, but doing the thing itself is what counts.[31]

July 1911, Century Magazine

Schoolhouses, electric light and newspapers, these three go together, and they mean progress.[32]

October 29, 1911, New York Times

What we should have is education by demonstration.[33]

January 11, 1914, New York Times

The advice above all that will do most good must begin at his mother's knee when he is a child. I still remember the advice and training given me by my good mother. Almost daily I apply it some way or other.[34]

February 12, 1914, New York Times

[A]nything which can be taught to the ear can be taught better to the eye. The moving object on the screen, the closest possible approximation to reality, is almost the same as bringing that object itself before the child or taking the child to that object.

Film teaching will be done without any books whatsoever. . . . The pupils will learn everything there is to learn, in every grade from the lowest to the highest. The long years now spent in cramming indigestible knowledge down unwilling young throats and in examining young minds on the subjects which they can never learn under the present system will be cut down marvelously, waste will be eliminated, and, the youth of every land will at last become actually educated.[35]

February 9, 1919, New York Times

[E]very classroom and every assembly hall [will become] a movie show, 100 per cent attendance [will be assured]. Why, you won't be able to keep boys and girls away from school then. They'll get there ahead of time and scramble for good seats, and they'll stay late, begging to see some of the films over again, when film teaching becomes universal.[36]

February 9, 1919, *New York Times*

The trouble is that boys' minds are atrophied before they reach college. This is due to the primary school system, which is repulsive. There is nothing to attract a boy who is taught by word instead of by eye. I have never seen a boy who liked to go to school, and I don't suppose I ever will, unless the method of teaching is changed.[37]

May 7, 1921, *New York Times*

If I had a man in my employ who was right only half of the time, or a little more than half the time, he would last just about long enough for me to find him out—and that would not take very long. But our schools consistently and persistently give passing grades to students who are right a bare 60 per cent. of the time. I consider this a disgraceful procedure.[38]

October 23, 1921, *New York Times*

Industry is the result of the efforts of man and I think a large part of the work of bettering industry will have to begin with the education of the boy.[39]

September 1923, *System*

Our educational system is not delivering enough either in its methods of teaching or in what it is teaching.[40]

January 1, 1925, *Boston Daily Globe*

At present most young people leave their schools only partially educated, and rapidly forget a large part even of that which they have been taught. I cannot believe that if they had been taught the right things in the right way this would be the case so frequently and notably. They fail to learn because the methods of teaching are wrong. They forget because the methods of instruction make them actually dislike knowledge.[41]

January 1927, *Forum*

Interest and simplicity should be the keynotes of all education, I believe. It is impossible to fascinate young minds with dull complexities.[42]

January 1927, *Forum*

I have been asked if I believe that girls and boys should be educated together. I am not very emphatic on this subject, but I think they better be kept apart during the school studying years. It may be that, together, they distract each other's attention. Whether coeducation always will be unwise is another matter.[43]

January 1927, *Forum*

The best service which maturity can render youth is to encourage and forward every worthy form of education.[44]

January 1927, *Forum*

To say our educators need education is merely to say of them what they are constantly proclaiming of themselves and everybody else in their own speeches. They know it and most of them are trying earnestly to get the education they need.[45]

January 1927, *Forum*

I am not an educational expert and can only guess with regard to a matter which has been, the world over, left too much to guess work.[46]

January 1927, *Forum*

Young men's desire for a technical education.[47]

On the greatest educational force.
February 12, 1930, *Fort Myers (Fla.) Press*

The future progress of science in [the] United States will be determined by the school boys of today.[48]

April 9, 1930, *Fort Myers (Fla.) Press*

On a College Education

When a man leaves college he is filled full of theory, but not an atom of practice. We encounter them every day and they have to start in and literally relearn what they think they have learned.[49]

December 31, 1894, *Ottumwa (Iowa) Courier*

The college man is not the practical man. Colleges are better than they once were, but they aren't practical yet. They are all right for lawyers, but this country needs engineers, not lawyers.[50]

December 6, 1911, *New York Times*

Colleges are for the social side and for the literary. Not worth while, generally.[51]

December 6, 1911, *New York Times*

Men who have gone through college I find to be amazingly ignorant. They don't seem to know anything.[52]

May 6, 1921, *New York Times*

I have been criticized by the college professors, who evidently misunderstand my purpose. I like college graduates. I want to get them to work for me, and I do get them, but the strange thing about it is that so small a number can answer simple questions.[53]

May 16, 1921, *New York Times*

I do not approve of the present day college graduate. My main object against a college graduate is that he objects to work, especially when it is dirty work. He does not want a job with much work to it. He expects to be appointed foreman at the end of his sixth week.[54]

November 18, 1922, *New York Times*

The American college is good in that it forces young men to learn something when they don't want to.[55]

February 11, 1924, *Boston Daily Globe*

What is a college? An institute of learning. What is a business? An institute of learning. Life, itself, is an institute of learning.[56]

January 1927, *Forum*

If the boy has ambition he doesn't need to go to college.[57]

February 11, 1929, *Tampa Tribune*

[T]o the Massachusetts Institute of Technology.[58]

Response to the question of where he would send a son to college. 1929 interview

You can learn much more in the laboratory right here than you can by going to college.[59]

Statement to his son Theodore

On the Body

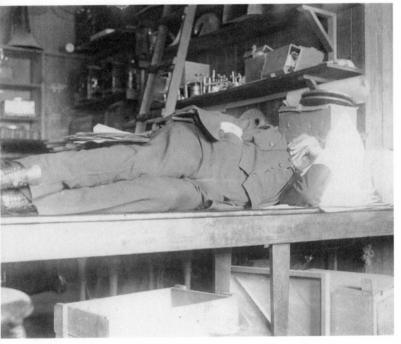

Edison was notorious for working for days at a time and taking naps to refresh himself. In this image, he is lying on a laboratory table. *Courtesy of the Thomas Edison National Historical Park, 14.220.27.*

Edison's perspectives on the body, health, medicine, and diet were reflective of his own childhood infirmities. He had scarlet fever as a boy, which likely caused, or contributed to, the chronic hearing loss that grew progressively worse during his life. As an adult, he underwent numerous operations to combat ear infections and improve his hearing, with limited success.

Edison generally distrusted the advice of doctors and had outright contempt for patent medicine's pills, tonics, and nostrums. He believed health would result from behaviors: He promoted eating the right foods—which in his case included large quantities of pie—and minimal sleeping. Individuals should avoid cigarettes—but not cigars. He also promoted nature's perfect food—milk—believing it would enable people to live long, healthy lives.

During the 1890s, Edison experimented with X-rays and developed a fluoroscope, which would become the standard for the medical profession. The inventor terminated his research around 1903, when one of his employee's excessive use of experimental X-rays resulted in his death. Despite this tragedy, when it came to the future of medicine, Edison was optimistic.

On the Medical Profession

If I were to follow your advice, take all the drugs you suggest or all that the physician you advise me to call in would prescribe, I would become worse.[1]

May 10, 1891, *New York Sun*

I don't believe in doctors or drugs. Doctors' theories are never to be relied on, and most of the drugs aren't worth anything.[2]

May 10, 1891, *New York Sun*

I believe heartily in the laws of common sense. If a physician prescribes a treatment that coincides with these laws then I approve of him; but if he comes with a lot of theories and drugs I won't have him.[3]

May 10, 1891, *New York Sun*

If one could only see into the future, and if modern physicians only understood what they practice, Jane might be living today.[4]

December 1, 1898, letter to his wife on the death of his sister-in-law

Medical science will save more lives this year than war will take, no matter how terrifically murderous that war may be.[5]

October 11, 1914, *New York Times*

Sickness is pretty hard on the workman now. It's hard for them to get a good doctor, and proper care is expensive. There is too much sickness. Something will have to be done about it and that is where biology and chemistry come in.[6]

December 24, 1930, *Fort Myers (Fla.) Press*

On Diseases and Medical Treatments

[Electricity] relieves neurologic [*sic*] pains, etc.[7]

April 11, 1878, marginalia on a letter from H. L. Leclare

I am convinced that the [yellow] fever germs must be either of two things—an animal organization or fungus growth.[8]

October 5, 1888, *Cranbury (N.J.) Press*

I've been experimenting a good deal with microbes, trying to understand the beast and see how they work. What I wanted was to get an idea of the germs of the yellow fever. . . . [I]f we could know how to catch them and take their fangs out they would be less harmful.[9]

November 4, 1888, *Brooklyn Citizen*

It's all very nice to get the X rays and to photograph the invisible; but the thing is to turn this wonderful discovery to practical account, to make use of it that will be a benefit and a blessing to mankind. This, of course, will be done when we make it a useful adjunct of the surgeon's profession.[10]

> On the invention of the fluoroscope.
> March 28, 1896, *New York Herald*

On the Human Body and His Theories of Its Workings

It has just occurred to me that the brain may digest certain portions of food, say the ethereal part, as well as the stomach. Perhaps dandruff is the excrete of the mind. The quantity of this material being directly proportional to the amount of reading one indulges in.[11]

> July 12, 1885, diary entry made in jest

Say, for example, a lot of cells git away from a toe and land 'way up in the nose. They don't know where they are or how in hell to act. So they go crazy and they start building toe, because that's all they know how to do—see? In this way a bit of toe grows up in the nose. We call it a wart, but it's nothing but a piece of toe in the wrong place. That's how warts come.[12]

> Circa 1903, quoted in September 1932, *Harper's Magazine*

You see, the laws of health are as simple as the laws of sound or electricity.[13]

> April 1904, *Outing*

I believe, for instance, that the time will come when a man with a bad kidney, if he has good money, will be able to go into the open market and purchase a good kidney of some one else who has a good one, but who needs the money more than he needs the kidney, and have it inserted in the place of his imperfect one.[14]

October 2, 1910, *New York Times*

All our mechanical engines are imperfect, but the engine of the human body is a competent machine. Some of our mechanical engines don't utilize more than 10 per cent. of the power which the fuel they consume should furnish, but the capabilities of the engine of the human body are far better.[15]

October 11, 1914, *New York Times*

I believe that the human body is vivified, made to function mentally and physically by myriads of infinitesimal entities, each in itself a unit of life. They work in communities or assemblies, as you like, each community performing its allotted task. They live in what we call "cells," and each cell is a commune. Cells may be seen with a microscope, but the entities are not visible even to the ultra microscope.[16]

October 30, 1920, *Scientific American*

The body is only a piece of machinery, and every practical man knows that to get good work out of a machine and keep it in repair at the same time one must know how to take care of it.[17]

April 13, 1912, *Health & Strength*

These entities are life; they rebuild our constantly wearing out tissues, watch over the functions of our various organs. If an organ is destroyed or becomes uninhabitable for its tenants, they leave it; if the body through disease or accident becomes no longer a habitable structure for the entities, they seek other work elsewhere.[18]

October 30, 1920, *Scientific American*

On Medicine and Patent Medicine

No sir, I shall not allow anything of this kind.[19]

> Response to a request to have a patent medicine
> sold under his name. December 11, 1879, marginalia
> on a letter from E. L. Jones & Co.

[T]hose people are nothin' but degenerates![20]

> On patent medicine makers. Circa 1903,
> quoted in September 1932, *Harper's Magazine*

I never give another man a dose of medicine I wouldn't take myself.[21]

> July 14, 1923, *Collier's Weekly*

On Sleep

Want of sleep is like the want of morphine. If a man once takes morphine he must have more of it, and it is so with sleep.[22]

> July 26, 1891, *New York Journal*

Sleep is an acquired habit. Cells don't sleep. Fish swim about in the water all night; *they* don't sleep. Even a horse don't sleep, he just stands still and rests. A man don't need any sleep.[23]

> Circa 1903, quoted in September 1932, *Harper's Magazine*

Men first learned to sleep because when darkness came they had nothing else to do. Through the ages their descendants, doing likewise, made sleep a custom—a matter of course. But if men had always lived in the land of perpetual light and sunshine, I don't suppose we would sleep at all.[24]

> December 10, 1910, *South Jersey Republican*

Too much sleep may be a national curse, may be among the greatest national dangers.[25]

October 29, 1911, *New York Times*

Everything which decreases the sum total of man's sleep increases the sum total of man's capabilities.[26]

October 11, 1914, *New York Times*

The average man who sleeps seven or eight or nine hours a day is continually oppressed by lassitude.[27]

October 11, 1914, *New York Times*

There really is no reason why men should go to bed at all, and the man of the future will spend far less time in bed than the man of the present does, just as the man of the present spends far less time in bed than the man of the past did.[28]

October 11, 1914, *New York Times*

As the race progresses in intelligence there will be less and less time wasted in unnecessary and injurious sleep, and less and less value and health wasted in unnecessary food consumption.[29]

October 11, 1914, *New York Times*

I have never overslept, and I have never had a dream, good or bad, so far as I know, in my life.[30]

October 11, 1914, *New York Times*.
His diary makes references to dreams.

Really, sleep is an absurdity, a bad habit.[31]

October 11, 1914, *New York Times*

We became known in the factory as the "insomnia squad," and we all were proud of that appellation.[32]

October 11, 1914, *New York Times*

Well, lack of sleep won't hurt anyone.[33]

August 19, 1924, *Boston Daily Globe*

What's the use of lying comatose until you have to, in the grave?[34]

February 27, 1927, *New York Times*

I sleep about seven or eight hours out of 24 now. I can't work as hard as I used to, but I can keep the other fellow busy. A person can learn to do without much sleep. It takes training.[35]

Comment made when he was eighty-three.
March 17, 1930, *Fort Myers (Fla.) Press*

On Food and Eating

[M]y imagination was getting into a coma. What I needed was pastry. That night I found a French pastry shop ... and filled up. My imagination got all right.[36]

Circa 1870s

Pastry, particularly apple pie.[37]

On what rejuvenated him. April 27, 1882, St. *Louis Post-Dispatch*

I do believe I have a big bump for cookies. The first entry made by the recording angel on my behalf was for stealing my mother's cookies.[38]

July 12, 1885, diary entry

I am a very light eater and always take care never to overload my stomach. For breakfast I eat a couple of eggs and a small slice of ham, with two or three slices of toast, and some tea or coffee, and for lunch and dinner about the same. Tea, coffee and water are the drinks that best agree with me.[39]

1890 interview

I am not a vegetarian at all; in fact just now I am not eating any vegetables to speak of.[40]

May 10, 1891, *New York Sun*

Oh, mince pies and such. I am very fond of mince pies.[41]

On the staples of his diet. February 1896, *Norwalk (Ohio) Reflector*

My diet consists of meat, vegetables, eggs—in fact, anything that I want, but in small quantities. I don't really care whether I eat or not; it is not my pleasure.[42]

April 1904, *Outing*

I don't know that the white bread we eat is bad, but I do not believe it is as good for us as [whole grain] bread would be, as good as us as German bread is for the Germans. I believe nature knows better than we do and we'd better not unbalance our grain rations.[43]

October 29, 1911, *New York Times*

All recipes should be based upon scientific experiment.[44]

March 1913, *Good Housekeeping*

Food should be to the body only what coal is to the boiler of a steam engine. It should be to the body what air and water are to the body. Who ever heard of perfuming air or flavoring water in order that the greater pleasure might be derived from breathing and drinking?[45]

March 1913, *Good Housekeeping*

Eating should not be a pleasure.[46]

March 1913, *Good Housekeeping*

The elimination of all stimulant would be a fine thing for the race. I lately have been using a coffee from which the caffeine has been extracted before it goes into the coffee-pot, and it has been a distinct advance.[47]

October 11, 1914, *New York Times*

Actually, a loaf of bread contains stored energy equal to one horse power operating through three hours, if it could all be utilized.[48]

October 11, 1914, *New York Times*

I boil everything except the water; no lettuce, celery or other raw things. The purpose is to guard me against bacterial invasion.[49]

Circa 1910–19

Fletcherize nothing, bolt. I bolt my food; that's the thing. Fletcherized food is too quickly digested. All animals bolt their food. To be sure, the cow chews later at its leisure, but that's because there is so little nutriment in the grass it eats. Our food, on the contrary, is concentrated and requires little mastication.[50]

Response to Fletcherism, a movement to increase the time spent chewing food. October 11, 1914, *New York Times*

I'm always the same. Always 185. If I weigh a little more I eat less and if I fall off a little I eat more and keep the balance even.[51]

February 13, 1923, *New York Times*

When I was a baby, I lived on milk and now that I am an old man I have gone back to that same practice. That's funny.[52]

March 17, 1930, *Fort Myers (Fla.) Press*

I have been experimenting with milk now for about eight years. For the last three years I have taken hardly anything else. I came in with milk and I guess I'll go out with it. It's the only balanced ration— balanced by the Great Chemist, who is far away.[53]

January 1931, *Review of Reviews*

On Diet

When she [Mina's sister, Jane] was stricken at Chautauqua had she taken to a milk diet? There is very little doubt that Nature would then had a chance [*sic*] to throw off the poisons of defective digestion and she would be strong + healthy today.[54]

> December 1, 1898, letter to his wife, Mina, about his
> sister-in-law, who died of heart problems at forty-three

You cannot beat the farm as a laboratory, commercially speaking. If we should dry up like Mars and couldn't raise vegetables on earth, we might turn to a chemical diet.[55]

> January 14, 1910, *Seattle Star*

It is not the laborer who has gout. A man must eat according to his work. A laborer needs more than a man of intellectual pursuits.[56]

> April 1904, *Outing*

If doctors would prescribe diet, instead of drugs, the ailments of the normal man would disappear.[57]

> April 1904, *Outing*

If you eat in the South you will get dyspepsia. If you eat at the big New York hotels, you will get Bright's disease or diabetes. The best cooking in the country is in the West—not in the great hotels, but in the homes of farmers and wage-workers.[58]

> March 1913, *Good Housekeeping*

On Overeating

It is simply appalling to know how professional men and others who do little physical work stuff themselves. There is no sense in it. It means dullness, disease and early death. It is an extraordinary thing to observe how great business men, lawyers, doctors and clergymen, men showing the highest intelligence in ordinary matters, continue to sin against nature by overeating.[59]

June 16, 1907, *New York Times*

Fully eighty per cent of the illness of mankind comes from eating improper food or too much food; people are inclined to overindulge themselves.[60]

October 3, 1907, *Fort Myers (Fla.) Press*

Food that tastes too good is dangerous. It leads to over-eating, and over-eating leads first to disease and then to premature death.[61]

March 1913, *Good Housekeeping*

On the average, men would get on better if they reduced their food consumption by two-thirds. They do the work of three horse-power engines and consume the fuel which should operate fifty horse-power engines.[62]

October 11, 1914, *New York Times*

Put too much fuel into the firebox of a locomotive and you will have a clogged furnace. Put too much food into the firebox of the human system—that is, into the stomach—and you will have a clogged human machine.[63]

October 11, 1914, *New York Times*

Anybody who is clogged with food and gives his stomach too much work can't do good work himself.[64]

February 12, 1920, *New York Times*

After the age of 21, a large variety and quantity of food is unnecessary. All those things crowd the stomach and cause poisons. It takes courage to learn restraint, but all that eating is unnecessary.[65]

December 24, 1930, *New York Times*

On Exercise

[T]he interest of to-day's young people in sport is inevitable and for their own good. It keeps their bodies healthy by compelling them to take good care of themselves or fail at sports; it disciplines them, and taken as a whole, it teaches them a great deal.[66]

January 1927, *Forum*

That girls as well as boys are going in systematically for sports will be of benefit to the race. The healthier girls are the stronger will be the women who must be the mothers of the race.[67]

January 1927, *Forum*

On Deafness

This deafness has been of great advantage to me in various ways. When in a telegraph office I could hear only the instrument directly on the table at which I sat, and, unlike the other operators, I was not bothered by the other instruments.[68]

Circa 1870s

Broadway is as quiet to me as a country village is to a person with normal hearing.[69]

Circa 1870s

I am so deaf that I am debarred from hearing all the finer articulations & have to depend on the judgement of others.[70]

Circa 1870s

Have heard of an ear trumpet for deaf people you invented. Can one be obtained?[71]

May 1879, telegram to Hamilton McKown Twombly

I wouldn't want to be cured for $10,000. . . . There are a lot of things I don't want to hear. Now I don't have to hear 'em.[72]

September 16, 1884, *New York Sun*

I need not hear a man when he wants to borrow money.[73]

September 16, 1884, *New York Sun*

I don't think it is human to make folks hear everything.[74]

September 16, 1884, *New York Sun*

It's nice to be a little deaf when traveling. You can ask everybody directions then pump the imagination for the answer, it strengthens this faculty.[75]

July 14, 1885, diary entry

I like the theatre, and should go very often were it not that my deafness makes it hard for me to hear what the actors say. With light opera I fare much better, and when I can get a seat in the front row, am able to hear the music without trouble.[76]

1890 interview

It's all right when it keeps in adjustment but it does not always do so.[77]

On an Acousticon hearing aid bought for him by his wife.
December 31, 1904, letter to Louis B. Schram

My hearing is becoming more difficult now, and I must hurry with the phonograph, so that I shall not be deprived of hearing it.[78]

February 11, 1907, *New York Times*

And I have a wonderfully sensitive inner ear . . . [that] has been protected from the millions of noises that dim the hearing of ears that hear everything. . . . [N]o one who has a normal ear can hear as well as I can.[79]

Circa 1910–19

I have discovered that the gray matter of the average person frazzies out before his voice does.[80]

On why he didn't use a device to improve his hearing.
June 29, 1913, *New York Sun*

Deafness has its advantages. My own deafness enables me to concentrate my thoughts as I'd never be able to do if distracted by noise and conversation. It helps me to sleep too.[81]

March 5, 1914, *Fort Myers (Fla.) Press*

My organism is built to withstand the demands of modern civilization and my nerves are intact because I don't hear well. People have to adapt themselves to their environment, and I guess we'll have to be deaf in time.[82]

On why he didn't use a device to improve his hearing.
Circa 1917

The deaf man can sleep in the noisiest quarters. They do not have to listen to bores. Their infirmity, furthermore, often gives them a reputation for wit.[83]

March 28, 1925, *Boston Daily Globe*

Nature, in making hearing less acute as outside noises increase, knows what she is doing. I am deaf, having been so since my boyhood. I am deafer now than I used to be. The noise of a city doesn't trouble me at all. . . . It saves me from many interruptions and much nerve strain.[84]

December 1926, *Forum*

Deaf people should take to reading. It beats the babble of ordinary conversation. The eye is the whole thing, and hearing a very minor affair. Its loss is not worth worrying about.[85]

February 20, 1927, *New York Times*

I'm only an outgoing station. I cannot receive.[86]

> January 19, 1928, *New York Times*

They have talking pictures now, but I can't hear them. There are 2,500,000 other deaf men in this country who can't hear them either. They'll have to do something about that.[87]

> January 18, 1929, *Fort Myers (Fla.) Press*

I have no doubt that my nerves are stronger and better today than they would have been if I had heard all the foolish, meaningless sounds that normal people hear.[88]

> September 8, 1929, *New York Times*

It's astounding how much more a deaf person can see.[89]

> January 21, 1930, *Fort Myers (Fla.) Press*

[D]on't forget about the talkies. For the deaf man, they're terrible.[90]

> January 21, 1930, *Fort Myers (Fla.) Press*

It takes a deaf man to hear music.[91]

> June 1932, *Etude*

Oh, no. I hear enough stupidity going on around me now the way it is.[92]

> On why he refused to wear a hearing aid. June 1932, *Etude*

On Smoking and Tobacco Products

Smoking too much makes me nervous—Must lasso my natural tendency to acquire such habits—Holding heavy cigar constantly in my mouth has deformed my upper lip, it has a sort of Havanna [*sic*] curl. . . . [C]ouldn't eat much, nerves of stomach too nicotiny [*sic*]. The roots of tobacco plants must go clear through to hell. Satans principal agent Dyspepsia must have charge of this branch of the vegitible [*sic*] kingdom.[93]

Stream-of-consciousness musings from his July 12, 1885, diary entry.

My old pipe beats all the cigars I ever tried.[94]

October 23, 1887, *New York Sun*

That's my little joke. I believe so thoroughly in [tobacco] that I smoke from ten to twenty cigars a day.[95]

November 17, 1889, *New York World*

I am a great smoker and smoke from ten to twenty strong cigars a day. I have never found that smoking hurts me; when I do I shall stop it.[96]

1890 interview

And the anti-cigarette law is another good thing. Tobacco's all right; it never hurt any one. But cigarettes are poison.[97]

January 12, 1908, *New York Times*

Cigarettes NOT TOLERATED, They Dull the Brain.[98]

Sign at Edison's West Orange plant. May 11, 1914, *New York Times*

That poison [in cigarettes] attacks the brain and works havoc with a man's mental activity.[99]

May 11, 1914, *New York Times*

If I wanted to live a hundred years I would use neither tobacco nor coffee. But you see I'd rather get a little really good work done than live long and do nothing to speak of. And so I spur what I am pleased to call my mind, at times with coffee and a good cigar—just pass the matches thank you![100]

Circa 1916

[I have] only one or two [cigars], usually after a meal. I don't know of any particular reason for cutting down, but I did. I chew all the time. It's a habit I learned when I was a telegrapher. I had no end of trouble with Mrs. Edison about it and was at the point of quitting when I found out that the Chief Justice of the United States Supreme Court used tobacco in that way. I told Mrs. Edison and that let me out.[101]

Circa 1917

Tobacco does not harm any one, except paper covered cigarettes which are harmful, especially to young people. This cigarette smoking is a fixed habit; the victims don't want tobacco; they want to smoke the paper. They ought to use tobacco wrappers only. But tobacco aside from cigarettes does no harm to society. It is not dangerous like narcotics and whisky and few smoke it to excess.[102]

August 13, 1921, *New York Times*

Yes, I chew tobacco. I learned to chew when I was an operator with the Western Union many years ago. I worked in an operating room where more than one hundred operators ticked off messages. A great number of them smoked and we nearly smothered. One day we held a meeting and decided that we would all quit smoking and take to the plug. I grew to like it and I never stopped. Yes, I have stomach trouble, have had it for 60 years. They say it comes from chewing too much tobacco but I don't believe them.[103]

March 7, 1927, St. *Petersburg (Fla.) Times*

The smoking of cigarettes in the laboratory building will not be tolerated and those disrespecting this order will be immediately dismissed from the company. [signed] Thomas A. Edison.[104]

July 20, 1928, *New York Times*

On the Arts

When he was not working, Edison was often found with a book in his hands.
He especially enjoyed detective stories. *Courtesy of the Thomas Edison
National Historical Park, 14.915.12.*

Edison's views on the arts reflect his humble beginnings and limited formal education. Given his scientific mind, he found the fine arts preposterous because they were not true to life. Though his tastes were not sophisticated, he was a great lover of music and a voracious reader.

On Music

Opera of Polly. We can com*parrot* with Sullivans.[1]

July 17, 1885, diary entry

I am fond of music, and used to be a pretty fair singer until I ruined my voice experimenting with the telephone and phonograph.[2]

1890 interview

In a short time it will be possible to produce within the humblest home the best music in the world, and to produce it there as perfectly as it was in its first form.[3]

October 12, 1912, *Good Housekeeping*

I have been studying music with as much intensity, of late, as I ever gave to any task, and I find few instruments and practically no human voices without glaring imperfections.[4]

October 12, 1912, *Good Housekeeping*

Heart songs. Yes, heart songs; they're the real music for me. . . . *Suwanee River*—oh, all of 'em. But I like all kinds of music. . . . I like all of Verdi, all of Brahms, all of Beethoven, ah, there was a composer! I like everything but cubish music which is hideous.[5]

On his favorite music. Circa 1917

Some of you may have been told that music is a non-essential. My views on the subject are probably well known to you. The time is not far distant when music will be recognized as a greater essential than books. Don't let anybody make you believe that music is a non-essential.[6]

June 8, 1918, *New York Times*

Music should be established upon so scientific a basis that anyone who can play at all can play a piece in precisely the time that the composer intended it should be played.[7]

April 1931, *Golden Book Magazine*

On Art

They are grand rot. I like modern pictures as much as I dislike antique stuff. I think nothing of pictures in the Louvre. They are wretched old things, and the pictures at the [1889 Paris] Exhibition are all modern as can be. They are good.[8]

September 8, 1889, *New York World*

The old masters are not in it. I had a tape line and measured some of the figures. No such human frames and proportions ever were born.[9]

1889, *New York Evening Sun*

Everything in this world should be done by machinery and measurement. [Things done otherwise are] not really very good.[10]

On his refusal to sit for a portrait. July 12, 1926, *Time*

To my mind the old masters are not art; their value is in their scarcity.[11]

April 1931, *Golden Book Magazine*

On Literature

[P]erhaps I am a literary barbarian and am not yet educated to the point of appreciating fine writing. 90 per cent of [Hawthorne's English Note Book] is descriptive of old churches and grave-yards. . . . He and Geo Slewyn ought to have been appointed perpetual coroners of London.[12]

July 12, 1885, diary entry

Don't like Dickens—don't know why.[13]

July 12, 1885, diary entry

[I bought] a work on Goethe + Schiller by Boynsen which is soggy literature, a little wit + anecdote in the style of literature would have the same effect as baking soda on bread, give pleasing results.[14]

July 13, 1885, diary entry

Do you know it is an odd thing but I like exciting novels, Indian stories, that sort of thing. . . . I like Poe's tales. He had a great imagination and wonderful ingenuity.[15]

July 26, 1891, New York Journal

Oh, I read everything. Not merely scientific works, but anything that helps the imagination. . . . But I like "Evangeline," "Enoch Arden," and things like that. These I call poetry.[16]

July 1911, Century Magazine

But ah, Shakespeare! That's where you get ideas. He would have been an inventor, a wonderful inventor, if he had turned his mind to it. He seemed to see inside of everything. Perfectly wonderful how many things he could think about. His originality in the way of expressing things has never been approached.[17]

July 1911, Century Magazine

Shakespeare [would be considered great] for his wonderful power in expression. But I do not think that he was a world mover.[18]

December 6, 1911, *New York Times*

I read Victor Hugo, for his poetical temperament. I like Bulwer and Charles Reed. I have read a few of the "best sellers," but I don't like them. I like the detective story. I like Emile Gaboriau better than Sherlock Holmes. I like Edgar A. Poe's prose works. Poe had a strange, unique ingenuity.[19]

December 6, 1911, *New York Times*

On Family

Edison spent so much of his time working at his laboratory that it was rare that he was in a formal photograph of his family. *Left to right*: Madeleine, Mina, Theodore, Charles, and Thomas Edison. Circa 1904. *Courtesy of the Thomas Edison National Historical Park, 021905032.*

Edison was married for the first time in 1871 to Mary Stilwell, a six-teen-year-old who had worked in his experimental shop. The marriage was challenging for both husband and wife. Edison worked long hours, leaving Mary feeling neglected and isolated. Mary was never his intellectual equal, and as the years passed, Edison found her difficult to relate to and emotionally needy.

The couple had three children, Marion, Thomas Jr., and William. When they were young, Edison had a close relationship with his daughter, Marion, but not with his sons. Thomas and William struggled and failed to live up to their father's and the public's expectations.

Mary Stilwell Edison died unexpectedly in 1884. Two years later, the inventor married twenty-year-old Mina Miller of Akron, Ohio. Mina, the daughter of inventor and Chautauqua cofounder Lewis Miller, was educated, well traveled, and had the support of her large family. She was also young, closer in age to her new stepdaughter than to her husband.

Though Mina tried to establish a relationship with Marion, the two clashed. Marion traveled to Europe, eventually marrying a German officer. Thomas Jr. and William had a better relationship with their stepmother, but felt estranged from Edison. After lackluster stints at boarding school, each tried his hand at business, with abysmal results. Thomas Jr. allowed his name to be used to promote inventions, provoking rage in his father. As Edison aged, Mina was able to broker peace among the children from his first marriage, but it was an uneasy truce.

During his second marriage, Thomas Edison and Mina had three children: Madeleine, Charles, and Theodore. Unlike their step-siblings, the children were well educated, all attending college. Madeleine married John Sloane in 1914 and eventually became mother to the Edisons' only grandchildren.

Charles Edison worked for his father's companies, becoming president of Thomas A. Edison, Inc., in 1926. In the years following his father's death, Charles was assistant secretary, then secretary of the United States Navy, and later the governor of New Jersey.

Theodore Edison graduated from the Massachusetts Institute of Technology with a physics degree. After working for his father, he began his own company, Calibron Industries. He earned eighty patents during his lifetime.

By today's standards, Edison would be characterized as a neglectful, perhaps even abusive, husband and father. His work consumed most of his time and energy, and he had little patience for day-to-day interactions. He expected his sons to be as accomplished as he. Yet he felt threatened when they were successful, and resentful when they failed.

By the standards of his own day, Edison would have been considered a better parent. He fulfilled his obligation to his children by providing them with food, clothing, shelter, and education. What they made of it was their own responsibility.

No nepotism. No answer.[1]

Note to a secretary to ignore his cousin's request for money and a job.
January 18, 1880, marginalia on a letter from John Edison

On Nancy Elliott Edison (1808?–1871), Edison's Mother

My mother was the making of me. She was so true, so sure of me; and I felt that I had some one to live for, some one I must not disappoint. . . . I did not have my mother very long, but in that length of time she cast over me an influence which has lasted all my life. The good effects of her early training I can never lose. If it had not been for her appreciation and her faith in me at a critical time in my experience, I should very likely never have been an inventor.[2]

August 10, 1908, *New York World*

On Mary Stilwell Edison (1855–1884),
Edison's First Wife

Midnight? Is that so? I must go home then, I was married today.[3]

> Though likely apocryphal, Edison, himself, told the story
> that he became so distracted by work that he forgot it
> was his wedding night. Circa 1871

Mrs. Mary Edison My wife Dearly Beloved Cannot invent worth a Damn!![4]
> February 1, 1872, technical notes and drawings

My Wife Popsy Wopsy Can't Invent.[5]
> February 14, 1872, technical notes and drawings

Inform wife will not be home tonight.[6]
> September 3, 1874, telegram to Charles Batchelor

My wife does not nor never can control me.[7]
> January 29, 1877, letter to his father

On Mina Miller Edison (1865–1947),
Edison's Second Wife, "Billy"

Saw a lady who looked like Mina, got thinking about Mina and came near being run over by a street car. If Mina interferes much more will have to take out an accident policy.[8]
> July 12, 1885, diary entry

Slept so sound that even Mina didn't bother me as It would stagger the mind of Raphael in a dream to imagine a being comparable to the Maid of Chataqua [*sic*] so I must have slept very sound.[9]

Since her father cofounded the Chautauqua movement, Edison called Mina the "Maid of Chautauqua." July 17, 1885, diary entry

Miss Mina Miller, of Akron, the most beautiful woman in Ohio, is to-day a guest of Mount Washington.[10]

August 1885 statement

Some months since, as you are aware, I was introduced to your daughter Miss Mina. The friendship which ensued became admiration as I began to appreciate her gentleness and grace of manner and beauty and strength of mind.

That admiration has on my part ripened into love, and I have asked her to become my wife.[11]

September 30, 1885, letter to Mina's father asking for permission to marry

Hoping you will have a very Merry Christmas and not watch me and Mina so closely when I come again.[12]

December 24, 1885, letter to Mina's younger brothers

Yes, I work all the time; my wife allows me.[13]

1888 interview

I would give $50000 to hug you for one hour.[14]

Note written between 1894 and 1898

I am longing to see you again with intimate love. I am your true lover to the limit.[15]

Note written between 1894 and 1898

Billy darling, you should not write so meanly about you being a small part of my life etc, that is all nonsense; You + the children and the Laboratory is all my life. I have nothing else, . . . I am your constant never changing Lover who thinks + knows he has the finest existing.[16]

Note written between 1894 and 1898

With a kiss like the swish of a 13 inch cannon projectile, I remain always your lover, sure, solid + unchangeable.[17]

August 11, 1895, note

Darling Edison you are the sweetest thing on earth and why should you ever get the *blues*. You have no earthly reason to get the blues except perhaps disappointment in having such a lover as myself or perhaps it is vain regrets after having gone to Chautauqua and seen George. I surmise that it is this that gave you the blues.[18]

August 12, 1895, letter with a reference to George Vincent, who at one time was Mina's suitor and a rival for her affections

There isn't 1 woman in 20000 that is really so smart as yourself. . . . Your lack of self confidence is the trouble, getting blue over such thing is rotten nonsense. Read the newspapers Darling Billy + stop novels.[19]

August 15, 1895, letter

I was carrying on a series of experiments with radium, but because of the danger in them my wife made me stop.[20]

February 11, 1907, *New York Times*

She is always near me, you know.[21]

April 1931, *Golden Book Magazine*

But just because letters don't swamp you don't get the idea I don't still love you to pieces in the same old way.[22]

Undated note

On Marion Estelle Edison Oeser (1873–1965), Edison's Daughter ("Dot")

Dot Edison angel Miss Marion Edison Sweetest of all.[23]

Circa 1880s

She has the judgment of a girl of 16 although only 12. . . . She laughed heartily when I told her about a church being a heavenly fire escape.[24]

July 12, 1885, diary entry

[Talk of Mina Miller] makes Dot jealous. She threatens to become an incipient Lucretia Borgia.[25]

Marion's threat to become like the Renaissance woman who allegedly poisoned and murdered her family's rivals set the foundation for her later relationship with Mina. July 17, 1885, diary entry

On Thomas Edison Jr. (1876–1935), Edison's Son

Tom is a *smart* one.[26]

October 21, 1877, letter to his father

I beg to state that the young man is my son. He has gone into business for himself but I know nothing of what he has got.[27]

December 16, 1897 letter to Spencer Borden

Tom is either crazy or a very bad character.[28]

1898 letter to his wife, Mina

He is being spoilt by the newspapers. His head is now so swelled that I can do nothing with him. He is being used by some sharp people for their own ends. I never could get him to go to school or work in the Laboratory. He is therefore absolutely illiterate scientifically + otherwise.[29]

> January 17, 1898, letter to Thomas Commerford Martin

I beg to say that should I become responsible for Thomas's debts, there would be no end to it and I will not hold myself responsible. . . . [P]ut it in hands of New York Sheriff, and if he can not in a reasonable time collect the money, let me know and I will see what I can do for him.[30]

> June 26, 1899, letter to Edward J. Redington

You must know that with your record of passing bad checks and use of liquor it would be impossible to connect you with any of the business prospects of mine.[31]

> July 21, 1903, marginalia on a letter from Thomas Edison Jr.

On William Edison (1878–1937), Edison's Son

William is going to study so he can get into College this year. He thinks he can do it.[32]

> 1896 letter to his wife, Mina

Please do not deliver anything to Wm. L. Edison, unless he pays for same or has an order signed by Mrs. Edison or myself.[33]

> June 27, 1898, letter to A. J. Miller in response to promissory notes given by Thomas and William without his permission

I see no reason whatever why I should support my son, he has done me no honor and has brought the blush of shame to my cheeks many times in fact he has at times hurt my feelings beyond measure.[34]

> December 1903 letter to Blanche Edison

On Madeleine Edison Sloane (1888–1979), Edison's Daughter

I have experimented with her. . . . I wanted to find out what made her cry. I discovered the reason. . . . I at last discovered that it was because she found out that being carried was more pleasant than lying in her cot.[35]

June 6, 1888, *Chicago Times*

We have two or three names selected for her, but have not decided what name we will give her.[36]

For the first few months of her life, she was named Grace, after Mina's sister. Edison changed her name to Madeleine just before her christening.
June 6, 1888, *Chicago Times*

That baby wouldn't cry for my phonograph and I just pinched her so she would. . . . But I've got that baby's howls right here on this wax cylinder.[37]

June 6, 1888, *New Brunswick (N.J.) Times*

Madeleine poured the tea like a little woman.[38]

Note to his wife, Mina, written between 1897 and 1898

I wanted my daughter to go to cooking school and tried my best to induce her to go. . . . But she did not seem to want to go and that ended it.[39]

March 1913, *Good Housekeeping*

I think now I have 3 children who know the value of money. I didn't know about my daughter but since you have had some experience + lessons you will be ok.[40]

April 1923 note to Madeleine

On Charles Edison (1890–1969), Edison's Son ("Toughy")

Charles was very obsequious.[41]

> Note to his wife, Mina, written between 1897 and 1898

Toughy was very much interested in the tools, the motor, and especially the typewriting machine.[42]

> July 1898 note to his wife, Mina

My son, Charles, managed the business during the two years I was engaged on war work and when I got back I was very much pleased to see how well he had handled things.[43]

> February 25, 1919, *Edison Herald*

On Theodore Edison (1898–1992), Edison's Son

[M]y "future laboratory assistant."[44]

> July 1898, letter to his wife, Mina

That boy's education shall be technical.[45]

> February 11, 1907, *New York Times*

Well, he is a student at the Massachusetts Institute of Technology. . . . I don't know how old Theodore is, but I guess he is twenty-one. At any rate he does original thinking.[46]

> December 13, 1921, *New York Times*

My son is a physicist and mathematician and I am no mathematician. If his mathematics are not too professional he can work with me, but if his mathematics shoot off in the Einstein direction he'll be practically no use at all.[47]

> February 11, 1923, *Boston Daily Globe*

On People

The automobile manufacturer Henry Ford and Edison on Edison's eightieth birthday in 1927. *Courtesy of the Thomas Edison National Historical Park, 14.110.61.*

E dison's opinions of others were influenced by his interests. He detested competitors like Bell, Tesla, and Westinghouse but admired those who achieved in fields outside his expertise.

Alexander Graham Bell (1847–1922), Telephone Inventor

You will find when the thing is sifted in the patent office how little Bell can claim except his magneto principle + even that is questioned . . . but I guess Bell is all right.[1]

October 12, 1877, letter to Franklin H. Badger

Under no circumstances will I have anything to do with Graham Bell. . . . They are a bunch of pirates.[2]

July 21, 1887, letter to George Edward Gouraud

Bell discovered the telephone, he did not invent it. He was making experiments on telegraphy by sound, and found out about the transmission of voice by a wire.[3]

November 4, 1888, *Brooklyn Citizen*

Bell was not a scientist.[4]

December 6, 1911, *New York Times*

Sarah Bernhardt (1844–1923), French Stage Actress

[She is] still full of pepper.[5]

February 12, 1922, *St. Louis Globe-Democrat*

Luther Burbank (1849–1926), Botanist and Horticulturalist

Burbank is one of the finest men living today, but he is getting out of his line when he dabbles in metaphysics. It is a sort of recreation with him, you might say, and he is not to be taken seriously.[6]

February 12, 1926, *New York Times*

Andrew Carnegie (1835–1919),
Steel Industrialist, Philanthropist

Mr. Carnegie stands for rapid American, for great outputs. He has brought the steel business to a high grade, perhaps not as to quality, but as to output, surely.[7]

December 6, 1911, *New York Times*

Calvin Coolidge (1872–1933), American President

Level headed fellow.[8]

September 25, 1930, interview

Marie Sklodowska Curie (1867–1934),
French Physicist and Chemist

Mme Curie hit on Becquerel's discoveries. She was a laboratory expert. Discovery, an accident, is the basis of the finding of radium. That is not invention.[9]

December 6, 1911, *New York Times*. (Antoine Henri Becquerel was the French winner of the 1903 Nobel Prize in Physics.)

Alexander Gustave Eiffel, (1832–1923),
Designer of the Eiffel Tower and Statue of Liberty

[T]he nicest fellow that I have met since I came to France, so simple and modest.[10]

Circa 1880s

Henry Ford (1863–1947),
Automobile Manufacturer and Industrialist

Henry Ford is no fool.[11]

> December 2, 1916, *Collier's Weekly*

Ford is the most humane man I ever saw.[12]

> December 2, 1916, *Collier's Weekly*

He is a natural-born mechanic if ever there was one.[13]

> December 2, 1916, *Collier's Weekly*

Henry Ford is a remarkable man in one sense and in another he's not. I would not vote for him for President, but as a director of manufacturing or industrial enterprises I'd vote for him—twice.[14]

> February 12, 1922, *New York Times*

I would hate to see Ford President because you would spoil a good man. He's more valuable where he is.[15]

> October 18, 1923, *New York Times*

I can only say to you that, in the fullest and richest meaning of the term—he is my friend.[16]

> October 22, 1929, *New York Times*

Benjamin Franklin (1706–1790), Founding Father and Inventor

I admire him as a sturdy patriot when patriotism meant more than mere words; as a diplomat, philosopher and correct observer; and as an apostle of hard work and sterling honesty. Long may his name be honored.[17]

> January 13, 1924, *New York Times*

Jason "Jay" Gould (1836–1892), Financier, Railroad Developer

He took no pride in building up an enterprise. He was after money, and money only. Whether the company was a success or a failure mattered not to him.[18]

Circa 1920s

Robert Ingersoll (1833–1899), American Freethinker

Some day when the veil of superstition is lifted Ingersoll will stand out as a great personality.[19]

Circa 1920s

Samuel Insull (1859–1938), Edison Employee and Electrical Magnate

Insull is as tireless as the tides.[20]

November 29, 1926, *Time*

Charles Lindbergh (1902–1974), Aviator and Explorer

Lindbergh is the product of our advanced civilization, admired for his fine character and achievements by all peoples, from the jungle-man up.[21]

January 1, 1928, *New York Times*

Guglielmo Marconi (1874–1937), Italian Inventor

If you are looking for a great inventor, take Marconi. *He* knew all the time what he was tryin' to git. It was a turribly hard thing to invent the wireless and it took lots of hard work and ingenuity to invent it, but he *invented* it.[22]

Circa 1903, quoted in September 1932, *Harper's Magazine*

I will say that I think that Marconi was a clever inventor. Very good. He was a practical man and is entitled to be called the "father of wireless."[23]

December 6, 1911, *New York Times*

Lewis Miller (1829–1899), Inventor, Educator, Edison's Father-in-Law

He grew up in the school of hard knocks. He invented some of the most useful labor-saving machines which had ever been brought out up to that time.

He contributed probably more to the cause of popular education that any other teacher of his time and helped to introduce more innovations into schools for higher education than many college presidents.[24]

July 25, 1929, *New York Times*

Benito Mussolini (1883–1945), Italian Dictator

Man of great executive abilities, probably a good man for the Italians.[25]

February 12, 1931, *Fort Myers (Fla.) Tropical News*

Thomas Paine (1737–1809), Revolutionary, Inventor, Writer

[M]y mother forced me to attend [church]—my father gave me Paine's Age of Reason.[26]

Circa 1880s

Thomas Paine was one of the greatest men of all time.[27]

May 31, 1925, *New York Times*

We never had sounder intelligence in this Republic. He was the equal of Washington in making American liberty possible. Where Washington performed Paine devised and wrote. . . . I consider Paine our greatest political thinker.[28]

June 7, 1925, *New York Times*

There was a great man, but he ran foul [*sic*] of the church people.[29]

September 25, 1930, interview

William Edward Sawyer (1850–1883), Lighting Systems Inventor

Regarding that despicable puppy Sawyer, I never believed a word he said. He's nothing but a bag of miasma under pressure.[30]

May 16, 1879, letter to Frederick W. Royce

Herbert Spencer (1820–1903), Philosopher

And Herbert Spencer [is a great man], for the meat in his books. He was a great generalizer. He proved things by statistics. . . . He based things on data. Spencer was a scientific thinker. And he was a good storyteller too.[31]

December 6, 1911, *New York Times*

Nikola Tesla (1856–1943), Inventor and Engineer

This is a damn good man.[32]

July 25, 1927, *Time*

If Tesla has a light why don't he show it?[33]

May 22, 1896, *New York Journal*

George Westinghouse (1846–1914), Entrepreneur and Rival

Westinghouse used to be a pretty solid fellow, but he has lately taken to shystering.[34]

October 7, 1889, *New York Herald*

On Himself

Edison reads the monument plaque on the site of his Menlo Park laboratory.
May 16, 1925. *Courtesy of the Thomas Edison National Historical Park, 14.130.54.*

Edison's comments on himself illustrate his sense of humor, single-mindedness, and eternal sense of optimism.

Ma, I'm a bushel of wheat. I weigh eighty pounds.[1]

> At the age of twelve. February 1890, *Harper's Magazine*

I have growed considerably. I don't look much like a boy now.[2]

> At nineteen. 1866 telegram to his parents

You ought to know me well enough to know that I am neither a dead beat or a selfish person, and that I always do as I agree[,] Without some damnable god damnable ill luck prevents. . . . However, I'll never give up for I may have a streak of luck before I die.[3]

> July 26, 1869, letter to Frank A. Hanaford

A barber told me yesterday that the roots of my hair were all coming out gray and that I would be gray in 10 months. My hair is now all sprinkled with them.[4]

> September 17, 1869, letter to Frank A. Hanaford

My hair is damnd near white. Man told me yesterday I was a walking churchyard.[5]

> 1870 letter to Frank A. Hanaford

I had more difficulty in holding a [job] than the world ever imagines. I drifted from one place to another and finally came to the conclusion that the possibility of success was to broaden out and devote my time more to the improvement of the telegraph services than to improving my ability as an operator.[6]

> June 4, 1892, *Bethlehem (Pa.) Times*

I am now what "you" Democrats call a "Bloated Eastern Manufacturer."[7]

> October 30, 1870, letter to his father

I hope to astonish the world yet with things more wonderful than this. I think the world is on the eve of grand and immense discoveries, before whose transcendent glories the record of the past will fade into insignificance.[8]

April 19, 1878, *Washington Post*

My business is experimenting. Without experimenting I am nothing.[9]

March 1880, *New York Herald*

Oh, I am young yet, and I think I have a few years yet before me. My grandfather died at the age of 103, my father is 78, and the youngest of four brothers.[10]

April 27, 1882, *St. Louis Post-Dispatch*

Only one night, [I got discouraged]. There was an evening that I quit work just disheartened, and feeling about as badly as a man could; but the next morning I gritted my teeth and went to work again more determined than ever to prove that I was right. After that I think I have reason to be grateful to my detractors and assailants, for they only stimulate me to greater efforts.[11]

May 3, 1885, *Tribuner*

I can't think about anything except when I'm experimenting. . . . How do I make calculations? Well, I don't know exactly. I can't do it on paper. I have to be moving around.[12]

July 16, 1885, *Salt Lake City Democrat*

By the way, I have played poker once or twice. It's a fine game.[13]

May 23, 1889, *Pittsburgh Dispatch*

After all, I am just as much of an American as ever; I wear the same sized hat now that I did when I left home. [The Spanish and the French] tried their best to spoil me, but my head is not a jot larger than it was, and this week you will see me back in harness as before.[14]

October 7, 1889, *New York Times*

I like to laugh, and I don't care for dancing, and I don't like a crowd, especially if I can't hide myself in it. I do like a good story, and I like the theatre. I go quite often and would enjoy it immensely if I could hear what the actors say, but I can't. I tell you. My best hold in the theatre is the light opera. There's where I get the fun. I can go there, you see, and get down in the bald heads' neighborhood and hear the music first rate.[15]

November 17, 1889, *New York World*

Oh, I don't like the city. There is too much jar and excitement there for me. I love the country and quietness. I never go into the city if I can help it.[16]

August 24, 1890, *New York Herald*

I like to begin at the large end of things; life is too short to begin at the small end.[17]

July 26, 1891, *New York Journal*

I have my own ideas, and I take my stand upon them, you know. A man who does that is always charged with eccentricity, inconsistency, and that kind of thing.[18]

July 1893, *Review of Reviews*

I am considered as sort of a museum freak.[19]

February 1896, *Norwalk (Ohio) Reflector*

I don't care for horses, I have no dogs or pets; my only pleasure out of doors is riding in my automobiles.[20]

April 1904, *Outing*

There are three things that I never could understand how any man could ever write a book, how any man could ever make a speech, and how any man could make the lightning mathematical calculations that those fellows in exhibitions do sometimes with a blackboard and a piece of chalk.[21]

May 19, 1907, *New York Times*

I always keep within a few feet of the earth's surface all the time. At least I never let my thought run up higher than the Himalayas. All my work is rather earthy.[22]

July 1911, *Century Magazine*

I have my own business problems to attend to, and I don't want to be set up as an authority on every question.[23]

August 13, 1921, *New York Times*

Well, if worse comes to worst, I've got a good trade. I can always make $75 a month as an expert telegraph operator and I can live comfortably on that.[24]

June 24, 1923, *New York Times*

My head has swelled an eighth of an inch.[25]

Edison on congratulatory telegrams and wishes for his eightieth birthday. February 13, 1927, *New York Times*

If I have spurred men to greater efforts, and if our work has widened the horizon of man's understanding even a little, and given a measure of happiness in the world, I am content.[26]

Edison's reluctant speech at the Golden Jubilee of Light. November 2, 1929, *Literary Digest*

On the Future

Henry Ford, Thomas Edison, and the botanist Luther Burbank surrounded
by a crowd in Santa Rosa, California, in 1915. *Courtesy of the Thomas
Edison National Historical Park, 14.130.100.*

Though Edison claimed not to be "much of a prophet," he often made predictions about the future. Some are surprisingly accurate, while others show Edison to be a man of his times.

You ask me about the future of electricity. It is the coming motive power. It will be used on all the railroads someday.[1]

June 12, 1889, *Pittsburgh Dispatch*

I am at work on an invention which will enable a man in Wall-street not only to telephone to a friend near Central Park, say, but to actually see that friend while speaking to him. . . . Of course, it is ridiculous to talk about seeing between New York and Paris; the rotundity of the earth, if nothing else, would render that impossible.[2]

September 1, 1889, *Levant Herald*

You listen to me. In twenty-five years from now electricity will have superseded horse power in New York in the performance of every sort of needful work. The horse will have become a luxury, a toy and a pet.[3]

November 17, 1889, *New York World*

If we could have a telephone from the earth to the sun—I mean a wire—we could send sounds there with perfect ease; and with the phonograph, were our language universal, we could make a speech here and have it recorded and reproduced in any of the great planetary bodies.[4]

December 31, 1891, unnamed newspaper

I believe that within thirty years nearly all railways will discard steam locomotives and adopt electric motors, and that the electric automobile will displace the horse entirely.[5]

August 12, 1902, *New York Times*

Ah, yes, you want to hear from me something about what the science of invention will do for the world fifty years hence. I wish I could tell you—but I am not much of a prophet.[6]

May 19, 1907, *New York Times*

New York and London will be in free communication by wireless telegraphy before long.[7]

October 19, 1907, *New York Times*

But if Americans keep on developing their nervous hurry, the one-hundred-mile-an-hour train will be a regular feature on our railroads.[8]

January 12, 1908, *New York Times*

The Trolley—that's a thing that's going to develop and spread wonderfully during the coming years. I expect to see Long Island and all the land about New York built up.[9]

January 12, 1908, *New York Times*

The work day, I believe, will be eight hours. Every man needs that much work to keep him out of mischief and to keep him happy. And it will be work with the brain, something men will be interested in and done in wholesome pleasant surroundings."[10]

January 14, 1910, *Seattle Star*

The clothes of the future will be so cheap that every woman will be able to follow the fashions promptly, and there will be plenty of fashions. Artificial silk that is superior to natural silk is now made of wood pulp. It shines better than silk. I think that the silk work barbarism will go in fifty years.[11]

January 28, 1910, *Independent*

Not individualism but social labor will dominate the future. Industry will constantly become more social and more independent. There will be no manual labor in the factories of the future. The men in them will be merely superintendents watching the machinery to see that it works right. Less and less man will be used as an engine or as a horse and his brain will be employed to benefit himself and his fellows.[12]

January 28, 1910, *Independent*

In the automatic shop of the future there will be no shopkeepers, no clerks, no boy to wrap up packages. On entering the shop, the intending purchaser will see no one, unless it be some other purchaser. There will be no counters, no scales, no shelves lined with goods, no showcases.

In the walls of the shop there will be dozens and dozens of little openings. Above every opening there will be a small sign. The sign will tell in a half dozen different languages what particular article that particular opening will deliver.... You see that in an automatic shop there will be no waiting time in talk, no pricing of articles, nor any sampling. Shopping will be an exact, speedy, and businesslike proposition.... [I]t will be a strictly cash proposition.... [A] man can't ask credit from a slot machine. If he wants the goods he's got to have a nickel.[13]

May 15, 1910, *New York Times*

I believe that the day is coming when it will be only necessary to heat a little water in order to prepare a meal. And I should add that the water will be heated by electricity. The old-fashioned cook stove will be a forgotten relic.[14]

May 15, 1910, *New York Times*

Nobody can tell what the conditions [of the future] will be. We may discover laws that will upset all our calculations. We discover what we think are fundamental laws, then they are upset by an-other discovery. The only thing to do is to work along and bring out every practical and useful fact we can.[15]

July 11, 1911, Century Magazine

The drudgery of life will, by and by, entirely disappear. In days to come, through a small outlay of money, both men and women will be gratified by an infinite variety of delightful sights, sounds, and experiences that today are unknown and unimagined.[16]

October 12, 1912, Good Housekeeping

We shall wake up presently to the dire fact that the world is get-ting settled at a rate which presently will occupy the total space. The less of that space which is occupied by the unfit and imperfect, certainly the better for the race. The development of women which has now begun and is progressing with such startling speed, will do more to solve this problem than any other thing can do.[17]

October 12, 1912, Good Housekeeping

I believe that in ten years cement roads will band the country from one end to the other to the exclusion of all other kinds.[18]

September 8, 1913, New York Times

Something [should be done] to save paper. If non-carbonized inks were used—inks that would bleach—papers could be run through the presses again by the aid of an invention or two and be used several times. It's bound to come to a proposition of this kind.[19]

September 8, 1913, New York Times

[B]y and by humanity will have to live in double shifts, so that there may be room upon the earth of all the people.[20]

October 11, 1914, New York Times

It will not be long till you can keep your submarines under water almost indefinitely without coming up for air.[21]

October 11, 1914, *New York Times*

Some day nearly everything will be done by electricity.[22]

December 2, 1916, *Collier's Weekly*

In twenty or thirty years there won't be any horse trucks left in the cities.[23]

December 2, 1916, *Collier's Weekly*

The future of the world? It appears to me to be fine and interesting, but somewhat complicated. The world is progressing and is moving along faster than ever. We have foreknowledge and the tools, so we can go ahead on new inventions. It is hard to say what the new inventions will be.[24]

February 12, 1921, *New York Times*

It's what is ahead that interests me, not the past.[25]

July 19, 1922, *New York Times*

I believe the great religious leaders of the future will not spend much time on teaching creeds, on participation in ceremonies, or on anything except the instruction of humanity in those details of Truth which have been fully established and the precise and cautious uncovering of new details.[26]

November 1926, *Forum*

The city of the future will be immensely affected by air travel. Sooner or later we shall get the helicopter . . . It does not require any very vivid imagination to help us realize that when the helicopter comes into being roofs of large buildings in our cities immediately will become very valuable parts of such structures. . . . Certain

new varieties of disaster will then develop, but it is useless to foretell these now.[27]

November 1926, *Forum*

My message to you is to be courageous. I have lived a long time. I
have seen history repeat itself again and again. I have seen depressions in business. Always America has come back stronger and
more prosperous. Be as brave as your fathers before you. Have faith.
Go forward.[28]

June 11, 1931, *Fort Myers (Fla.) Tropical News*

It's very beautiful over there.[29]

Reportedly Edison's last words before dying.
October 19, 1931, *New York Times*

Miscellaneous

Thomas Edison at bat with Connie Mack catching at Terry Park
in Fort Myers, Florida, on March 7, 1927. *Courtesy of the Thomas
Edison National Historical Park, 14.225.118.*

On Clothing

For the first time in my life I have bought a pair of premeditatedly tight shoes. . . . [I]t is pure vanity, conceit and folly to suffer bodily pains that one's person may have the graces the outcome of secret agony.[1]

July 20, 1885, diary entry

If I were to remove my clothing [to sleep] I would get up feeling out of shape and with all desire gone for continuing my labors. My train of thought would be lost.[2]

1890 interview

The dress of girls and women is becoming simpler and more beautiful. Simplicity and beauty of dress probably are signs of advancing civilization.[3]

January 1927, *Forum*

Fashion comes in waves. How they originate or why they pass, no one knows.[4]

February 11, 1928, *Fort Myers (Fla.) Press*

On Cooking

Cooking cannot be learned in the average home any more than mechanical engineering can be learned in the average home. Cooking can be successfully taught only in a great chemical laboratory, such as a good cooking school is.[5]

March 1913, *Good Housekeeping*

On Criticism

I believe in criticism because it brings out all the cold facts about a thing, and promotes discussion, which is always beneficial.[6]

September 17, 1878, *New York Sun*

On Dance

The "dancing" craze, as it is called, will keep on for it is perfectly natural. It really is by no means a "craze."[7]

January 1927, *Forum*

On Fame, Honors, and Awards

Autographs + Begging letters commencing to come in. My god how little they suspect.[8]

April 16, 1878, letter to Uriah Hunt Painter

My mail amounts to about 100 letters a day and is growing burdensome as I make it a rule to reply courteously to all who write me.[9]

November 8, 1878, letter to Theodore Puskas

I have no time for ordinary correspondence but am disposed at all times to give attention to communications from inventors or students.[10]

November 11, 1878, letter to Brewer & Jensen

I am the busiest man in America. This everlasting entertaining people from all over the world and from the farms hereabouts is fearful trying and murders one's time frightfully.[11]

December 4, 1878, letter to Clarence J. Blake

Oh, yes, now I remember; they did give me one of those things that you stamp butter with.[12]

On the honor of Italian Grand Officer of the Legion of Honor bestowed for his development of electrical power systems. April 1898, *Ladies' Home Journal*

It might make a good paper weight.[13]

On a 486-pound award received at the Electrical Exposition of 1911. October 12, 1911, *New York Times*

When you honor me, you are also honoring the vast army of workers but for whom my work would have gone for nothing.[14]

October 22, 1929, *Fort Myers (Fla.) Press*

I won't go in. I can't go in.[15]

Said to his wife at a dinner Henry Ford gave to honor him. October 21, 1929, *New York Times*

This experience [honorary dinner] makes me realize as never before that Americans are sentimental.[16]

On the fiftieth anniversary of the invention of the incandescent light. October 22, 1929, *New York Times*

I am tired of all the glory. I want to go back to work.[17]

Circa October 1929

On Luck

My reasoning mind revolts against the superstition of luck, my savage soul clings to it.[18]

September 1932, *Harper's Magazine*

And if there is such a thing as luck, then *I* must be the most unlucky fellow in the world. I've never once made a lucky strike in all my life.[19]

September 1932, *Harper's Magazine*

On Mathematicians

I have never been able to remember how much seven times seven are. I always have to count that seven times six is forty-two, and then add seven.[20]

April 1898, *Ladies' Home Journal*

[D]on't the mathematicians have any common sense at all?[21]

Circa 1903, quoted in September 1932, *Harper's Magazine*

I can always hire some mathematicians, but they can't hire me.[22]

Circa 1890s–1910

On Night Life

The nation whose inhabitants withdraw into their houses, as a turtle pulls into its shell, when darkness falls, is sure to be a very stupid nation. Night life and stupidity do not go together; a growing tendency toward night life means a growing mental spryness.[23]

October 29, 1911, *New York Times*

On Phrenology, the Reading of Character Based on Skull Shape

I never knew I had an inventive talent until Prof. O. S. Fowler examined my head and told me so. I was a stranger to myself until then.[24]

January 1904, *Phrenological Journal and Science of Health*

[A] pear shaped skull is the best type, [but a] pin head [is] not good for [an] inspector.[25]

Circa 1910–19

On Public Speaking

You can't get me to talk, even on a phonograph.[26]

On being asked to speak in front of movie cameras.
October 12, 1922, *New York Times*

A tendency toward stage fright, which has prevented me from becoming a dangerous rival of [actors Douglas] Fairbanks or [Rudy] Valentino, coupled with my extreme deafness, makes it impossible for me to speak in public.[27]

February 16, 1924, *New York Times*

Please do not expect a speech from me, as public speaking is entirely out of my line.[28]

September 18, 1928, *New York Times*

On the Red Cross

The Red Cross is the greatest organization in the world, and the people cannot do too much for it.[29]

February 14, 1921, *New York Times*

On Rotarians

From what I know of Rotarians, I rather imagine they must be imbued with the same spirit of mixing a little sentiment with business as they mingle together throughout the world, for the growth of the organization has been phenomenal from its modest beginnings twenty-five years ago to its world-wide prominence of the present day.[30]

July 10, 1930, *New York Times*

On Subways

If I were an insurance company, I'd like to issue a policy on the Subway. It would be an ideal risk, because the risk would be practically nil.[31]

January 7, 1906, *New York Times*

Miscellaneous

It is a mere stupidity to rob life of all its reservations.[32]

January 1927, *Forum*

We do not call apples a bad fruit because some have blemishes.[33]

January 1927, *Forum*

Others on Edison

Portrait of a confident Edison.
Courtesy of the Thomas Edison National Historical Park, 14.15.005.

Edison became nationally famous for the invention of the phonograph shortly after his thirtieth birthday. Two years later, his incandescent lamp transformed him into an American legend that to this day has no equal. During his own long life he was respected and lauded for his inventive genius, but he was also criticized for his religious views and personal flaws.

Rev. Orvis. T. Anderson (1881–1939), of the Thomas A. Edison Congregational Church, Fort Myers, Fla.

[T]hat man is no work of the dust and a co-worker with God.[1]

October 23, 1929, *Tropical News*

Dr. Henry van Dyke (1852–1933), Princeton Professor of English

On publicity he is an expert. On electricity he is good, but sometimes whimsical. On education as a process of teaching men to understand and think broadly, humanely he reminds one of a sub-freshman, coming up from the "prep" school where modesty is not in the curriculum.[2]

November 21, 1922, *New York Times*

Robert A. Carter, Expert Mechanic and Edison Employee in Newark

Mr. Edison had his desk in one corner, and after completing an invention he would jump up and do a kind of Zulu dance. He would swear something awful.[3]

October 18, 1931, *New York Times*

Calvin Coolidge (1872–1933), American President

To your energy, courage, industry and strong will the world owes a debt of gratitude which it is impossible to compute. Your inventions placing the forces of nature at the service of humankind have added to our comfort and happiness and are of benefit to all mankind for generations to come.[4]

February 12, 1927, *New York Times*

The life of Thomas Alva Edison, master of applied science, has been represented as a romance. He has been called a genius, a wizard. While these terms may well be used to describe his great abilities, yet this remarkably modest man has constantly refused to attribute such qualities to himself.[5]

October 21, 1928, *New York Times*

Daniel H. Craig (1811–1895), Telegraph Company Owner

Indeed, if you should tell me that you could *make babies by machines*, I shouldn't doubt it.[6]

February 13, 1871, letter to Edison

George Eastman (1854–1932), Photography Innovator

I regard him as the greatest inventor who ever lived, with nobody else even second.[7]

February 11, 1927, *New York Times*

Thomas A. Edison did more than any other man to make this world an easier, pleasanter, better world to live in. In him were combined a phenomenal mind, a tremendous energy, and even up to his declining years, an almost boyish enthusiasm for the successful solving of the problem of the moment. The world has lost one of its greatest men of all time.[8]

October 18, 1931, *New York Times*

Charles Edison (1890–1969), Edison's Son

Mr. Edison is one of those rare souls that stand as contradictions to the time worn adage that no man is a hero to those close to him. To know him is something, to actually know him is more, but to know him in the intimate relationship of father and son is to worship him.[9]

May 25, 1928, *New York Times*

Mina Miller Edison (1865–1947), Edison's Wife

He invents all the while, even in his dreams.[10]

May 25, 1888, *New York Sun*

He is absent-minded; yes but I suppose all men are. . . . So you see, he is like all other husbands. He forgets, but he expects me to understand.[11]

October 20, 1915, *San Francisco Examiner*

If there is any point about which you are sensitive, he dwells on it. He's a great tease, he will tell you what you don't like to hear.[12]

February 11, 1927, *New York Times*

Samuel Ogden Edison Jr. (1804–1896), Edison's Father

Did I foresee his destiny? No, I can't say that I did. I didn't think he amounted to very much when he left home and went to selling newspapers on the [railroad] cars.[13]

November 26, 1885, *New York World*

Harvey Firestone (1869–1938), Industrialist and Tire Manufacturer

Mr. Edison, we all know, had the greatest mind of any man in our generation.[14]

October 26, 1931, *Time*

Henry Ford (1863–1947), Auto Manufacturer and Industrialist

Well, I think Mr. Edison is the greatest man in the world and I guess everyone does.[15]

January 11, 1914, *New York Times*

They have called in Thomas Edison to help their war plans [by advising the U.S. Navy]. Let me say that Thomas Edison never has used, and, in my opinion, never will use his great brain to make anything that would destroy human life or human property. He could destroy nothing. His mind is a constructive mechanism that abhors destruction, and war is destruction. He is a man of peace, for he realizes the true meaning of war—wanton, unnecessary, and unreasoning destruction, death and disruption of all that peace has builded.[16]

August 23, 1915, *New York Times*

I have found Mr. Edison an inspiration. He is, I believe, the happiest man in the world.[17]

March 7, 1929, *New York Times*

Mr. Edison freed man from darkness, lengthened his day so that he could increase his production and his producing efficiency.[18]

November 1929, *Scientific American*

It might better be said we live in the age of Edison . . . in many ways, the greatest man since the world began.[19]

March 7, 1929, *New York Times*

Cardinal James Gibbons (1834–1921),
Catholic Archbishop of Baltimore

[H]e has maimed his own mind just as Darwin did, by a too one-sided exercise of its powers. He talks with great freedom, and, I may say, with not a little contempt, of theology; but one suspects that he has been too occupied, and perhaps too contemptuous, of theology, to devote much time to its study. One suspects that his acquaintance with it is almost limited to fragmentary reminiscences of sermons heard in boyhood days.... But here is a scientist who proclaims dogmas to the public; and he seems to ask us to believe them—because he believes them.[20]

February 19, 1911, *New York Times*

Hamilton Holt (1872–1951), President of Rollins College

[W]e are now in the presence of one of the immortals of all time.[21]

February 12, 1930, *Tropical News*

Herbert Hoover (1874–1964), American President

By inventing the electric lamp Mr. Edison did vastly more than provide a new lamp. He removed an untold burden for toil from the backs of men and women for all time.[22]

July 20, 1929, *New York Times*

Joseph Henry (1797–1878),
Scientist and Secretary of the Smithsonian Institution

[T]he most ingenious inventor in this country . . . or in any other.[23]

Circa 1870s

Sir Thomas Lipton (1850–1931), British Industrialist

I feel that we have had the greatest man in the whole world.[24]

January 6, 1899, *Dallas Morning News*

Emil Ludwig (1881–1948), German Writer and Historian

If we speculate as to the living being to whom the earth owes the greatest gratitude, no one can compete with Edison.[25]

February 10, 1928, *New York Times*

My estimate of Edison's genius went up after meeting him. He and Mrs. Edison are not only great, but great of heart.[26]

March 11, 1928, *New York Times*

There sits the uncrowned King of America.[27]

October 10, 1931, *New York Times*

Tomáš Garrigue Masaryk (1850–1937), President of Czechoslovakia

Whenever I am thinking of men who promoted real progress of mankind and the forces which were subservient to it, I always remember you and your creative work.[28]

August 13, 1927, *New York Times*

Benito Mussolini (1883–1945), Italian Dictator

The surmounting of obstacles which has always characterized you is an example to whoever has a wholesome conception of social duties and arouses the admiration of all.[29]

August 13, 1927, *New York Times*

Rabbi Louis I Newman (1893–1973),
Congregation Rodeph Shalom, New York City

Thomas Edison is included, [in his list of the ten greatest living men] because he is the father of our electrical era. He symbolized the spirit of America, relying upon machinery moved by natural power, which Edison harnessed. Edison, the inventor, is the supremely typical figure of American life.[30]

February 2, 1931, *New York Times*

Franklin D. Roosevelt (1882–1945), American President

He was not merely a great inventor—he was a great citizen who was constantly thinking in terms of the good of our country.[31]

October 18, 1931, *New York Times*

Charles Proteus Steinmetz, (1865–1923),
Mathematician and Electrical Engineer

From my experience I consider Edison today as the man best informed in all fields of human knowledge.[32]

October 11, 1914, *New York Times*

Nikola Tesla (1856–1943),
Inventor and Mechanical and Electrical Engineer

If he had a needle to find in a haystack he would stop to reason where it was most likely to be, but would proceed at once, with the feverish diligence of a bee, to examine straw after straw until he found the object of his search.[33]

October 19, 1931, *New York Times*

Francis R. Upton (1852–1921), Edison Employee, Electrical Systems Developer

I consider it no sacrilege to say that I think the genius of Mr. Edison is God-like in its infinite patience and industry.[34]

February 12, 1918, *New York Times*

The United States Congress

Edison is probably the last and the greatest of the heroic inventors ... the father of modern industrial research.[35]

October 21, 1928, *New York Times*

George Eastman invited Edison to his Rochester, New York, home in 1928. Eastman and Edison collaborated on motion film experimentation beginning in 1889. *Courtesy of the Thomas Edison National Historical Park, 14.225.041.*

Notes

Foreword

1. "Two Hours at Menlo Park, *New York Graphic*, Dec 28, 1878, The Thomas Edison Papers (hereafter TEP), [MBSB21091; TAEM 94:444].

2. "Of Thomas A. Edison: The Electrical Inventor and His Electrical Novel," *Lynchburg Virginian,* Nov 19, 1891, TEP, [SC91070A; TAEM 146:729].

Preface and Acknowledgments

Epigraph source: "Edison Defends Cigars," *New York Times* (hereafter *NYT*), Aug 13, 1921.

1. Ibid.

Chapter 1. On Inventing

1. "Tesla Says Edison Was an Empiricist," *NYT*, Oct 19, 1931.

2. Edison to Daniel H. Craig, Dec 7, 1870, TEP, [D7003F; TAEM 12:120].

3. Edison to George Harrington, July 22, 1871 [supplied date], TEP, [D7103L; TAEM 12:251].

4. Edison to Henry Bentley, Mar 7, 1878, TEP, [X001A1BG; TAEM 0:0]. (Courtesy of the Henry Ford Museum and Greenfield Village Research Center [hereafter HFMGV].)

5. "Edison's Thunder Stolen, Some English Electricians Laying Claim to His Discoveries," *New York Sun*, June 9, 1878, TEP, [MBSB10607; TAEM 94:230].

6. Conot, 139, quoting from laboratory notebook series, N78–12.20.3.

7. Edison to Theodore Puskas, Nov 13, 1878, TEP, [LB003487; TAEM 28:9130].

8. Edison to Freeman G. Lockhart, July 14, 1879, TEP, [LB004472; TAEM 80:99].

9. "Edison Still Sanguine," *Quincy (Ill.) Daily Whig*, quoting *Detroit Free Press*, Aug 31, 1883.

10. "Will Tackle a Flying Machine," *Dallas Morning News* quoting *New York Sun*, June 29, 1888.

11. "Edison's New Ideas," *Brooklyn Citizen*, Nov 4, 1888, TEP, [SMo38071; TAEM 25:580].

12. Marginalia by Edison on a Thomson-Houston Electric Co. report, Mar 23, 1889, p. 18, TEP, [HM89AAG; TAEM 144:198].

13. George Parsons Lathrop, "Talks with Edison," *Harper's Magazine*, Feb 1890, 431.

14. Ibid.

15. Ibid.

16. Ibid.

17. "Edison on Inventions," 1890 interview, published in Nov 1895 *Monthly Illustrator/Home & Country*, TEP, [SC90094A; TAEM 146:657].

18. "What Is This State Called Life?" *New York Herald*, Nov 8, 1891, TEP, [SC91069a; TAEM 146:728].

19. Ibid.

20. "Inventions of the Future," unnamed newspaper, Dec 31, 1891, TEP, [SC91074a; TAEM 146:733].

21. "Wizard Edison and His Wonderful Inventions," *Cincinnati Enquirer*, Jan 18, 1892, TEP, [SC92005; TAEM 146:739].

22. "A Talk with Edison," *Scientific American*, Apr 2, 1892, 216.

23. Charles D. Lanier, "Two Giants of the Electric Age," *Review of Reviews*, July 1893, 44.

24. "Edison in Town," *Philadelphia Bulletin*, Oct 10, 1895, TEP, [SC95051a; TAEM 146:978].

25. "Phonograph Improved," *NYT*, Apr 5, 1896.

26. "The Anecdotal Side of Edison," *Ladies' Home Journal*, April 1898, 8.

27. "Edison's Stories of His Inventions," *NYT*, Jan 20, 1901.

28. Circa 1903, quoted in "Edison in His Laboratory," *Harper's Magazine*, Sept 1932, 405. Edison was making cylinder phonograph records at the time of the statement.

29. Circa 1903, quoted ibid.

30. Circa 1903, quoted ibid.

31. Circa 1903, quoted ibid.

32. "Edison about to Give to the World His Greatest Wonder," *NYT*, Oct 21, 1906.

33. "Edison Is Sixty; Birthday To-Day," *NYT*, Feb 11, 1907.

34. "Edison at Sixty, Outlines Wonders of the Future," *NYT*, May 19, 1907.

35. Ibid.

36. "As Yet We Know Nothing," *NYT*, Jan 12, 1908.

37. Ibid.

38. Ibid.

39. Frederic J. Haskins, "Edison Is Sixty-one," *Dallas Morning News*, Feb 11, 1908.

40. "The Future's Possibilities," *NYT*, Oct 11, 1908.

41. Ibid.

42. Ibid.

43. "A Word from Edison," *Fort Myers (Fla.) Press*, Oct 15, 1908.

44. Statement from April 1909, in Meadowcroft, 301.

45. "No Immortality of the Soul Says Thomas A. Edison," *NYT*, Oct 2, 1910.

46. "Wizard with Amazing Powers Astounds Scientists," *NYT*, Nov 13, 1910.

47. "Edison on Invention and Inventors," *Century Magazine*, July 1911, 416.

48. Ibid.

49. Ibid.

50. Ibid.

51. Ibid.

52. Ibid.

53. "Edison Bars Poets from List of Great," *NYT*, Dec 6, 1911.

54. "Edison Sees 1912 Great, Minus Greed," *NYT*, Jan 3, 1912.

55. Hubbard, 18.

56. Oliver Simmons, "Edison and His Insomnia Squad," *Munsey's Magazine*, September 1916, 626.

57. "Edison Favors League," *NYT*, June 22, 1919.

58. "Experimenting Wins Success Says Edison Who Worked One Year to Reproduce a Word," *Fort Myers (Fla.) Press*, July 10, 1920.

59. "Edison and His Lamp Praised at Dinner," *NYT*, Sept 12, 1922.

60. "Edison Astonished as Science Wizards Show New Marvels," *NYT*, Oct 19, 1922.

61. "Edison against Ford's Election," *Boston Daily Globe*, Oct 18, 1923.

62. "Work Begins," *Time*, Mar 15, 1926.

63. "Edison at 80 Views a World He Changed," *NYT*, Feb 27, 1927.

64. "Edison Makes Debut in Radio Interview," *NYT*, Oct 22, 1927.

65. "Edison Foresees Healthier World," *NYT*, Dec 24, 1930.

66. "Titan of the Heroic Age of Invention; Edison Whose Name Symbolizes Electricity," *NYT*, Oct 25, 1931.

Chapter 2. On His Own Inventions

1. Notation made in Edison's Technical Notes and Drawings, July 19, 1871, TAED, [NE167001; TAEM 3:78].

2. Edison to William Henry Preece, Aug 2, 1877, Thomas A. Edison Papers, Digital edition at: http://edison.rutgers.edu/ (hereafter TAED), [Z005AB; TAEM 0:0]. (Courtesy of the Institution of Electrical Engineers Archive.)

3. Meadowcroft, 158.

4. "Wizard Edison and His Wonderful Inventions," *Cincinnati Enquirer*, Jan 18, 1892, TAED, [SC92005; TAEM 146:739].

5. Edison to Thomas B. A. David, Aug 15, 1877, TAED, [X012EH; TAEM 0:0]. (Courtesy of the AT&T Archives and History Center.)

6. Edison to Theodore Puskas, Feb 10, 1878, TAED, [Z400AE; TAEM 0:0]. (Courtesy of the Foundation of the Postal Communication Museum, Budapest, Hungary [hereafter PTM].)

7. Edison to Henry Bentley, Mar 7, 1878, TAED, [X001A1BG; TAEM 0:0]. (Courtesy of the HFMGV.)

8. Marginalia by Edison on letter from Eugenius H. Outerbridge, Aug 6, 1879, TAED, [D7937ZBW1; TAEM 52:89}.

9. "Edison and the Telephone," *Barnstable (Mass.) Patriot*, Nov 21, 1882.

10. "Thomas A. Edison Gives His Reasons Why He Prefers Being a Little Deaf," *Quincy (Ill.) Daily Whig*, quoting *New York Sun*, Sept 16, 1884.

11. "Inventions of the Future," unnamed newspaper, Dec 31, 1891, TAED, [SC91074a; TAEM 146:733].

12. "Edison Invents Phone Recorder," *NYT*, May 24, 1915.

13. "Send Greetings to Edison," *NYT*, Oct 22, 1915.

14. "A Marvellous Discovery," *New York Sun*, Feb 2, 1878, TAED, [MBSB 10378; TAEM 94:115].

15. Ibid.

16. Edison to Benjamin Franklin Butler, Feb 12, 1878, TAED, [X042AB; TAEM 0:0]. (Courtesy of the Manuscript Division, Library of Congress.)

17. Marginalia by Edison on letter from Henry W. Law, Feb 27, 1878, TAED, [D7802ABA; TAEM 15:289].

18. Edison to Alfred Marshall Mayer, Mar 2, 1878, TAED, [X095AC; TAEM 0:0]. (Courtesy of the Princeton University Libraries.)

19. Edison to George Samuel Nottage, Mar 23, 1878, TAED, [LB001462; TAEM 28:313].

20. "That Wonderful Edison," *New York World*, Mar 29, 1878, TAED, [SB031075; TAEM 27:776].

21. "The Papa of the Phonograph," *New York Graphic*, Apr 2, 1878, TAED, [MBSB10472; TAEM 94:151].

22. "The Man Who Invents," *Washington Post*, Apr 19, 1878, TAED, [MBSB10532; TAEM 94:169].

23. "The Phonograph at the Capitol," *Washington Star*, Apr 19, 1878, TAED, [MBSB10537; TAEM 94:171].

24. "Edison's Electric Light," *New York Sun*, Oct 20, 1878, TAED, [MBSB20963; TAEM 94:382].

25. Edison to Clarence J. Blake, Dec 4, 1878, TAED, [X011AE; TAEM 0:0]. (Courtesy of the Trustees of the Boston Public Library.)

26. "Two Hours at Menlo Park," *New York Graphic*, Dec 28, 1878, TAED, [MBSB21091; TAEM 94:444].

27. Statement made circa 1880, quoted in Conot, 245.

28. "Edison and the Telephone," *Barnstable (Mass.) Patriot*, Nov. 21, 1882.

29. "Edison's New Phonograph," *Scientific American*, Oct 29, 1887, 273, TAED, [SC87003A; TAEM 146:214].

30. Ibid.

31. "Edison's Phonograph," unnamed newspaper, likely *Wilmington Evening Journal*, Nov 10, 1887, TAED, [SC877003b; TAEM 146:215].

32. "Edison's Improved Phonograph," *Scientific American*, Nov 19, 1887.

33. Ibid.

34. "How It Grew into Its Present Usefulness," *Pittsburgh Chronicle Telegraph*, May 24, 1889, TAED, [SC89063; TAEM 146:428].

35. "Facetious Edison," *Quincy (Ill.) Daily Herald*, Aug 2, 1893.

36. "Phonograph Improved," *NYT*, Apr 5, 1896.

37. Ibid.

38. Ibid.

39. Ibid.

40. Israel, 437.

41. "Submarine Terror to End, Says Edison," *NYT*, Jan 3, 1915.

42. "Experimenting Wins Success Says Edison Who Worked One Year to Reproduce a Word," *Fort Myers (Fla.) Press*, July 10, 1920.

43. "Significant Sayings," *Current Opinion*, April 1922, 448.

44. "Edison on Air, Tells of First Phonograph," *NYT*, Aug 13, 1927.

45. "The Magic Edison Made for the World," *NYT*, Aug 12, 1928.

46. Conot, 121, quoting from a margin note from Dr. Alexander Schweichler, May 24, 1878.

47. "Edison's Newest Marvel," *New York Sun*, Sept 16, 1878, TAED, [MBSB20887; TAEM 94:354].

48. Edison to Theodore Puskas, Sept 22, 1878, TAED, [D7802ZZBL; TAEM 16:106].

49. Edison to Grosvenor Porter Lowrey, Oct 3, 1878, TAED, [LB003390; TAEM 28:824].

50. Edison to George Edward Gouraud, telegram, Oct 8, 1878, TAED, [D7821G; TAEM 18:139].

51. Edison to Henry Morton, Oct 10, 1878, TAED, [ZD012D1356; TAEM 47:502].

52. "Edison's Electric Light," *New York Sun*, Oct 20, 1878, TAED, [MBSB20963; TAEM 94:382].

53. "Edison's New Light," *New York Daily Graphic*, Oct 21, 1878, TAED, [MBSB20960; TAEM 94:380].

54. Ibid.

55. Edison to George G. Ward, telegram, Oct 24, 1878, TAED, [D7821X; TAEM 18:164].

56. "Edison a Lightning Inventor," *New York World*, Nov 17, 1878, TAED, [MBSB21012; TAEM 94:411].

57. "The New Electric Lights," *New York Sun*, Nov 25, 1878, TAED, [MBSB21021; TAEM 94:416].

58. Ibid.

59. "Edison's Light, Already Perfected, but Requiring to Be Cheapened," *New York Herald*, Jan 30, 1879, TAED, [MBSB21119; TAEM 94:455].

60. Ibid.

61. Edison to Theodore Puskas, Apr 8, 1879 [supplied date], TAED, [X098A002B; TAEM 0:0]. (Courtesy of the Smithsonian Institution, National Museum of American History Archives Center [NMAHAC].)

62. Marginalia by Edison on letter from John E. Watson, Sept 8, 1879, TAED, [D7905S; TAEM 49:632].

63. Ibid.

64. Marginalia by Edison on letter from Henry Cox to Edison, Nov 18, 1879, [D7922V; TAEM 50:350].

65. Edison to George Frederick Barker, Jan 1, 1880, TAED, [X106E; TAEM 0:0], Historical Society of Pennsylvania.

66. "The Electric Light," *Quincy (Ill.) Daily Whig*, Jan 2, 1880.

67. Edison to Joseph Medill, Apr 8, 1880, TAED, [D8020ZDN1; TAEM 53:720].

68. "Graphic Narrative of the Marvelous Menlo Park," *Quincy (Ill.) Daily Whig*, quoting *Cincinnati Enquirer*, Feb 24, 1881.

69. "The Doom of Gas," *St. Louis Post-Dispatch*, Apr 27, 1882, TAED, [MBSB52192; TAEM 95:191].

70. "Edison and His Light," Mar 13, 1883, interview with unnamed newspaper, probably in Ohio, TAED, [D8320D1; TAEM 66:21].

71. "The Electric Light," *Sunbury (Pa.) Democrat*, July 13, 1883, TAED, [SM016A; TAEM 24:82].

72. "Edison on Inventions," 1890 interview, published in Nov 1895 *Monthly Illustrator/Home & Country*, TAED, [SC90094A; TAEM 146:657].

73. "Mr. Edison Is Satisfied," *NYT*, Feb 21, 1892.

74. "Edison Is Delighted," unnamed newspaper, probably *New York Herald*, Oct 6, 1892, TAED, [SC92080d; TAEM 146:814].

75. "Edison Uses Sender for Banquet Speech," *NYT*, Feb 12, 1904.

76. "Where Europe Can Give America Valuable Points," *NYT*, Oct 29, 1911.

77. "'The Future Man Will Spend Less Time in Bed'—Edison," *NYT*, Oct 11, 1914.

78. Ibid.

79. "Edison at 80 Views a World He Changed," *NYT*, Feb 27, 1927.

80. Ibid.

81. "Edison Tours County Fair with Wife's Yellow Bunny; Goes Broke on Number 11," *Fort Myers (Fla.) Press*, Feb 12, 1930.

82. Edison to George Miller Beard, Apr 10, 1878, TAED, [X121AA; TAEM 0:0]. (Courtesy of the Yale University Library.)

83. Conot, 229, quoting *London Times*, Oct 12, 1878.

84. "The Genie of Menlo Park," *New York Sun*, Dec 19, 1878, TAED, [MBSB21066; TAEM 94:436].

85. Edison to Theodore Puskas, May 10, 1879, TAED, [Z400BR; TAEM 0:0], (Courtesy of PTM).

86. Marginalia by Edison on letter from M. E. Gates, May 24, 1879, TAED, [D7926A; TAEM 50:548].

87. Marginalia by Edison on letter from A. C. Carey, Jan 3, 1880, TAED, [D8006B; TAEM 53:289].

88. "The Doom of Gas," *St. Louis Post-Dispatch*, Apr 27, 1882, TAED, [MBSB52192; TAEM 95:191].

89. "Electricity Man's Slave: The Telegraph, the Telephone, the Electric Light and the Electric Motor," *New York Tribune*, Jan 18, 1885, 10.

90. "To Telegraph to Moving Trains," *New York Electrical Review*, May 23, 1885, TAED, [SB01710d; TAEM 89:693].

91. Edison's Diary, July 12, 1885, TAED.

92. "Thos. A. Edison," *Western Newspaper Union*, Sept 19, 1885, TAED, [SM062043; TAEM 89:28].

93. "Electric Light Patents," *San Francisco Chronicle*, Oct 1, 1885, TAED, [SB017068b; TAEM 89:676].

94. Untitled article, *New Orleans Times Democrat*, Feb 2, 1886, TAED, [SB017117c; TAEM 89:702].

95. "The Future of Electricity," *Dallas Morning News*, quoting *Pittsburgh Dispatch*, June 12, 1889.

96. "Mr. Edison and the Electric Millennium, *Levant Herald*, Sept 1, 1889, TAED, [SC89135c; TAEM 146:498].

97. Ibid.

98. "Edison's Remedy," *New York Sun*, Oct 14, 1889, TAED [SC89182A; TAEM 146:545].

99. "Electricity Made Safe," *New York World*, Oct 20, 1889, TAED [X098HC10; TAEM 0:0]. (Courtesy of the National Museum of American History Archives Center.)

100. Thomas A. Edison, "The Dangers of Electric Lighting," *North American Review*, Nov 1889, 633.

101. "The Orange Wizard," unnamed newspaper, Feb 16, 1891, TAED, [SC91016a; TAEM 146:676].

102. "Edison Has Tried to Fly," *Dallas Morning News*, Sept 10, 1893.

103. "Power to Be Derived Direct from the Sunshine," *Philadelphia Press*, Nov 22, 1896, TAED, [SC96071A1; TAEM 146:1069].

104. "Electricity in the Schools," *Dallas Morning News*, Jan 13, 1901.

105. "As Yet We Know Nothing," *NYT*, Jan 12, 1908.

106. "Edison on Future," *Wellsboro (Pa.) Gazette*, Jan 19, 1911.

107. Allan L. Benson, "Edison Tells How to Cook," *Good Housekeeping*, Mar 1913.

108. "Edison Will Aid 5-Cent Bus Line," *NYT*, Nov 30, 1913.

109. Hubbard, 18.

110. Ibid.

111. "Electricity Direct from Coal—Edison," *NYT*, June 6, 1914.

112. Ibid.

113. "Throngs Struggle for Sight of Edison," *NYT*, Oct 2, 1916.

114. "The Woman of the Future," *Good Housekeeping*, Oct 12, 1912, 436.

115. Ibid.

116. Ibid.

117. "Sees Horseless Farms," *Huntington Long Islander*, May 21, 1915.

118. Thomas H. Uzzell, "The Future of Electricity," *Collier's Weekly*, Dec 2, 1916, 7.

119. Ibid.

120. "Edison and His Lamp Praised at Dinner," *NYT*, Sept 12, 1922.

121. "Ford at Convention in Honor of Edison," *NYT*, June 7, 1929.

122. "Thomas Edison Talks on Invention in the Life of Today," *Review of Reviews*, Jan 1931, 39.

123. Edison's Technical Notes and Drawings, Oct 8, 1888, TAED, [PT031 AAA1; TAEM 113:238].

124. "Thomas A. Edison in Brooklyn," *Brooklyn Eagle*, May 9, 1891, TAED, [SC91031c; TAEM 146:691].

125. "Edison and the Big Fair," *Chicago Tribune*, May 14, 1891, TAED, [SC91039a; TAEM 146:699].

126. "The Edison Photophonokinetograph," *Electrical Engineer*, May 20, 1891, 584.

127. "The Wizard's Latest," *Quincy (Ill.) Daily Journal*, June 11, 1891.

128. "Edison Has Tried to Fly," *Dallas Morning News*, Sept 10, 1893.

129. Edison to Eadweard Muybridge, Feb 21, 1894, TAED [D9425AAF; TAEM 135:262].

130. "Edison Reproduces Moving Figures in Photographs," *Quincy (Ill.) Daily Herald*, March 15, 1894.

131. "Edison's Invention for Stage," *Quincy (Ill.) Daily Whig*, June 18, 1904.

132. Ibid.

133. Ibid.

134. "Edison at Sixty, Outlines Wonders of the Future," *NYT*, May 19 1907.

135. Conot, 397, referencing a letter from Edison to Hawenstein, Aug 2, 1910.

136. "Moving Pictures Are Made to Talk," *NYT*, Aug 27, 1910.

137. "Edison Sees 1912 Great, Minus Greed," *NYT*, Jan 3, 1912.

138. "Edison's Pictures Talk and Perform," *NYT*, Jan 4, 1913.

139. "The Coming of the Talking Picture," *Munsey's Magazine*, Mar 1913, 960.

140. Ibid.

141. Ibid.

142. "Picture Men at Odds," *NYT*, July 12, 1913.

143. Ibid.

144. Conot, 398, referencing the Kinetophone, Jan 14, 1914.

145. "Edison Submarine Coming," *NYT*, Nov 9, 1914.

146. "First Motion Pictures," *NYT*, June 9, 1921.

147. "Edison at 75 Still a Two-Shift Man," *NYT*, Feb 12, 1922.

148. "Edison Honored by Movie Leaders," *NYT*, Feb 16, 1924.

149. Ibid.

150. "Rubber Grows Here Naturally Says Thomas A. Edison Who Visits Friends in La Belle This Week," *Hendry County (Fla.) News*, Feb 16, 1926.

151. "Americans Don't Want Talking Movies; Prefer Silent Film Shows, Says Edison," *NYT*, May 21, 1926.

152. "Edison Frowns on Radio World," *St. Petersburg Times*, Mar 7 1927.

153. "Edison a Passenger in a New Ford Car," *NYT*, Dec 20, 1927.

154. "Edison Warns Boys Test Today Is Hard," *NYT*, Aug 1, 1929.

155. "Edison Sees Poor Acting in Talkies," *Fort Myers (Fla.) Press*, Jan 21, 1930.

156. "Mrs. Thomas A. Edison Tells You in This Intimate and Sparkling Story," *American Magazine*, Feb 1930, 25.

157. "Edison Lauds Hays on New Film Ethics," *NYT*, Apr 2, 1930.

158. "New Rubber Mill Ready for Testing," *Fort Myers (Fla.) Press*, Apr 11, 1930. (A *NYT* article dating from the next day omits "Hebrew" from Edison's statement.)

159. Ibid.

160. "Edison Has Tried to Fly," *Dallas Morning News*, Sept 10, 1893.

161. Tate, 279.

162. Edison to Richard Rogers Bowker [supplied or conjectured], Aug 6, 1897, TAED, [LM245410; TAEM 154:454].

163. Theodore Waters, "Edison's Revolution in Iron Mining," *McClure's Magazine*, Nov 1897, 84.

164. "Wireless Wonders Are Yet to Come," *NYT*, Oct 19, 1907.

165. Ibid.

166. Editorial, unnamed newspaper, Oct 1909, TAED, [X109B; TAEM 0:0]. (Courtesy of Webb Shadle Memorial Library.)

167. "Edison's Cement House," *Huntington Long Islander*, Dec 3, 1909.

168. "Edison on Future," *Wellsboro (Pa.) Gazette*, Jan 19, 1911.

169. "Edison's Concrete Furniture," *Huntington Long Islander*, Dec 15, 1911.

170. "Mr. Edison on Storage Batteries," *Boston Herald*, Jan 28, 1883, TAED, [CB016275; TAEM 96:804].

171. "Edison Says His New Battery Is a Success," *NYT*, May 29, 1902.

172. "Storage Battery Test Satisfies Mr. Edison," *NYT*, July 29, 1905.

173. "Wireless Wonders Are Yet to Come," *NYT*, Oct 19, 1907.

174. "Edison Battery Solves Old Problems, *Oakland Tribune*, June 27, 1909.

175. Ibid.

176. Meadowcroft, 275.

177. "Electricity Direct from Coal—Edison," *NYT*, June 6, 1914.

178. "Ford Firestone and Edison Unite to Break Rubber Monopoly Now Held by Great Britain," *Fort Myers (Fla.) Press*, Apr 7, 1925.

179. Ibid.

180. "Edison, Backed by Ford, in South Inventing Machinery to Revolutionize Rubber Industry," *NYT*, Feb 27, 1927.

181. "Edison Strives to Wrest Secret of Rubber from Florida Soils," *Venice (Fla.) News*, Mar 18, 1927.

182. "Edison Aids the Hunt for American Rubber," *NYT*, Mar 20, 1927.

183. "Edison Has Hard Time with Rubber Plants," *NYT*, July 27, 1927.

184. "More Rubber," *Time*, Aug 1, 1927.

185. "Edison Hunting for Rubber in Weeds," *Literary Digest*, Nov 26, 1927.

186. Ibid.

187. "The Magic Edison Made for the World," *NYT*, Aug 12, 1928.

188. "Edison Says Cost Bars Synthetic Rubber Making," *Tampa (Fla.) Tribune*, Feb 11, 1929.

189. "Edison on Newsreel," *NYT*, Feb 17, 1930.

190. "Edison, to Stay on Job Till He Makes Rubber," *NYT*, Mar 18, 1930.

191. "Edison Prepares Mill for Giant Goldenrod," *NYT*, Apr 12, 1930.

192. Ibid.

193. "Edison Discusses His Rubber Tests," *NYT*, Apr 13, 1930.

194. "Goldenrod Ban Ends; Edison against It," *NYT*, Aug 2, 1930.

195. "Edison Sees Rubber Fake," *NYT*, May 8, 1931.

196. "Edison Says His Rubber Progress Is 'Satisfactory,'" *Fort Myers (Fla.) Press*, May 8, 1931.

197. Firestone, 79.

Chapter 3. On Inventions of Others and the Machine Age

1. Meadowcroft, 155.

2. "Edison against Ford's Election," *Boston Daily Globe*, Oct 18, 1923.

3. "Will Tackle a Flying Machine," *Dallas Morning News*, quoting *New York Sun*, June 29, 1888.

4. Ibid.

5. Ibid.

6. Ibid.

7. "Edison and Air Ships," *Chicago Mail*, Feb 11, 1888, TAED, [SC88003C; TAEM 146:231].

8. Edison's Wonderful Inventions, Ships of the Air," *Times of India*, Dec 25, 1895, TAED, [SC95066a; TAEM 146:994].

9. "Mysterious Airship," *Arkansas Democrat*, May 11, 1897, TAED, [SC 97009B1; TAEM 146:1101].

10. "Edison Sticks to Electricity," *Brooklyn Daily Eagle*, Aug 11, 1902.

11. Circa 1903, quoted in "Edison in His Laboratory," *Harper's Magazine*, Sept 1932, 414.

12. "Men and Women of the Outdoor World, *Outing*, Apr 1904, 60.

13. "The Future's Possibilities," *NYT*, Oct 11, 1908.

14. Ibid.

15. "A Word from Edison," *Fort Myers (Fla.) Press*, Oct 15, 1908.

16. Ibid.

17. Editorial, unnamed newspaper, Oct 1909, TAED, [X109B; TAEM 0:0]. (Courtesy of Webb Shadle Memorial Library.)

18. Ibid.

19. "Edison Invents His Own Aeroplane," *NYT*, Dec 1, 1910.

20. Ibid.

21. "Edison on Future," *Wellsboro (Pa.) Gazette*, Jan 19, 1911.

22. "Edison, 66, Works On," *NYT*, Feb 12, 1913.

23. "Edison Tests Coal to Get Electricity," *NYT*, June 4, 1914.

24. "Electricity Direct from Coal—Edison," *NYT*, June 6, 1914.

25. "No Flying Machines for Thomas Edison" *Fort Myers (Fla.) Tropical News*, Feb 16, 1926.

26. Edward Marshall, "Youth of To-Day and To-Morrow," *Forum*, Jan 1927, 51.

27. "Edison on Air, Tells of First Phonograph," *NYT*, Aug 13, 1927.

28. "Ford and Edison to Go South Today," *NYT*, Jan 12, 1928.

29. "Edison Visits First Airport; Eager to Fly," *NYT*, Sept 19, 1930.

30. "Edison Astonished by Autogiro Planes," *NYT*, Sept 22, 1930.

31. "Thomas Edison Talks on Invention in the Life of Today," *Review of Reviews*, Jan 1931, 40.

32. "Edison Works Hard on his 73D Birthday," *NYT*, Feb 12, 1920.

33. "Edison Still Busy on the Phonograph," *NYT*, July 19, 1922.

34. "Edison Astonished as Science Wizards Show New Marvels," *NYT*, Oct 19, 1922.

35. Israel, 457.

36. "Edison Opens Work on Paine Memorial," *NYT*, May 22, 1925.

37. "Edison at Loss for Words in His First Talk over Radio," *NYT*, May 20, 1926.

38. "Edison Calls Radio a Failure for Music; Thinks Phonograph Will Regain Its Own," *NYT*, Sept 23, 1926.

39. Edward Marshall, "Youth of To-Day and To-Morrow," *Forum*, January 1927, 51.

40. "Edison Began at 8 as an Inventor," *NYT*, Feb 12, 1927.

41. "Edison Frowns on Radio World," *St. Petersburg (Fla.) Times*, Mar 7, 1927.

42. "Edison in Radio Deal," *NYT*, June 16, 1928.

43. "Mr. Edison's Radio Broadcast Talk," *Tampa (Fla.) Tribune,* Feb 11, 1929.

44. "Groups in 3 Nations Linked by the Radio," *NYT*, June 19, 1930.

45. "Edison Tests Flare as Aid in Fog-Flying," *NYT*, Nov 26, 1930.

46. "Radio v. Phonograph," *Time*, Oct 4, 1931.

47. Ibid.

48. Ibid.

49. "One of Edison's Prophecies," *Quincy (Ill.) Daily Herald*, quoting *Brooklyn Eagle*, Dec 22, 1886.

50. "Edison on the Horseless Carriage," *Electrical Review*, Nov 27, 1895, 307, TAED, [SC95065a; TAEM 146:993].

51. "Edison in Town," *Philadelphia Bulletin*, Oct 10, 1895, TAED, [SC95051a; TAEM 146:978].

52. Ibid.

53. Conot, 377, quoting from *Rochester (N.Y.) Times*, May 30, 1902.

54. "Edison Perfects His Storage Battery," *Fort Myers (Fla.) Press*, June 5, 1902, quoting *New York World*, May 29, 1902.

55. "The Storage Battery," *Brooklyn Daily Eagle*, June 27, 1902.

56. Thomas Edison, "The Storage Battery and the Motor Car," *North American Review*, July 1902, 4.

57. "Edison about to Give to the World His Greatest Wonder, *NYT*, Oct 21, 1906.

58. "Edison Is Sixty; Birthday To-Day," *NYT*, Feb 11, 1907.

59. Untitled article, *South Jersey Republican*, June 4, 1910, 2.

60. "The Scientific City of the Future," *Forum*, Dec 1926, 824.

61. "Edison a Passenger in a New Ford Car," *NYT*, Dec 20, 1927.

62. Ibid.

63. "Edison at Home," *Denver Tribune*, Apr 25, 1880, TAED, [SM015018].

64. "Edison Sticks to Electricity," *Brooklyn Daily Eagle*, Aug 11, 1902.

65. "Edison Began at 8 as an Inventor," *NYT*, Feb 12, 1927.

66. Interview with Edison, 1929 (supplied year), TAED, [X001A5AY; TAEM 0:0]. (Courtesy of the HFMGV.)

67. "Edison Foresees Healthier World," *NYT*, Dec 24, 1930.

68. "The Speaking Phonograph," *Scientific American Supplement*, Mar 16, 1878, 1828.

69. "Edison Forecasts 'Eye' for Fog Flying," *NYT*, Oct 3, 1930.

70. "Edison on the Labor Question," *Scientific American*, Nov 5, 1887, 289.

71. "Edison on Inventions," 1890 interview, published in Nov 1895 *Monthly Illustrator/Home & Country*, TAED, [SC90094A; TAEM 146:657].

72. "Edison Plans an Automatic Clerkless Shop," *NYT*, May 15, 1910.

73. Ibid.

74. "Edison Praises Machine," *NYT*, Jan 11, 1914.

75. "Edison Works Hard on his 73D Birthday," *NYT*, Feb 12, 1920.

76. "Edison Wants His Portrait Made Only with Machinery," *NYT*, July 4, 1926.

77. Edward Marshall, "Machine-Made Freedom," *Forum*, Oct 1926, 492.

78. Ibid.

79. Ibid.

80. Ibid.

81. Ibid.

82. Ibid.

83. Ibid.

84. "Thomas A. Edison: Philosopher," *Golden Book Magazine*, Apr 1931, 79.

Chapter 4. On the Sciences

1. See Edison to Charles Robert Darwin, TEP, [Z002AA; TAEM 0:0]. (Courtesy the Syndics of Cambridge University Library.)

2. "Mr. Edison's New Force," *Scientific American*, Feb 12, 1876, 101.

3. Edison's Diary, July 12, 1885.

4. "Edison's Religious Belief," *Salt Lake City Democrat*, July 16, 1885, TEP, [SB017039b; TAEM 89:661].

5. "What Is This State Called Life?" *New York Herald*, Nov 8, 1891, TEP, [SC91069a; TAEM 146:728].

6. Ibid.

7. Ibid.

8. "Unsolved Problems That Edison Is Studying," *Scientific American*, July 8, 1893, 25.

9. Edison to Mina Miller Edison, his wife, Dec 1, 1898, TEP, [B037ABU; TAEM 0:0].

10. Ibid.

11. "Edison about to Give to the World His Greatest Wonder," *NYT*, Oct 21, 1906.

12. "Edison at Sixty, Outlines Wonders of the Future," *NYT*, May 19, 1907.

13. Ibid.

14. "The Future's Possibilities," *NYT*, Oct 11, 1908.

15. Ibid.

16. Ibid.

17. Ibid.

18. "No Immortality of the Soul Says Thomas A. Edison," *NYT*, Oct 2, 1910.

19. Ibid.

20. "Edison Views the World at Seventy, *Edison Diamond Points*, excerpted from *New York Sun*, Feb 1917, 14–16.

21. Austin C. Lescarboura, "Edison's Views on Life and Death," *Scientific American*, Oct 30, 1920, 446.

22. "Edison Father of New Act to Patent Plants," *Fort Myers (Fla.) Press*, May 30, 1930.

23. "Thomas A. Edison: Philosopher," *Golden Book Magazine*, Apr 1931, 78.

24. Conot, 133

25. "The Man Who Invents," *Washington Post*, Apr 19, 1878, TEP, [MBSB 10532; TAEM 94:169].

26. "Mr. Edison at Home Unspoiled by Glory," *New York Herald*, Oct 7, 1889, TEP, [MBSB62465; TAEM 95:244].

27. "Arrival of Thomas A. Edison," *Chicago Globe*, May 13, 1891, TEP, [SC91036a; TAEM 146:696].

28. "Edison Posers Tax Brains of 49 Boys," *NYT*, Aug 1, 1930.

29. "Thomas Edison Talks on Invention in the Life of Today," *Review of Reviews*, Jan 1931, 40.

30. Edison's Diary, July 12, 1885, TEP.

31. "Only One Element," *New York Herald*, Nov 29, 1896, TEP, [SC96080A1; TAEM 146:1078].

32. "Edison Injured by Radium," *Fort Myers (Fla.) Press*, Jul 6, 1905.

33. "'The Future Man Will Spend Less Time in Bed'—Edison," *NYT*, Oct 11, 1914.

34. "Edison Views the World at Seventy," *Edison Diamond Points*, excerpted from *New York Sun*, Feb 1917, 15.

35. "Edison Discusses His Philosophy," *NYT*, Feb 12, 1921.

36. Israel, 460.

37. "Mr. Edison and the Electric Millennium, *Levant Herald*, Sept 1, 1889, TEP, [SC89135c; TAEM 146:498].

38. "To Utilize Niagara," *Brooklyn Daily Eagle*, Nov 9, 1889.

39. "Power to Be Derived Direct from the Sunshine," *Philadelphia Press*, Nov 22, 1896, TEP, [SC96071A1; TAEM 146:1069].

40. Ibid.

41. "Mr. Edison's Ideas on Fuel from Trees," *Denver Rocky Mountain News*, Jan 1, 1897, TEP, [SC97003A1; TAEM 146:1095].

42. "Edison at Sixty, Outlines Wonders of the Future," *NYT*, May 19, 1907.

43. "The Future's Possibilities," *NYT*, Oct 11, 1908.

44. Ibid.

45. Ibid.

46. "The Kingdom of Labor Is at Hand, Declares Edison," *Seattle Star*, Jan 14, 1910.

47. Hubbard, 18.

48. Ibid.

49. Ibid.

50. Ibid.

51. "We'll Harness the Sun, Says Edison," *Boston Daily Globe*, Sept 21, 1924.

52. "Edison Says Power Is Not Vital Issue," *NYT*, Nov 2, 1928.

53. 1929 *Mining and Metallurgy*, 54; *Saturday Evening Post*, June 14, 1929.

54. Edison to Henry Draper, Aug 8, 1877, TEP, [X120BAL; TAEM 0:0]. (Courtesy of the New York Public Library, Astor, Lenox, and Tilden Foundations.)

55. Untitled article, *Pittsburgh Times*, July 30, 1888, TEP, [SC88044; TAEM 146:272].

56. "A Telephone to the Sun," *Quincy (Ill.) Daily Whig*, Sept 7, 1890.

57. "The Wizard's Latest," *Quincy (Ill.) Daily Journal*, quoting *Chicago Tribune*, June 14, 1891.

58. Ibid.

59. "What Thomas Edison Thinks Will Be Science's Next Most Vital Discovery," *NYT*, Jan 7, 1906.

60. "We Are Animals Says Mr. Edison," *Decatur (Ill.) Review*, quoting *Independent*, Jan 28, 1910.

61. "Edison on Invention and Inventors," *Century Magazine*, July 1911, 417.

62. Ibid.

63. Allan Benson, *Hearst's International Magazine*, 1924, quoted in *NYT*, Oct 15, 1926.

64. "Edison Will Spend Remainder of Life on Rubber Project," *Fort Myers (Fla.) Press*, Mar 17, 1930.

Chapter 5. On Work and Business

1. Miller, 55.

2. "Four Hours with Edison," *New York Sun*, Aug 29, 1878, TAED, [MBSB10859; TAEM 94:339].

3. "Two Hours at Menlo Park," *New York Graphic*, Dec 28, 1878, TAED, [MBSB21091; TAEM 94:444].

4. "An Interview with Thomas A. Edison," *New York World*, Mar 28, 1887, quoted in *Fort Myers (Fla.) Press*, Apr 19, 1887.

5. "Edison's Motto," *Quincy (Ill.) Daily Whig*, quoting *New York Sun*, Oct 2, 1890.

6. "A Day with Edison," *New York Journal*, July 26, 1891, TAED, [MBSB62499; TAEM 95:257].

7. Ibid.

8. From Charles D. Lanier, "Two Giants of the Electric Age," *Review of Reviews*, July 1893, 44.

9. "Mr. Edison on Electricity as a Profession," *Ottumwa (Iowa) Courier*, Dec 31, 1894, TAED, [SC94032a; TAEM 146:926].

10. "Edison and Tesla Rivals," *New York Journal*, May 22, 1896, TAED, [SC96038A1; TAEM 146:1036].

11. Edison's definition of genius. "Anecdotes of Edison," *American Monthly Review of Reviews,* Apr 1898, 458.

12. Ibid.

13. Edison to Mina Miller Edison, his wife, Dec 1, 1898, TAED, [B037ABU; TAEM 0:0], Swann Galleries, Inc., New York.

14. Circa 1903, quoted in "Edison in His Laboratory," *Harper's Magazine*, Sept 1932, 403.

15. Circa 1903, ibid.

16. Circa 1903, ibid.

17. "Edison Improves on Saying," *American Eagle*, July 9, 1904.

18. *Good Stories*, 13.

19. "Edison's Birthday Just a Work Day," *NYT*, Feb 12, 1911.

20. Meadowcroft, 24.

21. "The Woman of the Future," *Good Housekeeping*, Oct 12, 1912, 441.

22. "Edison Wants a Good Chew," *NYT*, Apr 6, 1914.

23. "Electricity Direct from Coal—Edison," *NYT*, June 6, 1914.

24. "Men and Methods," *System*, Nov 1914, 522.

25. "Edison Views the World at Seventy, *Edison Diamond Points*, excerpted from *New York Sun*, Feb 1917, 14–16.

26. "Mr. Edison Interviewed," *Edison Herald*, Feb 25, 1919, 7.

27. Ibid.

28. "Thomas Edison, 73, Will Work All Day," *NYT*, Feb 11, 1920.

29. "Edison Works Hard on His 73D Birthday," *NYT*, Feb 12, 1920.

30. "Experimenting Wins Success Says Edison Who Worked One Year to Reproduce a Word," *Fort Myers (Fla.) Press*, July 10, 1920.

31. Ibid.

32. "Why Do So Many Men Never Amount to Anything?" *American Magazine,* Jan 1921, 10.

33. "Edison Says Work 18 Hours a Day," *Dallas Morning News*, Feb 12, 1921.

34. Edison's advice to fellow inventor, Edouard Belin. "Master Inventors Discuss Some Revolutionizing Projects," *Current Opinion*, January 1922, 121.

35. "Edison Astonished as Science Wizards Show New Marvels," *NYT*, Oct 19, 1922.

36. "Edison Talks of Immortality and the Basis of Life," *NYT,* Oct 7, 1923.

37. "Edison Opposes Ford for President," *NYT,* Oct 18, 1923.

38. "Double Shift Makes Edison 120, Feels 50 on 79 Birthday," *Tropical News*, Feb 12, 1926.

39. Edward Marshall, "Machine-Made Freedom," *Forum*, Oct 1926, 493.

40. Ibid.

41. Edward Marshall, "Youth of To-Day and To-Morrow," *Forum*, January 1927, 42.

42. "Edison Began at 8 as an Inventor," *NYT*, Feb 12, 1927.

43. "Edison at 80 Views a World He Changed," *NYT*, Feb 27, 1927.

44. "4,000 School Children Attend Edison Party," *Fort Myers (Fla.) Press*, Feb 11, 1928.

45. "Ford in Florida; Sees Edison First," *NYT*, Feb 8, 1929.

46. "Edison Urges Work as Key to Success," *NYT*, July 31, 1930.

47. Ibid.

48. "Thomas A. Edison: Philosopher," *Golden Book Magazine*, Apr 1931, 78.

49. Ibid.

50. "Edison Predicts Oil in Florida or Sulphur, as in Texas," *NYT*, May 9, 1931.

51. "Edison's Laboratory in War Time," *Science*, Jan 15, 1932, 70.

52. "Edison in His Laboratory," *Harper's Magazine*, Sept 1932, 404.

53. Henry Ford, "Thinking Out Loud," *American Magazine*, October 1934.

54. Edison to Samuel Ogden Edison, his father, July 24, 1871 [supplied year], TAED, [X001A1AS; TAEM 0:0]. (Courtesy of the HFMGV.)

55. Edison to Ebenezer Baker Welch, Oct 12, 1878, TAED, [W600U; TAEM 0:0]. (Courtesy of the National Archives.)

56. "Content at Menlo Park," *New York World*, Dec 5, 1878, TAED [MBSB 21057; TAEM 94:434].

57. Edison to George H. Bliss, Mar 18, 1879, regarding John M. Griest and the electric pen and mimeograph, TAED, [LB004222A; TAEM 80:64].

58. "Graphic Narrative of the Marvelous Menlo Park," *Quincy (Ill.) Daily Whig*, quoting Cincinnati *Enquirer*, Feb 24, 1881.

59. Circa 1903, quoted in "Edison in His Laboratory," *Harper's Magazine*, Sept 1932, 406.

60. "Men and Women of the Outdoor World," *Outing*, Apr 1904, 60.

61. "Edison's Birthday Just a Work Day," *NYT*, Feb 12, 1911.

62. "What Edison Learned in Germany, *Literary Digest*, June 1, 1912, 1157.

63. Ibid.

64. "Edison Discovers He's a Bull Mooser," *NYT*, Oct 7, 1912.

65. Israel, 438.

66. Edison to Henry Villard, Feb 8, 1890, TAED, [LB037198; TAEM 140:510].

67. Edison to William Dennis Marks, April 7, 1891, TAED, [D9124AAI1; TAEM 131:145].

68. Edison to Sigmund Bergmann, Nov 23, 1888, TAED, [D8802ABY; TAEM 121:116].

69. Interview with Edison, probably by reporter from *Cincinnati Enquirer*, 1888, TAED, [D8807ADK; TAEM 121:793].

70. "Edison on Inventions," 1890 interview, published in Nov 1895 *Monthly Illustrator/Home & Country*, TAED, [SC90094A; TAEM 146:657].

71. Conot, 387, referencing a letter to N. F. Brady, Dec 4, 1910.

72. "Edison Discovers He's a Bull Mooser," *NYT*, Oct 7, 1912.

73. "Edison Praises Machines," *NYT*, Jan 11, 1914.

74. Ibid.

75. "Edison Sees Prosperity," *NYT*, Nov 24, 1918.

76. "Edison for Square Deal," *NYT*, June 28, 1919.

77. Ibid.

78. "Thomas Edison, 73, Will Work All Day," *NYT*, Feb 11, 1920.

79. Ibid.

80. "Turned Down Edison," *Boston Herald*, Feb 12, 1923 [supplied year], TAED, [X065AL; TAEM 0:0]. (Courtesy of the North Carolina Division of Archives and History, Raleigh.)

81. "Edison at Ad Show, Looking for Ideas," *NYT*, Nov 16, 1923.

82. Edward Marshall, "Machine-Made Freedom," *Forum*, Oct 1926, 497.

83. "Edison Will Urge Second Term on Hoover," *NYT*, June 11, 1930.

84. Edison to Ebenezer Baker Welch, May 8, 1869, TAED, W600Q; TAEM 0:0]. (Courtesy of the National Archives.)

85. Edison's earliest accounting system (Meadowcroft, 134).

86. Document by Edison, Aug 15, 1875 [supplied date], TAED, [D7512N1; TAEM 13:507].

87. Edison to Albert B. Chandler, note, Nov 11, 1875, TAED, [B056BA; TAEM 0:20]. (Courtesy of the Gallery of History, Inc.)

88. Edison to Theodore Puskas, Nov 11, 1879, TAED [Z400BV; TAEM 0:0]. (Courtesy of the PTM.)

89. Marginalia by Edison on letter from George H. Bliss, Mar 26, 1880, TAED, [D8004ZCF; TAEM 53:136].

90. Marginalia by Edison on letter from Edward Hibberd Johnson to Charles Henry Coster and Edison, July 6, 1887, TAED, [D8739AAA; TAEM 120:29].

91. Edison to Henry Villard, Feb 8, 1890, TAED, [LB037198; TAEM 140:510].

92. "Edison on Inventions," 1890 interview, published in Nov 1895 *Monthly Illustrator/Home & Country*, TAED, [SC90094A; TAEM 146:657].

93. Dyer, 504–5.

94. "Edison about to Give to the World His Greatest Wonder," *NYT*, Oct 21, 1906.

95. Conot, 367, quoting a letter from Edison to A. Dalgleish, June 2, 1909.

96. "Edison Sees 1912 Great, Minus Greed," *NYT*, Jan 3, 1912.

97. "Edison's Invention for Stage," *Quincy (Ill.) Daily Whig*, June 18, 1904.

98. "Edison Sees Luxury War-Winning Force," *NYT*, June 8, 1918.

99. "Monetary Sayings of Thomas A. Edison," *NYT*, July 16, 1922.

100. Ibid.

101. Ibid.

102. Ibid.

103. Ibid.

104. Ibid.

105. Ibid.

106. "Edison Knocks off Work, Takes His Wife to Fair," *Fort Myers (Fla.) Press*, Feb 22, 1929.

107. "Monetary Sayings of Thomas A. Edison," *NYT*, July 16, 1922.

108. "Edison's Very Latest Idea," *Rolla (Mo.) New Era*, Oct 7, 1891.

109. "Ford Sees Wealth in Muscle Shoals," *NYT*, Dec 6, 1921.

110. Ibid.

111. Ibid.

112. "What Edison Thinks of Gold," *Mentor*, Jan 1, 1922, 29.

113. "Monetary Sayings of Thomas A. Edison," *NYT*, July 16, 1922.

114. Ibid.

115. Ibid.

116. Ibid.

117. Ibid.

118. Ibid.

119. Ibid.

120. Ibid.

121. Ibid.

122. "Mr. Edison Further Explains," *NYT*, July 23, 1922.

123. Ibid.

124. "Edison Still Thinks His Farm Plan Best," *NYT*, June 18, 1929.

125. "Edison Sees Prosperity," *NYT*, Nov 24, 1918.

126. "Grit Edison's Cure for Upset Times," *NYT*, Sept 29, 1921.

127. Ibid.

128. Ibid.

129. Ibid.

130. Ibid.

131. Ibid.

132. Ibid.

133. "Monetary Sayings of Thomas A. Edison," *NYT*, July 16, 1922.

134. "Edison Urges Work as Key to Success," *NYT*, July 31, 1930.

135. "Edison Won't Predict," *Fort Myers (Fla.) Press*, Jan 21, 1931.

136. Ibid.

137. Remsen Crawford, "Did Thomas Edison Die a Poor Man?" *Modern Mechanics and Inventions*, Jan 1932, 57.

138. "The Anecdotal Side of Edison," *Ladies' Home Journal*, April 1898, 8.

139. "Edison Sees This Age Destroying Myths," *NYT*, Oct 7, 1927.

140. "Edison Still Hard at Work," *New York Graphic*, Apr 11, 1879, TAED, [MBSB21163; TAEM 94:747].

141. Conot, 302, quoting from 1911 Edison personal correspondence.

142. "Edison Sees His Vast Plant Burn," *NYT*, Dec 10, 1914.

143. Hubbard, 18.

144. "Why Do So Many Men Never Amount to Anything?" *American Magazine*, Jan 1921, 89.

145. "Edison on Birthday Feels More Than 83," *Fort Myers (Fla.) Press*, Feb 12, 1930.

146. "Thomas Edison Talks on Invention in the Life of Today," *Review of Reviews*, Jan 1931, 40.

Chapter 6. On Religion

1. Edison's Diary, July 12, 1885.

2. "Edison's Religious Belief," *Salt Lake City Democrat*, July 16, 1885, TAED, [SB017039b; TAEM 89:661].

3. Edison's Diary, July 20, 1885.

4. Ibid.

5. Ibid., July 21, 1885.

6. "Edison on Inventions," 1890 interview, published in Nov 1895 *Monthly Illustrator/Home & Country*, TAED, [SC90094A; TAEM 146:657].

7. Ibid.

8. Edison to Mina Miller Edison, his wife, Dec 1, 1898, TAED, [B037ABU; TAEM 0:0].

9. "Edison's Religion," *Paduca (Ky.) Sun*, quoting the *Cincinnati Enquirer*, July 9, 1900.

10. "Newest Anecdotes about Noted Men and Women," *Brooklyn Daily Eagle*, July 13, 1902.

11. Circa 1903, quoted in "Edison in His Laboratory," *Harper's Magazine*, Sept 1932, 414.

12. Ibid.

13. "Men and Women of the Outdoor World," *Outing*, Apr 1904, 60.

14. "No Immortality of the Soul Says Thomas A. Edison," *NYT*, Oct 2, 1910.

15. "Edison Invents His Own Aeroplane," *NYT*, Dec 1, 1910.

16. "Edison on Invention and Inventors," *Century Magazine*, July 1911, 417.

17. Miller, 32, quoting a letter from Edison to Joseph Metagon, June 24, 1916.

18. "Edison Convinced the Soul Lives On," *NYT*, Aug 11, 1923.

19. Allan Benson, *Hearst's International Magazine*, 1924, quoted in the *NYT*, Oct 15, 1926.

20. "Ford, Edison, Firestone Jolly Coolidge Callers," *Boston Daily Globe*, Aug 20, 1924.

21. "Double Shift Makes Edison 120, Feels 50 on 79th Birthday," *Fort Myers (Fla.) Tropical News*, Feb 12, 1926.

22. Edward Marshall, "Has Man an Immortal Soul?" *Forum*, Nov 1926, 643.

23. Ibid, 645.

24. Ibid, 646.

25. Ibid.

26. Ibid, 646–47.

27. Ibid, 647.

28. Ibid.

29. Ibid, 648.

30. Ibid.

31. Ibid.

32. Ibid.

33. Ibid, 649.

34. Ibid.

35. Ibid, 650.

36. "Edison Began at 8 as an Inventor," *NYT*, Feb 12, 1927.

37. "Edison at 80 Views a World He Changed," *NYT*, Feb 27, 1927.

38. "Edison Is Happy on 81st Birthday," *NYT*, Feb 12, 1928.

39. "Edison Predicts Hoover's Victory," *NYT*, July 30, 1928.

40. "Edison Says America Must Catch up Spiritually," unnamed newspaper. dated 1929, Mina Edison's clipping book, Edison-Ford Winter Estates.

41. "Providence Youth Wins Edison Award," *NYT*, Aug 2, 1930.

42. "Mr. Edison's Views of Life and Work," *Review of Reviews*, Jan 1932, 31.

43. Edison's Diary, July 16, 1885.

44. "Mr. Edison Wants to Fly," *Albany (N.Y.) Telegram*, Nov 3, 1893, TAED, [SC93047b; TAEM 146:883].

45. "No Immortality of the Soul Says Thomas A. Edison," *NYT*, Oct 2, 1910,

46. "Wizard with Amazing Powers Astounds Scientists," *NYT*, Nov 13, 1910.

47. Austin C. Lescarboura, "Edison's Views on Life and Death," *Scientific American*, Oct 30, 1920, 446.

48. Ibid.

49. Ibid.

50. "Mr. Edison's 'Life Units,'" *NYT*, Jan 21, 1921.

51. "Edison at 75 Still a Two-Shift Man," *NYT*, Feb 12, 1922.

52. "Edison at 80 Views a World He Changed," *NYT*, Feb 27, 1927.

53. Edison to Mina Miller Edison, his wife, Dec 1, 1898, on the occasion of her sister's death, TAED, [B037ABU; TAEM 0:0].

54. "No Immortality of the Soul Says Thomas A. Edison," *NYT*, Oct 2, 1910.

55. Ibid.

56. Ibid.

57. "Edison Invents His Own Aeroplane," *NYT*, Dec 1, 1910.

58. Austin C. Lescarboura, "Edison's Views on Life and Death," *Scientific American*, Oct 30, 1920, 446.

59. "Edison Discusses His Philosophy," *NYT*, Feb 12, 1921.

60. "Edison Convinced the Soul Lives On," *NYT*, Aug 11, 1923.

61. Ibid.

62. "Edison Talks of Immortality and the Basis of Life," *NYT*, Oct 7, 1923.

63. Ibid.

64. Edward Marshall, "Has Man an Immortal Soul," *Forum*, Nov 1926, 641.

65. Ibid.

66. Edward Marshall, "Youth of To-Day and To-Morrow," *Forum*, January 1927, 52.

67. Ibid.

68. "Edison Began at 8 as an Inventor," *NYT*, Feb 12, 1927.

69. Ibid.

70. Ibid.

71. "4,000 School Children Attend Edison Party," *Fort Myers (Fla.) Press*, Feb 11, 1928.

72. "Edison Predicts Hoover's Victory," *NYT*, July 30, 1928.

73. "Providence Youth Wins Edison Award," *NYT*, Aug 2, 1930.

74. "Thomas A. Edison: Philosopher," *Golden Book Magazine*, Apr 1931, 78.

75. Conversation related by Edison's physician, Dr. Hubert S. Howe. "Inventor Thought Soul Might Live On," *NYT*, Oct 18, 1931.

Chapter 7. On Politics and Government

1. "Edison Will Vote," *New York Advertiser*, Nov 4, 1892, TAED, [SC92097b; TAEM 146:831].

2. "A Young Man at 90 Years," unnamed newspaper, likely the *New York Mail*, Aug 5, 1893, TAED, [SC93033a; TAEM 146:869].

3. "Edison Discovers He's a Bull Mooser," *NYT*, Oct 7, 1912.

4. Ibid.

5. Ibid.

6. Ibid.

7. Untitled article, *Suffolk County (N.Y.) News*, Oct 25, 1912, 4.

8. "Edison for Wilson as against Hughes," *NYT*, Sept 4, 1916.

9. "Edison Tells Why He Will Vote for Wilson," *NYT*, Sept 10, 1916.

10. Thomas H. Uzzell, "The Future of Electricity," *Collier's Weekly*, Dec 2, 1916, 7.

11. "Edison Favors League," *NYT*, June 22, 1919.

12. "Edison for Square Deal," *NYT*, June 28, 1919.

13. Ibid.

14. "Hoover Candidacy Espoused by Edison," *NYT*, May 12, 1920.

15. "Best Lost, Edison Says," *NYT*, June 20, 1920.

16. Ibid.

17. "Edison at 75, Talks of Tut-ankh-Amen Also Ruhr and Girls," *NYT*, Feb 13, 1923.

18. "Ford, Edison, Firestone Jolly Coolidge Callers," *Boston Daily Globe*, Aug 20, 1924.

19. "The Scientific City of the Future," *Forum*, Dec 1926, 828.

20. Ibid.

21. "Edison Makes Debut in Radio Interview," *NYT*, Oct 22, 1927.

22. "Wet Hoover Allies Reconcile Stand to Nominee's Views," *NYT*, Aug 14, 1928.

23. "Where Lurks the Real Danger," *Davis County (Utah) Clipper*, June 28, 1929.

24. "Edison Sounds Warning," *NYT*, Dec 31, 1929.

25. "Edison on Birthday Feels More Than 83," *Fort Myers (Fla.) Press*, Feb 12, 1930.

26. "Edison Lauds Hays on New Film Ethics," *NYT*, Apr 2, 1930.

27. "Edison Will Urge Second Term on Hoover," *NYT*, June 11, 1930.

28. "Edison, 84, Thinks Up-Trend Has Begun," *NYT*, Feb 12, 1931.

29. "Thomas A. Edison: Philosopher," *Golden Book Magazine*, Apr 1931, 78.

30. "Edison Says His Rubber Progress Is 'Satisfactory,'" *Fort Myers (Fla.) Press*, May 8, 1931.

31. "Edison Discovers He's a Bull Mooser," *NYT*, Oct 7, 1912.

32. Ibid.

33. Ibid.

34. "Tom. Edison Is for Teddy," *Suffolk County (N.Y.) News*, Oct 11, 1912.

35. "Submarine Terror to End, Says Edison," *NYT*, Jan 3, 1915.

36. "Sees Horseless Farms," *Huntington Long Islander*, May 21, 1915.

37. "Edison Tells Why He Will Vote for Wilson," *NYT*, Sept 10, 1916.

38. Ibid.

39. "Edison Hopes for Wilson," *NYT*, Nov 7, 1916.

40. "Hoover Candidacy Espoused by Edison," *NYT*, May 12, 1920.

41. "Edison Prizes Chewing Tobacco from Harding," *NYT*, Aug 12, 1922.

42. "Ford, Edison, Firestone Jolly Coolidge Callers," *Boston Daily Globe*, Aug 20, 1924.

43. Ibid.

44. Ibid.

45. "Edison '20 Years Younger,'" *NYT*, May 5, 1927.

46. "National Affairs," *Time*, Jan 28, 1929, 10.

47. "Edison Sees Hoover as Next President," *NYT*, June 14, 1928.

48. "Edison Has Picture Taken but Ducks Inquiring Writers," *Fort Myers (Fla.) Press*, Jan 18, 1929.

49. "Edison Criticizes Morrow," *NYT*, Dec 9, 1930.

50. "Edison Will Vote," *New York Advertiser*, Nov 4, 1892, TAED, [SC92097b; TAEM 146:831].

51. "Edison Discovers He's a Bull Mooser," *NYT*, Oct 7, 1912.

52. "New Sugar Industry at Clewiston Visited by Edison and Ford," *Fort Myers (Fla.) Press*, Feb 17, 1929.

53. "Edison Urges Tariff Protection for Farmers; Commends Plant-Bill as Aid to Crops," *NYT*, May 30, 1930.

54. "Wizard Edison at Home," *New York World*, Nov 17, 1889, TAED, [MBSB62500; TAEM 95:261].

55. Ibid.

56. "Edison on Inventions," 1890 interview, published in Nov 1895 *Monthly Illustrator/Home & Country*, TAED, [SC90094A; TAEM 146:657].

57. Edison to his wife, Mina Miller Edison, note, Sept 1901, TAED, [B037 ABZ; TAEM 0:0].

58. Oral History of Madeleine Edison, Thomas Edison National Historical Park.

59. "As Yet We Know Nothing," *NYT*, Jan 12, 1908.

60. "The Kingdom of Labor Is at Hand, Declares Edison," *Seattle Star*, Jan 14, 1910.

61. "'The Future Man Will Spend Less Time in Bed'—Edison," *NYT*, Oct 11, 1914.

62. "Edison on Birthday Urges Milder Beer," *NYT*, Feb 12, 1916.

63. "Edison's Laboratory Tests for Human Nature," *Literary Digest*, Mar 9, 1918, 52.

64. "Edison Works Hard on his 73D Birthday," *NYT*, Feb 12, 1920.

65. "Edison Defends Cigars," *NYT*, Aug 13, 1921.

66. "Double Shift Makes Edison 120, Feels 50 on 79th Birthday," *Tropical News*, Feb 12, 1926.

67. "W.C.T.U. Urges State Enforcement of Code," *Huntington Long Islander*, Nov 29, 1929.

68. "Drys Portray Prohibition as Basis of Prosperity; Edison and Ford for Law," *NYT*, Mar 6, 1930.

69. "Edison Criticizes Morrow," *NYT*, Dec 9, 1930.

70. "Edison Sees Boon in Prohibition Law," *NYT*, Dec 18, 1930.

71. "Edison Gives His Reasons for Backing Prohibition," *Fort Myers Press*, Dec 18, 1930.

72. "Know-Nothing," *Time*, Dec 22, 1930.

73. "The Future of Electricity," *New York World*, Jan 1, 1897, TAED, [SC97000A1; TAEM 146:1090].

74. Edison to Mina Miller Edison, his wife, note, July 1898, TAED, [B037ABT; TAEM 0:0].

75. "Where Europe Can Give America Valuable Points," *NYT*, Oct 29, 1911.

76. Ibid.

77. "Edison Bars Poets from List of Great," *NYT*, Dec 6, 1911.

78. "No Intervention—Edison, *NYT*, Jan 19, 1914.

79. "'The Future Man Will Spend Less Time in Bed'—Edison," *NYT*, Oct 11, 1914.

80. Ibid.

81. Ibid.

82. "Edison Won't Invent Man-Killing Devices," *NYT*, Oct 26, 1914.

83. Ibid.

84. Ibid.

85. "Submarine Terror to End, Says Edison," *NYT*, Jan 3, 1915.

86. Ibid.

87. Ibid.

88. "Edison Lessens Submarine Peril," *NYT*, Apr 18, 1915.

89. "Boycott Germany Edison Advises," *NYT*, May 22, 1915.

90. Ibid.

91. Ibid.

92. Ibid.

93. Ibid.

94. Ibid.

95. Ibid.

96. "Edison Despairs of Peace," *NYT*, May 30, 1915.

97. "Edison's Plan for Preparedness," *NYT*, May 30, 1915.

98. Ibid.

99. Ibid.

100. Ibid.

101. Ibid.

102. Ibid.

103. Ibid.

104. Ibid.

105. Ibid.

106. "Edison's Will Head Navy Test Board," *NYT*, July 13, 1915.

107. "Machine Fighting Is Edison's Idea," *NYT*, Oct 16, 1915.

108. Ibid.

109. Ibid.

110. Ibid.

111. "Edison Despairs of Peace," *NYT*, Nov 6, 1915.

112. "Edison's Plan for Preparedness," *NYT*, Nov 6, 1915.

113. "Our Navy Torpedo Called the Best," *NYT*, Feb 10, 1916.

114. "Secret Safe, Edison Says, Inventor Denies Divulging Hidden Submarine Battery Details, *NYT*, Mar 9, 1916.

115. "Edison for Wilson as against Hughes," *NYT*, Sept 4, 1916.

116. "Edison Tells Why He Will Vote for Wilson," *NYT*, Sep 10, 1916.

117. Thomas H. Uzzell, "The Future of Electricity," *Collier's Weekly*, Dec 2, 1916, 7.

118. Ibid.

119. Ibid.

120. Ibid.

121. Edison speech encouraging participation in the Liberty Loan program. "Edison Rallies Men for Loan," *NYT*, May 25, 1917.

122. "Edison Sees Luxury War-Winning Force," *NYT*, June 8, 1918.

123. Ibid.

124. Ibid.

125. Ibid.

126. "Ford Nominated, Newberry Also," *NYT*, Aug 28, 1918.

127. "New Liberty Loan Slogan," *NYT*, Sept 18, 1918.

128. "Edison, Hale at 74 Sifts World's Ills," *NYT*, Feb 10, 1921.

129. "Ford Sees Wealth in Muscle Shoals," *NYT*, Dec 6, 1921.

130. "Horrors of Future Wars," *Wellsboro (Pa.) Gazette*, Dec 21, 1921.

131. Ibid.

132. "Edison Will Live 15 More Years, He Says, on 75th Birthday," *St. Louis Globe-Democrat*, Feb 12, 1922.

133. Josephson, 454, referencing the *New York World*, Feb 13, 1923.

134. "Edison Reaches 78, Says He Feels Fine," *NYT*, Feb 12, 1925.

135. Edward Marshall, "Youth of To-Day and To-Morrow," *Forum*, Jan 1927, 52.

136. "Edison Hunting for Rubber in Weeds," *Literary Digest*, Nov 26, 1927.

137. "Edison Thinks Hoover Would Aid Dry Law," *NYT*, Sept 28, 1928.

138. "Thomas A. Edison: Philosopher," *Golden Book Magazine*, Apr 1931, 78.

Chapter 8. On the Press

1. "Edison's Electric Light," *New York Sun*, Oct 20, 1878, TAED, [MBSB20963; TAEM 94:382].

2. "Two Hours at Menlo Park," *New York Graphic*, Dec 28, 1878, TAED, [MBSB21091; TAEM 94:444].

3. Ibid.

4. "What Edison Has Done," *New York World*, Apr 30, 1879, TAED, [MBSB21174; TAEM 94:480].

5. Untitled article, *Lancaster (Pa.) New Era*, Sept 8, 1885, TAED, [SB017022b; TAEM 89:652].

6. "Edison in Town," *Philadelphia Bulletin*, Oct 10, 1895, TAED, [SC95051a; TAEM 146:978].

7. "Thomas Edison, The Distinguished Electrician, a Man of Charming Per-

sonality," *Norwalk (Ohio) Reflector*, Feb 1896 [supplied date], TAED, [SC9600A1; TAEM 146:1004].

8. Edison to *New York Sun*, Jan 11, 1898, TAED, [LB059641; TAEM 143:601].

9. "The Influence of the Press," *Dallas Morning News*, Feb 24, 1901.

10. "What Thomas Edison Thinks Will Be Science's Next Most Vital Discovery," *NYT*, Jan 7, 1906.

11. Ibid.

12. "Wireless Wonders Are Yet to Come," *NYT*, Oct 19, 1907.

13. "Edison Discovers He's a Bull Mooser," *NYT*, Oct 7, 1912.

14. Hubbard, 18.

15. "Edison at 75, Talks of Tut-ankh-Amen Also Ruhr and Girls," *NYT*, Feb 13, 1923.

16. Ibid.

17. "Edison, Sunburned, Back from Florida," *NYT*, June 16, 1929.

18. Ibid.

19. "The Wizard's Chat," *Pittsburgh Dispatch*, May 23, 1878. "Food from Dirt and Water," unnamed newspaper, Feb 13, 1878, TAED, [SC87001A; TAEM 146:208].

20. Edison to *New York Graphic*, May 10, 1878, TAED, [D7805ZAX1; TAEM 162:1046].

21. "Wanted Edison's Gelatine Shirt," *Quincy (Ill.) Daily Whig*, quoting *New York Sun*, Aug 25, 1886.

22. "Edison Now Admits the Soul May Exist," *NYT*, Oct 12, 1926.

Chapter 9. On the Law

1. Meadowcroft, 131.

2. Edison to George G. Ward [supplied or conjectured], Nov 14, 1879, TAED, [LB005338B; TAEM 80:179].

3. Edison to George Edward Gouraud, Apr 3, 1880, TAED, [D8049ZDC; TAEM 56:577].

4. Edison's Diary, July 13, 1885.

5. "Edison's Quadruplex," *Quincy (Ill.) Daily Herald*, Mar 29, 1893.

6. "Edison on Witness Stand," *NYT*, Dec 5, 1902.

7. Conot, 318, quoting the *New York Herald*, Dec 5, 1902.

8. Ibid.

9. "Edison's Forty Years of Litigation," *Literary Digest*, Sept 13, 1913, 450.

10. Hubbard, 18.

11. Edison to William Fletcher Barrett, Oct 7, 1878, TAED, [D7802ZZDZ; TAEM 161:194].

12. Edison to Benjamin Franklin Butler, Feb 17, 1879, TAED, [X042AD; TAEM 0:0]. (Courtesy of the Manuscript Division, Library of Congress.)

13. "Graphic Narrative of the Marvelous Menlo Park," *Quincy (Ill.) Daily Whig*, quoting Cincinnati *Enquirer*, Feb 24, 1881.

14. "About Patents," *New Haven Palladium*, quoting *New York Post*, Jan 7, 1888, TAED, [SM085052].

15. Marginalia on a letter from the National Electrical Light Association and Arthur Steuart to Edison, July 2, 1888, TAED, [D8846ABA; TAEM 124:34].

16. Interview with Edison, probably by the *Cincinnati Enquirer*, 1888, TAED, [D8807ADK; TAEM 121:793].

17. Edison to Samuel Insull, June 18, 1890, TAED, [LB041463; TAEM 141:160].

18. "Edison on Inventions," 1890 interview, published in Nov 1895 *Monthly Illustrator/Home & Country*, TAED, [SC90094A; TAEM 146:657].

19. Ibid.

20. "A Day with Edison," *New York Journal*, July 26, 1891, TAED, [MBSB 62499; TAEM 95:257].

21. Ibid.

22. "Are Patents Worthless?" *New York Journal*, Nov 9, 1891, TAED, [SC 91043C; TAEM 146:703].

23. Untitled article, *Cranbury (N.J.) Press*, Mar 18, 1892, 1.

24. "Wizard of the World," unnamed newspaper, likely the *Akron (Ohio) Beacon Journal*, TAED, Apr 22, 1892, [SC92045a; TAEM 146:779].

25. "Edison's Gold Mine," unnamed newspaper, probably the *Butte City (Mont.) Miner*, May 18, 1895, TAED, [SC95032a; TAEM 146:959].

26. "Edison, the Wizard, Talks about Patents," *St. Louis Star*, Dec 26, 1897, TAED, [SC97061A1; TAEM 146:1153].

27. Hubbard, 18.

28. Ibid.

29. "Edison Urges Tariff Protection for Farmers; Commends Plant-Bill as Aid to Crops," *NYT*, May 30, 1930.

30. Remsen Crawford, "Did Thomas Edison Die a Poor Man?" *Modern Mechanics and Inventions*, Jan 1932, 56.

31. Edison's Diary, July 13, 1885.

32. "He Never Knew Temptation," *Davis County (Utah) Clipper*, quoting the *New York Mail*, Jan 5, 1917.

33. "If the Answer Is Easy It's Wrong." *Collier's Weekly*, Dec 6, 1924, 6.

34. "The Scientific City of the Future," *Forum*, Dec 1926, 828.

35. "Edison Thinks Hoover Would Aid Dry Law," *NYT*, Sept 28, 1928.

36. Edison to A. P. Southwick, Dec 19, 1887, TAED, [LB026116; TAEM 138:355].

37. "Electricity as a Life Taker," *New York Sun*, Nov 4, 1888, TAED, [SC88126A; TAEM 146:353].

38. Ibid.

39. Ibid.

40. "Edison's New Ideas," *Brooklyn Citizen*, Nov 4, 1888, TAED, [SM038071; TAEM 25:580].

41. "Westinghouse and Edison," *Pittsburgh Post*, May 23, 1889, TAED, [SM085107; TAEM 89:235].

42. "Certain Death," *Brooklyn Daily Eagle*, July 23, 1889.

43. Edison's response when asked if electrocution was painful. "Does Electricity Kill?" *Buffalo Times*, Aug 8, 1895, TAED, [SC95043b; TAEM 146:970].

44. Interview with Edison, 1929 [supplied year], TAED [X001A5AY; TAEM 0:0]. (Courtesy of the HFMGV.)

Chapter 10. On the United States

1. "We're Still Ahead, Says Mr. Edison, *NYT*, Oct 8, 1911.

2. "No People So Progressive As We Are—Edison," *NYT*, Oct 22, 1911.

3. Ibid.

4. Ibid.

5. "Where Europe Can Give America Valuable Points," *NYT*, Oct 29, 1911.

6. Ibid.

7. Ibid.

8. Ibid.

9. Ibid.

10. "Edison, 67, Feels Like a Boy, He Says," *NYT*, Feb 12, 1914.

11. "Edison's Plan for Preparedness," *NYT*, May 30, 1915.

12. Ibid.

13. "Machine Fighting Is Edison's Idea," *NYT*, Oct 16, 1915.

14. "Speed up Industry, Edison's Warning," *NYT*, July 15, 1917.

15. 1918 radio address, Michigan State University Libraries, VVL Call No.: DB504.

16. Edward Marshall, "Machine-Made Freedom," *Forum*, Oct 1926, 497.

17. "Thomas A. Edison: Philosopher," *Golden Book Magazine*, Apr 1931, 78.

18. "Beauty of Fort Myers Is Praised to All America When Edison Talks Over Radio," *Fort Myers (Fla.) News-Press*, Jun 11, 1931.

19. "Edison Views the World at Seventy, *Edison Diamond Points*, excerpted from *New York Sun*, Feb 1917, 14–16.

20. "Edison at Ad Show, Looking for Ideas," *NYT*, Nov 16, 1923.

21. Josephson, 134

22. Ibid., 311.

23. "Wizard Edison in Florida," *New York World Magazine*, Mar 1887, reprinted in Gonzalez.

24. "Thomas A. Edison Rapidly Improving," *Fort Myers (Fla.) Press*, Apr 2, 1908.

25. "There is Only One Fort Myers . . ." *Fort Myers (Fla.) Press*, Mar 25, 1914.

26. "Thomas Edison Has New Slogan for City," *Fort Myers (Fla.) Press*, May 3, 1923.

27. "Bright Future Is Predicted," *Fort Myers (Fla.) Press*, Apr 24, 1916.

28. "Double Shift Makes Edison 120, Feels 50 on 79th Birthday," *Tropical News*, Feb 12, 1926.

29. Capt. Jack DeLysle, "The Thomas Edison I Know," *Fort Myers (Fla.) Palm Leaf*, May 29, 1926.

30. "Edison Will Spend Remainder of Life on Rubber Project," *Fort Myers (Fla.) Press*, Mar 17, 1930.

31. Ibid.

32. "Come in Special as Friends Wait at Wrong Depot," *Fort Myers (Fla.) Press*, Jan 22, 1931.

Chapter 11. On Other Nations and Their Populations

1. "No People So Progressive As We Are—Edison," *NYT*, Oct 22, 1911.

2. Ibid.

3. Ibid.

4. Ibid.

5. Ibid.

6. "Where Europe Can Give America Valuable Points," *NYT*, Oct 29, 1911.

7. Ibid.

8. Ibid.

9. Ibid.

10. Ibid.

11. Ibid.

12. "Submarine Terror to End, Says Edison," *NYT*, Jan 3, 1915.

13. Untitled article, *Cranbury Press*, May 26, 1916, 2.

14. 1918 radio address, Michigan State University Libraries, VVL Call No.: DB504.

15. "Edison at 75, Talks of Tut-ankh-Amen Also Ruhr and Girls," *NYT*, Feb 13, 1923.

16. "No People So Progressive As We Are—Edison," *NYT*, Oct 22, 1911.

17. "Thomas A. Edison: Philosopher," *Golden Book Magazine*, Apr 1931, 78.

18. Edison to Theodore Puskas, Feb 10, 1878, TEP, [Z400AE; TAEM 0:0]. (Courtesy of the PTM.)

19. "Edison Talks about Paris," *New York World*, Sept 8, 1889, TAED, [SC89112b; TAEM 146:477].

20. "No People So Progressive As We Are—Edison," *NYT*, Oct 22, 1911.

21. Ibid.

22. Ibid.

23. Ibid.

24. Ibid.

25. "We're Still Ahead, Says Mr. Edison, *NYT*, Oct 8, 1911.

26. "No People So Progressive As We Are—Edison," *NYT*, Oct 22, 1911.

27. Ibid.

28. Ibid.

29. Ibid.

30. Ibid.

31. Ibid.

32. "Where Europe Can Give America Valuable Points," *NYT*, Oct 29, 1911.

33. Ibid.

34. "Edison Sees Luxury War-Winning Force," *NYT*, June 8, 1918.

35. Ibid.

36. Circa 1903, quoted in "Edison in His Laboratory," *Harper's Magazine*, Sept 1932, 415.

37. "Edison on Invention and Inventors," *Century Magazine*, July 1911, 416.

38. Edison to Isaac Markens, Nov 15, 1911. (Courtesy of the American Jewish Historical Society, Isaac Markens Papers, P-47, Box 1, Folder 10.)

39. Ibid.

40. Ibid.

41. "The Woman of the Future," *Good Housekeeping*, Oct 12, 1912, 441.

42. "No Intervention—Edison, *NYT*, Jan 19, 1914.

43. "Edison Bans Cigarettes," *NYT*, May 11, 1914.

44. "Thomas Edison Talks on Invention in the Life of Today," *Review of Reviews*, Jan 1931, 40.

45. Shands, 12.

46. "No People So Progressive As We Are—Edison," *NYT*, Oct 22, 1911.

47. "Where Europe Can Give America Valuable Points," *NYT*, Oct 29, 1911.

Chapter 12. On Gender, Humanity, and Youth

1. Edison's Diary, July 12, 1885.

2. "Edison's in Chicago," *Chicago Evening Post*, May 12, 1891, TAED, [SC91035a; TAEM 146:695].

3. "Electricity to Do All Chores Eventually," *Dallas Morning News*, Aug 11, 1908.

4. "Edison Sees 1912 Great, Minus Greed," *NYT*, Jan 3, 1912.

5. Richard Cole Newton, M.D., "How Can a Man Keep Well and Grow Old; Thomas A. Edison Tells Why He Is Never Sick," *Health & Strength*, April 13, 1912, 364.

6. "The Woman of the Future," *Good Housekeeping*, Oct 12, 1912, 437.

7. Allan L. Benson, "Edison Tells How to Cook," *Good Housekeeping*, Mar 1913.

8. "The Woman of the Future," *Good Housekeeping*, Oct 12, 1912, 440.

9. Ibid.

10. Ibid.

11. Ibid.

12. Ibid.

13. Ibid.

14. Ibid.

15. Ibid.

16. Allan L. Benson, "Edison Tells How to Cook," *Good Housekeeping*, Mar 1913.

17. "'The Future Man Will Spend Less Time in Bed'—Edison," *NYT*, Oct 11, 1914.

18. "Thomas A. Edison, Paying Tribute to Wife, Says Women Should Have Vote," *Wellsboro (Pa.) Gazette*, Aug 19, 1915.

19. "Edison Favors Suffrage," *Suffolk County News*, Oct 15, 1915.

20. "Edison on Birthday Urges Milder Beer," *NYT*, Feb 12, 1916.

21. "Throngs Struggle for Sight of Edison," *NYT*, Oct 2, 1916.

22. "Hoover Candidacy Espoused by Edison," *NYT*, May 12, 1920.

23. "Edison Admits his Famous Questionnaire Is Failure," *Boston Daily Globe*, Feb 11, 1924.

24. "Edison, 77, Finds World Improving," *NYT*, Feb 12, 1924.

25. "Edison Tours County Fair with Wife's Yellow Bunny; Goes Broke on Number 11," *Fort Myers (Fla.) Press*, Feb 12, 1930.

26. "Thomas A. Edison: Philosopher," *Golden Book Magazine*, Apr 1931, 78.

27. Ibid.

28. Israel, 157, quoting the *New York World*, Apr 23, 1878.

29. Meadowcroft, 47.

30. "The Woman of the Future," *Good Housekeeping*, Oct 12, 1912, 440.

31. "Edison Discusses His Philosophy," *NYT*, Feb 12, 1921.

32. "Edison Makes Debut in Radio Interview," *NYT*, Oct 22, 1927.

33. "4,000 School Children Attend Edison Party," *Fort Myers (Fla.) Press*, Feb 11, 1928.

34. "Edison Says Cost Bars Synthetic Rubber Making," *Tampa (Fla.) Tribune*, Feb 11, 1929.

35. "Men Efficient at 80, Edison, 82, Declares," *NYT*, Sept 8, 1929.

36. "Thomas A. Edison: Philosopher," *Golden Book Magazine*, Apr 1931, 78.

37. Edison's Diary, July 12, 1885.

38. Edison to his wife, Mina, note, 1897–1898, TAED, [B037ABR; TAEM 0:0].

39. "The Woman of the Future," *Good Housekeeping*, Oct 12, 1912, 444.

40. Mar 25, 1918 [supplied year, month, and day], TAED, [X104DC; TAEM 0:0]. (Courtesy of the Edison and Ford Winter Estates.)

41. Edward Marshall, "Youth of To-Day and To-Morrow," *Forum*, Jan 1927, 50.

42. Ibid.

43. "We are Animals Says Mr. Edison," *Decatur (Ill.) Review*, quoting the *Independent*, Jan 28, 1910.

44. "Good Stories and Where They Come From," *NYT*, Mar 13, 1910.

45. "Edison Plans an Automatic Clerkless Shop," *NYT*, May 15, 1910.

46. "Edison on Invention and Inventors," *Century Magazine*, July 1911, 417.

47. "Edison Sees 1912 Great, Minus Greed," *NYT*, Jan 3, 1912.

48. "'The Future Man Will Spend Less Time in Bed'—Edison," *NYT*, Oct 11, 1914.

49. Ibid.

50. Ibid.

51. Ibid.

52. "The Scientific City of the Future," *Forum*, Dec 1926, 823.

53. "Edison Sees This Age Destroying Myths," *NYT*, Oct 7, 1927.

54. "Edison Predicts Hoover's Victory," *NYT*, July 30, 1928.

55. "Edison Thinks Hoover Would Aid Dry Law," *NYT*, Sept 28, 1928.

56. "Edison Says Cost Bars Synthetic Rubber Making," *Tampa (Fla.) Tribune*, Feb 11, 1929.

57. "Edison Warns Boys Test Today Is Hard," *NYT*, Aug 1, 1929.

58. "Thomas A. Edison: Philosopher," *Golden Book Magazine*, Apr 1931, 78.

59. "Mr. Edison's Views of Life and Work," *Review of Reviews*, Jan 1932, 31.

60. Edward Marshall, "Youth of To-Day and To-Morrow," *Forum*, Jan 1927, 41.

61. Ibid.

62. Ibid.

63. Ibid.

64. Ibid.

65. Ibid.

66. Ibid.

67. "Edison Says Cost Bars Synthetic Rubber Making," *Tampa (Fla.) Tribune*, Feb 11, 1929.

68. "Edison Warns Boys Test Today Is Hard," *NYT*, Aug 1, 1929.

Chapter 13. On the Brain

1. "Edison at Sixty, Outlines Wonders of the Future," *NYT*, May 19 1907.

2. "The Future's Possibilities," *NYT*, Oct 11, 1908.

3. "No Immortality of the Soul Says Thomas A. Edison," *NYT*, Oct 2, 1910.

4. "Wizard with Amazing Powers Astounds Scientists," *NYT*, Nov 13, 1910.

5. Ibid.

6. "Edison on Invention and Inventors," *Century Magazine*, July 1911, 418.

7. Thomas H. Uzzell, "The Future of Electricity," *Collier's Weekly*, Dec 2, 1916, 8.

8. Hubbard, 18.

9. "Edison Working on How to Communicate with the Next World," *American Magazine*, Oct 1920, 10.

10. Ibid.

11. "Why Do So Many Men Never Amount to Anything?" *American Magazine*, Jan 1921, 10.

12. Ibid.

13. Ibid.

14. Ibid.

15. Ibid.

16. Ibid.

17. "Edison Stands by His Questionnaires," *NYT*, June 26, 1921.

18. "Ford Sees Wealth in Muscle Shoals," *NYT*, Dec 6, 1921.

19. Edward Marshall, "Youth of To-Day and To-Morrow," *Forum*, Jan 1927, 46.

20. "Edison Foresees Healthier World," *NYT*, Dec 24, 1930.

21. "Thomas A. Edison: Philosopher," *Golden Book Magazine*, Apr 1931, 78.

22. Marginalia by Edison on a letter from Henry Augustus Rowland to Edward Dean Adams, Oct 27, 1889, TAED, [D8933ACA; TAEM 126:114].

23. "Mr. Edison on Electricity as a Profession," *Ottumwa Courier*, Dec 31, 1894, TAED, [SC94032a; TAEM 146:926].

24. Ibid.

25. Ibid.

26. "Electricity in the Schools, *Dallas Morning News*, Jan 13, 1901.

27. "Edison in His Laboratory," *Harper's Magazine*, Sept 1932, 405.

28. Ibid.

29. "Edison on Invention and Inventors," *Century Magazine*, July 1911, 418.

30. Ibid.

31. Ibid.

32. "Where Europe Can Give America Valuable Points," *NYT*, Oct 29, 1911.

33. "Edison Praises Machines," *NYT*, Jan 11, 1914.

34. "Edison, 67, Feels Like a Boy, He Says," *NYT*, Feb 12, 1914.

35. "Edison on Educationals," *NYT*, Feb 9, 1919.

36. Ibid.

37. "Edison Condemns the Primary School," *NYT*, May 7, 1921.

38. "Edison Answers Some of His Critics," *NYT*, Oct 23, 1921.

39. "How I Would Double the Volume of a Business," *System: The Magazine of Business* 44 (Sept 1923): 268.

40. "Thinks Faculty Would Quarrel," *Boston Daily Globe*, Jan 1, 1925.

41. Edward Marshall, "Youth of To-Day and To-Morrow," *Forum*, Jan 1927, 46.

42. Ibid.

43. Ibid.

44. Ibid.

45. Ibid.

46. Ibid.

47. "Edison on Birthday Feels More Than 83," *Fort Myers (Fla.) Press*, Feb 12, 1930.

48. "Scholarship Is Outlined by Inventor," *Fort Myers (Fla.) Press*, Apr 9, 1930.

49. "Mr. Edison on Electricity as a Profession," *Ottumwa (Iowa) Courier*, Dec 31, 1894, TAED, [SC94032a; TAEM 146:926].

50. "Edison Bars Poets from List of Great," *NYT*, Dec 6, 1911.

51. Ibid.

52. "Edison on College Men," *NYT*, May 6, 1921.

53. "Edison Asserts He Wants College Men if He Can Get Them," *NYT*, May 16, 1921.

54. "College Men Shirk Work, Says Edison," *NYT*, Nov 18, 1922.

55. "Edison Admits His Famous Questionnaire Is Failure," *Boston Daily Globe*, Feb 11, 1924.

56. Edward Marshall, "Youth of To-Day and To-Morrow," *Forum*, Jan 1927, 49.

57. "Edison Says Cost Bars Synthetic Rubber Making," *Tampa (Fla.) Tribune*, Feb 11, 1929.

58. Interview with Edison, 1929 supplied year, TAED, [X001A5AY; TAEM 0:0, HFMGV].

59. Recalled by his son Theodore. Oct 12, 1972, interview with Theodore Edison conducted by Kenneth Goldstein. (Courtesy of Thomas Edison National Historical Park.)

Chapter 14. On the Body

1. "Edison His Own Doctor," *New York Sun*, May 10, 1891, TAED, [SC91034a; TAEM 146:694].

2. Ibid.

3. Ibid.

4. Edison to Mina Miller Edison, his wife, Dec 1, 1898, TAED, [B037ABU; TAEM 0:0].

5. "'The Future Man Will Spend Less Time in Bed'—Edison," *NYT*, Oct 11, 1914.

6. "Edison Predicts Next Inventions in Health Field," *Fort Myers (Fla.) Press*, Dec 24, 1930.

7. Marginalia on a letter from H. L. Leclare, Apr 11, 1878, TAED, [D7833B; TAEM 19:347].

8. "Edison's Remedy," *Cranbury (N.J.) Press*, Oct 5, 1888.

9. "Edison's New Ideas," *Brooklyn Citizen*, Nov 4, 1888, TAED, [SM038071; TAEM 25:580].

10. "Fluoroscope Is a Success," *New York Herald*, Mar 28, 1896, TAED, [SC96008A1; TAEM 146:1007].

11. The comment was likely made in jest. Edison's Diary, July 12, 1885.

12. "Edison in His Laboratory," *Harper's Magazine*, Sept 1932, 405.

13. "Men and Women of the Outdoor World," *Outing*, Apr 1904, 60.

14. "No Immortality of the Soul Says Thomas A. Edison," *NYT*, Oct 2, 1910.

15. "'The Future Man Will Spend Less Time in Bed'—Edison," *NYT*, Oct 11, 1914.

16. Austin C. Lescarboura, "Edison's Views on Life and Death," *Scientific American*, Oct 30, 1920, 446.

17. Richard Cole Newton, M.D., "How Can a Man Keep Well and Grow Old; Thomas A. Edison Tells Why He Is Never Sick," *Health & Strength*, April 13, 1912, 363.

18. Austin C. Lescarboura, "Edison's Views on Life and Death," *Scientific American*, Oct 30, 1920, 446.

19. Despite disparaging comments about patent medicine, Edison established his own patent medicine company, Polyform, during the 1870s. Marginalia on letter to Edison from E. L. Jones & Co, Dec 11, 1879, TAED, [D7903ZLZ; TAEM 49:560].

20. Circa 1903, quoted in "Edison in His Laboratory," *Harper's Magazine*, Sept 1932, 405.

21. "Edison Himself Answers a Questionnaire," *Collier's Weekly*, July 14, 1923, 10.

22. "A Day with Edison," *New York Journal*, July 26, 1891, TAED, [MBSB62499; TAEM 95:257].

23. Circa 1903, quoted in "Edison in His Laboratory," *Harper's Magazine*, Sept 1932, 407.

24. "'Four Hours' Sleep Enough for Anyone,' Says Edison," *South Jersey Republican*, Dec 10, 1910.

25. "Where Europe Can Give America Valuable Points," *NYT*, Oct 29, 1911.

26. "'The Future Man Will Spend Less Time in Bed'—Edison," *NYT*, Oct 11, 1914.

27. Ibid.

28. Ibid.

29. Ibid.

30. Ibid. (Edison's diary makes references to his dreams.)

31. Ibid.

32. Ibid.

33. "Coolidge Gives Sap Bucket to Ford," *Boston Daily Globe*, Aug 19, 1924.

34. "Edison at 80 Views a World He Changed," *NYT*, Feb 27, 1927.

35. "Edison Will Spend Remainder of Life on Rubber Project," *Fort Myers (Fla.) Press*, Mar 17, 1930.

36. Meadowcroft, 143.

37. "The Doom of Gas," *St. Louis Post-Dispatch*, Apr 27, 1882, TAED, [MBSB52192; TAEM 95:191].

38. Ibid.

39. "Edison on Inventions," 1890 interview, published in Nov 1895 *Monthly Illustrator/Home & Country*, TAED, [SC90094A; TAEM 146:657].

40. "Edison His Own Doctor," *New York Sun*, May 10, 1891, TAED, [SC91034a; TAEM 146:694].

41. "Thomas Edison, the Distinguished Electrician, a Man of Charming Personality," *Norwalk (Ohio) Reflector*, Feb 1896 [supplied date], TAED, [SC9600A1; TAEM 146:1004].

42. "Men and Women of the Outdoor World," *Outing*, Apr 1904, 60.

43. "Where Europe Can Give America Valuable Points," *NYT*, Oct 29, 1911.

44. Allan E. Benson, "Edison Tells How to Cook," *Good Housekeeping*, Mar 1913.

45. Ibid.

46. Ibid.

47. "'The Future Man Will Spend Less Time in Bed'—Edison," *NYT*, Oct 11, 1914.

48. Ibid.

49. "Edison Views the World at Seventy, *Edison Diamond Points*, excerpted from *New York Sun*, Feb 1917, 14–16.

50. Ibid.

51. "Edison at 75, Talks of Tut-ankh-Amen Also Ruhr and Girls," *NYT*, Feb 13, 1923.

52. "Edison Will Spend Remainder of Life on Rubber Project," *Fort Myers (Fla.) Press*, Mar 17, 1930.

53. "Thomas Edison Talks on Invention in the Life of Today," *Review of Reviews*, Jan 1931, 39.

54. Edison to Mina Miller Edison, his wife, Dec 1, 1898, TAED, [B037ABU; TAEM 0:0].

55. "The Kingdom of Labor Is at Hand, Declares Edison," *Seattle Star*, Jan 14, 1910.

56. "Men and Women of the Outdoor World," *Outing*, Apr 1904, 60.

57. Ibid.

58. Allan L. Benson, "Edison Tells How to Cook," *Good Housekeeping*, Mar 1913.

59. "Light Breakfasts the Secret of Efficiency," *NYT*, June 16, 1907.

60. "Edison Injured by Radium," *Fort Myers (Fla.) Press*, Oct 3, 1907.

61. Allan L. Benson, "Edison Tells How to Cook," *Good Housekeeping*, Mar 1913.

62. "'The Future Man Will Spend Less Time in Bed'—Edison," *NYT*, Oct 11, 1914.

63. Ibid.

64. "Edison Works Hard on His 73D Birthday," *NYT*, Feb 12, 1920.

65. "Edison Foresees Healthier World," *NYT*, Dec 24, 1930.

66. Edward Marshall, "Youth of To-Day and To-Morrow," *Forum*, Jan 1927, 42.

67. Ibid.

68. Meadowcroft, 39.

69. Ibid.

70. Israel, 134.

71. Edison to Hamilton McKown Twombly, telegram, May 1879 [supplied date], TAED, [D7901A1; TAEM 49:7].

72. "Thomas A. Edison Gives His Reasons Why He Prefers Being a Little Deaf," *Quincy (Ill.) Daily Whig*, quoting *New York Sun*, Sept 16, 1884.

73. Ibid.

74. Ibid.

75. Edison's Diary, July 14, 1885.

76. "Edison on Inventions," 1890 interview, published in Nov 1895 *Monthly Illustrator/Home & Country*, TAED, [SC90094A; TAEM 146:657].

77. Edison to Louis B. Schram, Dec. 31, 1904, TAED, [LB071229A; TAEM 197: 197].

78. "Edison Is Sixty; Birthday To-Day," *NYT*, Feb 11, 1907.

79. Israel, 435.

80. Edison explains why he didn't use a device to improve his hearing. "When Edison Was Peeved," *Dallas Morning News*, quoting *New York Sun*, June 29, 1913.

81. "Edison on Deaf Wit," *Fort Myers (Fla.) Press*, Mar 5, 1914.

82. "Edison Views the World at Seventy, *Edison Diamond Points*, excerpted from *New York Sun*, Feb 1917, 14–16.

83. "A Blessing in Disguise," *Boston Daily Globe*, Mar 28, 1925.

84. "The Scientific City of the Future," *Forum*, Dec 1926, 827.

85. "All May Lose Hearing Edison Tells the Deaf," *NYT*, Feb 20, 1927.

86. "Edison Off to Florida but Ford Is Detained," *NYT*, Jan 19, 1928.

87. "Edison Has Picture Taken but Ducks Inquiring Writers," *Fort Myers (Fla.) Press*, Jan 18, 1929.

88. "Men Efficient at 80, Edison, 82, Declares," *NYT*, Sept 8, 1929.

89. "Edison Sees Poor Acting in Talkies," *Fort Myers (Fla.) Press*, Jan 21, 1930.

90. Ibid.

91. Victor Young, "Edison and Music," *Etude*, June 1932, 399.

92. Ibid.

93. Edison's Diary, July 12, 1885.

94. "Edison and His Pipe," *Quincy (Ill.) Daily Whig*, quoting *New York Sun*, Oct 23, 1887.

95. "Wizard Edison at Home, *New York World*, Nov 17, 1889, TAED, [MBSB 62500; TAEM 95:261].

96. "Edison on Inventions," 1890 interview, published in Nov 1895 *Monthly Illustrator/Home & Country*, TAED, [SC90094A; TAEM 146:657].

97. "As Yet We Know Nothing," *NYT*, Jan 12, 1908.

98. Sign at Edison's West Orange Plant. "Edison Bans Cigarettes," *NYT*, May 11, 1914.

99. Ibid.

100. Hubbard, 18.

101. "Edison Views the World at Seventy," *Edison Diamond Points*, excerpted from *New York Sun*, Feb 1917, 14–16.

102. "Edison Defends Cigars," *NYT*, Aug 13, 1921.

103. "Edison Frowns on Radio World," *St. Petersburg Times*, Mar 7, 1927.

104. "Edison Bans Cigarettes," *NYT*, July 20, 1928.

Chapter 15. On the Arts

1. Edison's Diary, July 17, 1885.

2. "Edison on Inventions," 1890 interview, published in Nov 1895 *Monthly Illustrator/Home & Country*, TAED, [SC90094A; TAEM 146:657].

3. "The Woman of the Future," *Good Housekeeping*, Oct 12, 1912, 441.

4. Ibid.

5. On his favorite kind of music. "Edison Views the World at Seventy," *Edison Diamond Points*, excerpted from *New York Sun*, Feb 1917, 14–16.

6. "Edison Sees Luxury War-Winning Force," NYT, Jun 8, 1918.

7. "Thomas A. Edison: Philosopher," *Golden Book Magazine*, Apr 1931, 78.

8. "Edison Talks about Paris," *New York World*, Sept 8, 1889, TAED, [SC89112b; TAEM 146:477].

9. Untitled article, *New York Evening Sun*, 1889, TAED, [SC89151; TAEM 146:514].

10. "Maladie du siecle," *Time*, July 12, 1926.

11. "Thomas A. Edison: Philosopher," *Golden Book Magazine*, Apr 1931, 79.

12. Edison's Diary, July 12, 1885.

13. Ibid.

14. Ibid.

15. "A Day with Edison," *New York Journal*, July 26, 1891, TAED, [MBSB 62499; TAEM 95:257].

16. "Edison on Invention and Inventors," *Century Magazine*, July 1911, 417.

17. Ibid.

18. "Edison Bars Poets from List of Great," *NYT*, Dec 6, 1911.

19. Ibid.

Chapter 16. On Family

1. Marginalia by Edison on letter from John Edison, Jan 18, 1880, TAED, [D8015B; TAEM 53:531].

2. "Edison Says His Mother Made Him," *Dallas Morning News* quoting *New York World*, Aug 10, 1908.

3. Josephson, 99.

4. Edison's Technical Notes and Drawings, Feb 1, 1872, TAED, [NE167603A; TAEM 3:93].

5. Edison's Technical Notes and Drawings, Feb 14, 1872, TAED, [NE1678059; TAEM 3:35].

6. Edison to Charles Batchelor, telegram, Sept 3, 1874, TAED, [SB1677128; TAEM 27:426].

7. Edison to Samuel Ogden Edison, his father, Jan 29, 1877, TAED, [X001A1AW; TAEM 0:0]. (Courtesy of the HFMGV.)

8. Edison's Diary, July 15, 1885.

9. Ibid., July 17, 1885.

10. "The Anecdotal Side of Edison," *Ladies' Home Journal*, April 1898, 8. (The statement was uttered in August 1885.)

11. Edison to Lewis Miller, Mina's father, Sept 30, 1885, TAED, [B037AAA; TAEM 0:0].

12. Edison to Theodore Westwood and John Vincent Miller, Mina's younger brothers, Dec 24, 1885, TAED, [D8514ZAG; TAEM 77:480].

13. Interview with Edison, probably by reporter from *Cincinnati Enquirer*, 1888, TAED, [D8807ADK; TAEM 121:793].

14. Edison to his wife, note, written between 1894 and 1898, TAED, [B037AAE1; TAEM 0:0].

15. Ibid.

16. Ibid.

17. Edison to his wife, note, Aug 11, 1895, TAED, [B037AAXZ; TAEM 0:0].

18. Edison to his wife, note, Aug 12, 1895, TAED, [B037ABA; TAEM 0:0].

19. Edison to his wife, note, Aug 15, 1895 [supplied year and month], TAED, [B037ABB; TAEM 0:0].

20. "Edison Is Sixty; Birthday To-Day," *NYT*, Feb 11, 1907.

21. "Thomas A. Edison: Philosopher," *Golden Book Magazine*, Apr 1931, 79.

22. Edison to his wife, note, undated, TAED, [X104GC; TAEM 0:0]. (Courtesy of the Edison-Ford Winter Estates.)

23. Israel, 234.

24. Edison's Diary, July 12, 1885.

25. Ibid., July 17, 1885.

26. Edison to Samuel Ogden Edison, his father, Oct 21, 1877 [supplied year], TAED, [X001A1BD; TAEM 0:0]. (Courtesy of the HFMGV.)

27. Edison to Borden Spencer, in Fall River, Mass., Dec 16, 1897, TAED, [LB059620; TAEM 143:592].

28. Edison to Mina Miller Edison, his wife, 1898 [supplied or conjectured], TAED, [B037ABY; TAEM 0:0].

29. Edison to Thomas Commerford Martin, Jan 17, 1898, TAED, [D9807AAB; TAEM 137:107].

30. Edison to Edward J. Redington, June 26, 1899, TAED, [LB063570; TAEM 143:1021].

31. Conot, 363, quoting from marginalia on letter from Thomas Edison Jr. to his father, July 21, 1903.

32. Edison to Mina Miller Edison, his wife, 1896 [supplied year], TAED, [B037ABK; TAEM 0:0].

33. Edison to A. J. Miller, Mar 15, 1899, TAED, [LB063403; TAEM 143:987].

34. Israel, 393, quoting from a draft from Edison to Blanche Edison, Dec 1903.

35. "Experimenting with a Baby," *Chicago Times*, June 6, 1888, TAED, [SC88026C; TAEM 146:254].

36. Ibid.

37. "The Baby at the Phonograph," *New Brunswick (N.J.) Times*, June 6, 1888, TAED, [SC88040; TAEM 146:254].

38. Edison to his wife, note, 1897–1898 [supplied range of years], TAED, [B037ABR; TAEM 0:0].

39. Allan L. Benson, "Edison Tells How to Cook," *Good Housekeeping*, Mar 1913. Madeleine did eventuallly take a course in housecare and cooking at Columbia University a few months after Edison made the comment.

40. Edison to his daughter Madeleine, note, Apr 1923 [supplied year and month], TAED, [B037ACI; TAEM 0:0].

41. Edison to his wife, note, 1897–1898 [supplied range of years], TAED, [B037ABR; TAEM 0:0].

42. Edison to his wife, note, July 1898, TAED, [B037ABT; TAEM 0:0].

43. "Mr. Edison Interviewed," *Edison Herald*, Feb 25, 1919, 7.

44. Edison to Mina, July 1898, TAED, [B037ABT; TAEM 0:0].

45. "Edison Is Sixty; Birthday To-Day," *NYT*, Feb 11, 1907.

46. "Edison Takes Pride in Son's Invention," *NYT*, Dec 13, 1921.

47. "Edison's Son Gets Tech Degree Today," *Boston Daily Globe*, Feb 11, 1923.

Chapter 17. On People

1. Edison to Franklin H. Badger, Oct 13, 1877, TEP, [X001A1BC; TAEM 0:0]. (Courtesy of the HFMGV.)

2. Edison to George Edward Gouraud, July 21, 1887, TAED, [D8751AAB; TAEM 120:277].

3. "Edison's New Ideas," *Brooklyn Citizen*, Nov 4, 1888, TAED, [SM038071; TAEM 25:580].

4. "Edison Bars Poets from List of Great," *NYT*, Dec 6, 1911.

5. "Edison Will Live 15 More Years, He Says, on 75th Birthday," *St. Louis Globe-Democrat*, Feb 12, 1922.

6. "Edison Is Jolly on 79th Birthday," *NYT*, Feb 12, 1926.

7. "Edison Bars Poets from List of Great," *NYT*, Dec 6, 1911.

8. Interview with Edison, Sept 25, 1930, TAED, [X166A; TAEM 0:0. (Courtesy of Lilly Library.)

9. "Edison Bars Poets from List of Great," *NYT*, Dec 6, 1911.

10. Israel, 321.

11. Thomas H. Uzzell, "The Future of Electricity," *Collier's Weekly,* Dec 2, 1916, 7.

12. Ibid.,

13. Ibid.

14. "Edison at 75 Still a Two-Shift Man," *NYT*, Feb 12, 1922.

15. "Edison Opposes Ford for President," *NYT*, Oct 18, 1923.

16. "Edison Accepts Honor as Paid to His Life Purpose, Advancing Human Understanding and Happiness," *NYT,* Oct 22, 1929.

17. "Nations Tribute Again to Benjamin Franklin," *NYT*, Jan 13, 1924.

18. Meadowcroft, 153.

19. Israel, 8.

20. "Tsar," *Time*, November 29, 1926.

21. "Edison Praises Deeds of Lindbergh in 1927," *NYT*, Jan 1, 1928.

22. Circa 1903, quoted in "Edison in His Laboratory," *Harper's Magazine*, Sept 1932, 415.

23. "Edison Bars Poets from List of Great," *NYT*, Dec 6, 1911.

24. "Chautauqua Pays Honor to Founder," *NYT*, July 25, 1929.

25. "Edison in Birthday Interview Says He Feels 'Pretty Good,'" *Fort Myers (Fla.) Tropical News*, Feb 12, 1931.

26. Israel, 8.

27. "Edison Opens Work on Paine Memorial," *NYT*, May 31, 1925.

28. "Edison Speaks for Tom Paine," *NYT*, June 7, 1925.

29. Interview with Edison, Sept 25, 1930, TAED, [X166A; TAEM 0:0]. (Courtesy of Lilly Library.)

30. Edison to Frederick W. Royce, May 16, 1879, [X060AB; TAEM 0:0]. (Courtesy of the Filson Club Historical Society.)

31. "Edison Bars Poets from List of Great," *NYT*, Dec 6, 1911.

32. "Damn Good Man," *Time*, Jul 25, 1927.

33. "Edison and Tesla Rivals," *New York Journal*, May 22, 1896, TAED, [SC96038A1; TAEM 146:1036].

34. "Mr. Edison at Home Unspoiled by Glory," *New York Herald*, Oct 7, 1889, TAED, [MBSB62465; TAEM 95:244].

Chapter 18. On Himself

1. George Parsons Lathrop, "Talks with Edison," *Harper's Magazine*, Feb 1890, 431.

2. Edison to his parents, telegram, 1866, sent when he was nineteen years old, TAED, [X001A1AC; TAEM 0:0].

3. Edison to Frank A. Hanaford, July 26, 1869, TAED, [D6901E; TAEM 12:23].

4. Edison to Frank A. Hanaford, Sep 17, 1869, TAED.

5. Edison to Frank A. Hanaford, 00/26/1870, TAED, [D7001C; TAEM 12:42]. The date of the letter illegible; *The Thomas Edison Papers* give the date as shown here.

6. "Edison Isn't Proud," *Bethlehem (Pa.) Times*, June 4, 1892, TAED, [SC 92055; TAEM 146:789].

7. Edison to Samuel Ogden Edison, his father, Oct 30, 1870, TAED, [X001A1AR; TAEM0:0]. (Courtesy of the HFMGV.)

8. "The Man Who Invents," *Washington Post*, Apr 19, 1878, TAED, [MBSB 10532; TAEM 94:169].

9. "Edison's Big Bonanza," *New York Herald*, Mar 1880 [supplied month], TAED, [MBSB21483; TAEM 94:593].

10. Edison, at the age of thirty-five. "The Doom of Gas," *St. Louis Post-Dispatch*, Apr 27, 1882, TAED, [MBSB52192; TAEM 95:191].

11. "Electric Light Patents," *Tribuner* [possibly *Chicago Tribune*], May 3, 1885, TAED, [SB017003; TAEM 89:642].

12. "Edison's Religious Belief," *Salt Lake City Democrat*, July 16, 1885, TAED, [SB017039b; TAEM 89:661].

13. "The Wizard's Chat," *Pittsburgh Dispatch*, May 23, 1889.

14. "Edison Back from Paris," *NYT*, Oct 7, 1889.

15. "Wizard Edison at Home, *New York World*, Nov 17, 1889, TAED, [MBSB 62500; TAEM 95:261].

16. "Edison's Latest Work, Inventions and Improvements," *New York Herald*, Aug 24, 1890, TAED, [SC90055A; TAEM146:618].

17. "A Day with Edison," *New York Journal*, July 26, 1891, TAED, [MBSB 62499; TAEM 95:257].

18. Charles D. Lanier, "Two Giants of the Electric Age," *Review of Reviews*, July 1893, 42.

19. "Thomas Edison, the Distinguished Electrician, a Man of Charming Personality," *Norwalk Reflector*, Feb 1896 [supplied date], TAED, [SC9600A1; TAEM 146:1004].

20. "Men and Women of the Outdoor World," *Outing*, Apr 1904, 60.

21. "Edison at Sixty, Outlines Wonders of the Future," *NYT*, May 19, 1907.

22. "Edison on Invention and Inventors," *Century Magazine*, July 1911, 416.

23. "Edison Defends Cigars," *NYT*, Aug 13, 1921.

24. "Value of Edison's Genius Is Put at Fifteen Billions," *NYT*, June 24, 1923.

25. "Head Swelled, Edison Says by Felicitations on Birthday; Mussolini Joins in Tribute," *NYT*, Feb 13, 1927.

26. "Edison's Golden Days," *Literary Digest*, Nov 2, 1929, 11.

Chapter 19. On the Future

1. "The Future of Electricity," *Dallas Morning News* quoting *Pittsburgh Dispatch*, June 12, 1889.

2. "Mr. Edison and the Electric Millennium, *Levant Herald*, Sept 1, 1889, TAED, [SC89135c; TAEM 146:498].

3. "Wizard Edison at Home," *New York World*, Nov 17, 1889, TAED, [MBSB62500; TAEM 95:261].

4. "Inventions of the Future," unnamed newspaper, Dec 31, 1891, TAED, [SC91074a; TAEM 146:733].

5. "A Prediction by Mr. Edison," *NYT*, Aug 12, 1902.

6. "Edison at Sixty, Outlines Wonders of the Future," *NYT*, May 19 1907.

7. "Wireless Wonders Are Yet to Come," *NYT*, Oct 19, 1907.

8. "As Yet We Know Nothing," *NYT*, Jan 12, 1908.

9. Ibid.

10. "The Kingdom of Labor Is at Hand, Declares Edison," *Seattle Star*, Jan 14, 1910.

11. "We are Animals Says Mr. Edison," *Decatur (Ill.) Review*, quoting *Independent*, Jan 28, 1910.

12. Ibid.

13. "Edison Plans an Automatic Clerkless Shop," *NYT*, May 15, 1910.

14. Ibid.

15. "Edison on Invention and Inventors," *Century Magazine*, July 1911, 419.

16. "The Woman of the Future," *Good Housekeeping*, Oct 12, 1912, 441.

17. Ibid.

18. "Edison Looks into Future," *NYT*, Sept 8, 1913.

19. Ibid.

20. "'The Future Man Will Spend Less Time in Bed'—Edison," *NYT*, Oct 11, 1914.

21. "Edison Tells How Submarine May Stay Submerged," *NYT*, Oct 11, 1914.

22. Thomas H. Uzzell, "The Future of Electricity," *Collier's Weekly*, Dec 2, 1916, 7.

23. Ibid.

24. "Edison Discusses His Philosophy," *NYT*, Feb 12, 1921.

25. "Edison Still Busy on the Phonograph," *NYT*, July 19, 1922.

26. Edward Marshall, "Has Man an Immortal Soul," *Forum*, Nov 1926, 646.

27. "The Scientific City of the Future," *Forum*, Dec 1926, 826.

28. "Beauty of Fort Myers Is Praised to All American When Edison Talks Over Radio," *Fort Myers (Fla.) Tropical News*, June 11, 1931.

29. "Edison Courageous as End Approached," *NYT*, Oct 19, 1931.

Chapter 20. Miscellaneous

1. Edison's Diary, July 20, 1885.

2. "Edison on Inventions," 1890 interview, published Nov 1895 *Monthly Illustrator/Home & Country*, TAED, [SC90094A; TAEM 146:657].

3. Edward Marshall, "Youth of To-Day and To-Morrow," *Forum*, Jan 1927, 43.

4. "4,000 School Children Attend Edison Party," *Fort Myers (Fla.) Press*, Feb 11, 1928.

5. Allan L. Benson, "Edison Tells How to Cook," *Good Housekeeping*, Mar 1913.

6. "Power Flashed by Wire," *New York Sun*, Sept 17, 1878, TAED, [SB032124; TAEM 27:915].

7. Edward Marshall, "Youth of To-Day and To-Morrow," *Forum*, January 1927, 44.

8. Edison to Uriah Hunt Painter, Apr 16, 1878, TAED, [X154A2BC; TAEM 0:0], Historical Society of Pennsylvania.

9. Edison to Theodore Puskas, Nov 8, 1878, TAED, [Z400BB; TAEM 0:0]. (Courtesy of the PTM.)

10. Edison to Brewer & Jensen, Nov 11, 1878, TAED, [D7828ZDP; TAEM 18:807].

11. Edison to Clarence J. Blake, Dec 4, 1878, TAED, [X011AE; TAEM 0:0]. (Courtesy of the Trustees of the Boston Public Library.)

12. "The Anecdotal Side of Edison," *Ladies' Home Journal*, April 1898, 8.

13. "Electrical Show Opened by Edison," *NYT*, Oct 12, 1911.

14. "Hoover Lauds Edison at Light Celebration," *Fort Myers (Fla.) Press*, Oct 22, 1929.

15. "Edison Tries to Flee Dinner; Returns When Wife Insists," *NYT*, Oct 21, 1929.

16. "Edison Accepts Honor as Paid to His Life Purpose, Advancing Human Understanding and Happiness," *NYT*, Oct 22, 1929.

17. Josephson, 481.

18. Circa 1903, quoted in "Edison in His Laboratory," *Harper's Magazine*, Sept 1932, 406.

19. Ibid.

20. "The Anecdotal Side of Edison," *Ladies' Home Journal*, April 1898, 8.

21. Circa 1903, quoted in "Edison in His Laboratory," *Harper's Magazine*, Sept 1932, 405.

22. Meadowcroft, 20.

23. "Where Europe Can Give America Valuable Points," *NYT*, Oct 29, 1911.

24. "How We Can Improve Your Income," *Phrenological Journal and Science of Health*, Jan 1904, 5.

25. Israel, 445.

26. "Edison Astonished as Science Wizards Show New Marvels," *NYT*, Oct 19, 1922.

27. "Edison Honored by Movie Leaders," *NYT*, Feb 16, 1924.

28. "Firestone and Ford with Edison at Fair," *NYT*, Sept 18, 1928.

29. "Edison Gives His Birthday Cake for Sale to Aid Relief Fund," *NYT*, Feb 14, 1931.

30. "Edison Receives Rotary Club Medal," *NYT*, July 10, 1930.

31. "What Thomas Edison Thinks Will Be Science's Next Most Vital Discovery," *NYT*, Jan 7, 1906.

32. Edward Marshall, "Youth of To-Day and To-Morrow," *Forum*, January 1927, 46.

33. Ibid.

Chapter 21. Others on Edison

1. "Fort Myers Rotary Club Honors Edison Invention of Light," *Fort Myers (Fla.) Tropical News*, Oct 23, 1929.

2. "Dr. Van Dyke Chides Edison on Colleges," *NYT*, Nov 21, 1922.

3. "Edison Never 'Mad,' Says One of His Men," *NYT*, Oct 18, 1931.

4. "Edison, at 80, Finds Work a Pleasure," *NYT*, Feb 12, 1927.

5. "Edison Is Decorated by Nation and Hailed by the President," *NYT*, Oct 21, 1928.

6. Daniel H. Craig to Edison, Feb 13, 1871, TAED, [D7110D; TAEM 12:447].

7. "Eastman Pays a Tribute," *NYT*, Feb 11, 1927.

8. "Edison Is Eulogized in World Tributes," *NYT*, Oct 18, 1931.

9. "Son Accepts Medal in Honor of Edison," *NYT*, May 25, 1928.

10. Conot, 263, quoting *New York Sun*, May 25, 1888.

11. "Wife's Task Is to Care of Husband," *San Francisco Examiner*, Oct 20, 1915.

12. "Mrs. Edison Describes Husband," *NYT*, Feb 11, 1927.

13. "Edison's Father," *Quincy (Ill.) Daily Whig*, quoting *New York World*, Nov 26, 1885.

14. "Death of a Titan," *Time*, Oct 26, 1931.

15. "Edison Batteries for New Ford Cars," *NYT*, Jan 11, 1914.

16. "Ford to Start Peace Campaign," *NYT*, Aug 23, 1915.

17. "Ford Calls Edison 'The Happiest Man,'" *NYT*, Mar 7, 1929.

18. "Ford's Friend Edison," *Scientific American*, Nov 1929, 377.

19. "Death of a Titan," *Time*, Oct 26, 1931.

20. "Gibbons Answers Edison's Soul Talk," *NYT*, Feb 19, 1911.

21. "City Unveils Plaque in Honor of Edisons," *Fort Myers (Fla.) Tropical News*, Feb 12, 1930.

22. "Hoover Says Edison Removed Untold Toil from the World," *NYT*, July 20, 1929.

23. Israel, 153.

24. "Thomas Edison a Guest," *Dallas Morning* News, Jan 6, 1899.

25. "Ludwig Picks Four Greatest Americans," *NYT*, Feb 10, 1928.

26. "Ludwig Sails Home Eulogizing Edison," *NYT*, Mar 11, 1928.

27. "Ludwig Saw in Edison Our 'Uncrowned King,'" *NYT*, Oct 18, 1931.

28. "Edison on Air, Tells of First Phonograph," *NYT*, Aug 13, 1927.

29. Ibid.

30. "Rabbi Newman Picks 10 Greatest Living Men; Edison, Einstein, Gandhi, Shaw Head His List," *NYT*, Feb 2, 1931.

31. "Edison Is Eulogized in World Tributes," *NYT*, Oct 18, 1931.

32. "'The Future Man Will Spend Less Time in Bed'—Edison," *NYT*, Oct 11, 1914.

33. "Tesla Says Edison Was an Empiricist," *NYT*, Oct 19, 1931.

34. "Edison, 71, Honored by Old Associates," *NYT*, Feb 12, 1918.

35. "Congress Honors Edison," *NYT*, Oct 21, 1928.

Bibliography

Published Sources

Baldwin, Neil. *Edison: Inventing the Century*. New York: Hyperion, 1995.

Conot, Robert. *A Streak of Luck*. New York: Seaview Books, 1979.

Dyer, Frank Lewis, and Thomas Commerford Martin. *Edison, His Life and Inventions*. New York: Harper and Brothers, 1910.

Edison, Thomas. Diary. The inventor's diary can be viewed in the original form through the Thomas Edison Papers [TEP] at edison.rutgers.edu [MA001; TAEM 90:3].

Firestone, Harvey S., Jr. *The Romance and Drama of the Rubber Industry*. Akron, Ohio: Firestone Tire and Rubber Company, 1932.

Gonzalez. *The Caloosahatchee*. Fort Myers, Fla.: Southwest Florida Historical Society, 1982.

Hubbard, Elbert. *Little Journeys to the Homes of the Great*. East Aurora, N.Y.: Roycrofters, 1916.

Israel, Paul. *Edison, A Life of Invention*. New York: John Wiley and Sons, 1998.

Josephson, Matthew. *Edison: A Biography*. New York: John Wiley and Sons, 1959.

Meadowcroft, William H. *The Boy's Life of Edison*. New York: Harper and Brothers, 1911.

Miller, Francis Trevelyan. *Thomas A. Edison, Benefactor of Mankind: The Romantic Life Story of the World's Greatest Inventor*. New York: John C. Winston, 1931.

Shands, A. L. *The Real Life of Thomas A. Edison*. Girard, Kans.: Haldeman-Julius, 1929.

Tate, Alfred O. *Edison's Open Door: The Life Story of Thomas A. Edison, A Great Individualist*. New York: Dutton, 1938.

———. *Good Stories Reprinted from the "Ladies' Home Journal" of Philadelphia*. Philadelphia: Henry Altemus Company, 1907.

———. "How We Can Improve Your Income." *Phrenological Journal and Science of Health* 117 (January 1904).

Libraries, Museums, and Other Repositories

American Jewish Historical Society, New York, N.Y.

AT&T Archives and History Center, Warren, N.J., through the TEP.

Boston Public Library, Boston, Massachusetts, through the TEP.

Charles Edison Fund, West Orange, N.J.

Edison and Ford Winter Estates, Fort Myers, Fla.

Edison National Historical Park, West Orange, N.J.

Filson Club Historical Society, Louisville, Ky.

Foundation of the Postal and Telecommunication Museum, Budapest, Hungary, through the TEP.

Gallery of History, Inc., Las Vegas, Nev., through the TEP.

Henry Ford Museum and Greenfield Village Research Center [HFMGV], Dearborn, Mich., through the TEP.

Historical Society of Pennsylvania, Philadelphia, through the TEP.

Institution of Electrical Engineers Archive, London, through the TEP.

Library of Congress, Manuscript Division, through the TEP.

Lilly Library, Indiana University, through the TEP.

Michigan State University Libraries, Vincent Voice Libraries.

National Archives, Washington, District of Columbia, through the TEP.

National Museum of American History Archives Center.

New York Public Library, Astor, Lenox and Tilden Foundations, New York, through TEP.

North Carolina Division of Archives and History, Raleigh, through the TEP.

Princeton University Libraries, Princeton, N.J., through the TEP.

Smithsonian Institution, National Museum of American History Archives Center, Washington, D.C., through the TEP.

Swan Galleries, Inc., New York, N.Y.

Thomas A. Edison Papers [TEP]. Digital edition is at Edison.rutgers.edu

Webb Shadle Memorial Library, Pleasantville, Iowa, through the TEP.

Yale University Library, Manuscripts and Archives, New Haven, Ct., through the TEP.

Index

Page numbers in italics refer to illustrations

country, 159; housekeeping, 175; human body as, 201, 208

Machine gun, 131

Machinist, 136, 159

Mack, Connie, *250*

Magnet, 72

"Make babies by machines," 259

Management, 121

Manhattan, 18. *See also* New York

Mankind, 104, 153, 259

Manufacturers, 93, 151

Manufacturing, 95, 233

Marconi, Guglielmo, 234–235

Mark, William Dennis, 89

Markens, Isaac, 171

Marriage, 181, 182, 221, 224

Mars, 57, 144, 207

Martin, Thomas Commerford, 227

Mary Had a Little Lamb, 22

Masaryk, Tomáš Garrigue, 263

Mass, 111

Massachusetts Institute of Technology (MIT), 196, 222, 229

Master, 63

Maternity, 31

Mathematicians, 229, 253–254

Mathematics, 229; calculations, 242

Matter, 67, 68

Maturity, 185

Maxim, Hiram and Hudson (brothers), 131

Mayer, Alfred Marshall, 19

McKinley, William, 105

Measurement, 217

Meat, 146, 188

Media, 112

Medical men, 73. *See also* Physicians

Medicine, 202

Medieval nonsense, 129

Medill, Joseph, 26

Men, 11, 12, 68, 78, 81, 82, 86, 176, 177, 178, 180–181, 183, 189, 190, 191, 202, 203, 247, 262; competent, 180; greatest, 260, 261, 263; industrial man, 125; laboring, 45; modest, 259; of peace, 261; professional, 207; of science, 105; southern, 180; young, 180

Mendel, Gregor, 166

Menlo Park, New Jersey, xiv, xx, 160, *238*

Merchant, 120

Mercy, 106

Messenger boys, 136

Metaphysics, 231

Method, practical, 190

Metropolitan Opera, 37

Mexicans, 164, 172

Mexico, 130, 172

Miasma, 236

Microbe, 199

Microphone, 2

Milan, Ohio, xiii, xix

Military, 129–141; caste, 166; establishments, 135; gangs, 131; nation, 137; nonsense, 129

Milk, 101, 206, 207; synthetic, 73

Miller, A. J., 227

Miller, Lewis (father-in-law), 221, 235

Miller, Mina. *See* Edison, Mina Miller

Millionaires, 153, 172

Mimeograph, 6, 16

Mind, 2, 188, 259; greatest, 261; reading, 104, 111; young, 194. *See also* Brains

Miner, 98

Michele Wehrwein Albion is a former curator of the Edison and Ford Winter Estates in Fort Myers, Florida. She has worked at several museums, including the U.S. Holocaust Memorial Museum in Washington, D.C., and the Maine State Museum. Albion is the author of the award-winning *The Florida Life of Thomas Edison* (2008). She lives with her family in New Hampshire.